They Walked
with God

ALSO BY MAX LUCADO

They Walked with God

40 BIBLE CHARACTERS WHO INSPIRE US

MAX LUCADO

THOMAS NELSON
Since 1798

Published in Nashville, Tennessee, by Thomas Nelson. Thomas Nelson is a registered trademark of HarperCollins Christian Publishing, Inc.

Thomas Nelson titles may be purchased in bulk for educational, business, fundraising, or sales promotional use. For information, please e-mail SpecialMarkets@ThomasNelson.com.

Scripture quotations marked CEV are taken from the Contemporary English Version. Copyright © 1991, 1992, 1995 by American Bible Society. Used by permission.

Scripture quotations marked ESV are taken from the ESV® Bible (The Holy Bible, English Standard Version®). Copyright © 2001 by Crossway, a publishing ministry of Good News Publishers. Used by permission. All rights reserved.

Scripture quotations marked GNT are taken from the Good New Translation in Today's English Version—Second Edition. Copyright 1992 American Bible Society. Used by permission

Scripture quotations marked KJV are taken from the King James Version. Public domain.

Scripture quotations marked MSG are taken from THE MESSAGE. Copyright © 1993, 2002, 2018 by Eugene H. Peterson. Used by permission of NavPress. All rights reserved. Represented by Tyndale House Publishers, a Division of Tyndale House Ministries.

Scripture quotations marked NASB are taken from the New American Standard Bible® (NASB). Copyright © 1960, 1962, 1963, 1968, 1971, 1972, 1973, 1975, 1977, 1995 by The Lockman Foundation. Used by permission. www.lockman.org

Scripture quotations marked NCV are taken from the New Century Version®. Copyright © 2005 by Thomas Nelson. Used by permission. All rights reserved.

Scripture quotations taken from The Holy Bible, New International Version®, NIV®. Copyright © 1973, 1978, 1984, 2011 by Biblica, Inc.® Used by permission of Zondervan. All rights reserved worldwide. www.Zondervan.com. The "NIV" and "New International Version" are trademarks registered in the United States Patent and Trademark Office by Biblica, Inc.®

Scripture quotations marked NKJV are taken from the New King James Version®. Copyright © 1982 by Thomas Nelson. Used by permission. All rights reserved.

Scripture quotations marked NLT are taken from the Holy Bible, New Living Translation. © 1996, 2004, 2015 by Tyndale House Foundation. Used by permission of Tyndale House Publishers, Inc., Carol Stream, Illinois 60188. All rights reserved.

The Scripture quotations marked NRSV are taken from the New Revised Standard Version Bible. Copyright © 1989 National Council of the Churches of Christ in the United States of America. Used by permission. All rights reserved worldwide.

Scripture quotations marked PHILLIPS are from The New Testament in Modern English by J. B. Phillips. Copyright © 1960, 1972 J. B. Phillips. Administered by the Archbishops' Council of the Church of England. Used by permission.

Scripture quotations marked RSV are taken from the Revised Standard Version of the Bible. Copyright © 1946, 1952, and 1971 National Council of the Churches of Christ in the United States of America. Used by permission. All rights reserved worldwide.

Scripture quotations marked TLB are taken from The Living Bible. Copyright © 1971. Used by permission of Tyndale House Publishers, Inc., Carol Stream, Illinois 60188. All rights reserved.

Any internet addresses, phone numbers, or company or product information printed in this book are offered as a resource and are not intended in any way to be or to imply an endorsement by Thomas Nelson, nor does Thomas Nelson vouch for the existence, content, or services of these sites, phone numbers, companies, or products beyond the life of this book.

ISBN 978-0-7852-9461-0 (audiobook)
ISBN 978-0-7852-9460-3 (eBook)
ISBN 978-0-7852-9459-7 (HC)

Library of Congress Cataloging-in-Publication Data on File

Printed in the United States of America

22 23 24 25 26 LSC 10 9 8 7 6 5 4 3 2 1

CONTENTS

CONTENTS

A WORD FROM THE AUTHOR

Dear Friend,

Somewhere in your mind is a novel—your novel. Your novel about your future. You don't have all the details worked out, but you've got some pretty good ideas about characters and storyline. You envision a spouse or dear friend, kids, maybe grandkids. Your story includes good health, ample income, honest love, early retirement. We've all got a story we're working on.

But just when we're ready for the manuscript to be bound and published, God exercises editorial authority.

He adds a character with a surprise pregnancy.

He removes a character through a sudden tragedy.

He reverses the order of events. The manuscript you wrote called for retirement, then old age. The manuscript you are living has you aging, with no sign of retirement.

In your story you lead a long and happy life. How would you feel if he gave you the happy life but edited out the long part?

What do you do when God edits your story?

That's no small question. Indeed, it is *the* question. Every person knows the challenge of an edited storyline. When God edits yours, how do you react? Fear or faith? Anger or trust? Do you turn away from God or turn toward him?

To help us choose the latter, God tells us stories. He chronicles life after life of people who faced what you and I face. He packed the Bible full of personalities and profiles, all written so that you and I would know how to respond when our own stories take unexpected turns.

Are you struggling with guilt? Then meet Peter, the apostle who bailed on Jesus.

Facing an impossible challenge? So was a boy named David.

Have you exhausted your box of second chances? Then consider the plight of the woman found in the act of adultery.

For every person, Scripture has a story. For every problem, God has a promise. For each occasion when we feel our story is coming undone, God steps in with a message: "Just trust me. I'm the author and the finisher of your life!"

My prayer for all who hold this book is simple. May you remember that your story is being written by a good Father who knows and loves you. In his hands, your story will have an amazing ending.

ABIGAIL

ABIGAIL

BEFORE YOU BEGIN

Read 1 Samuel 25:18-25, 32-35 MSG

Abigail flew into action. She took two hundred loaves of bread, two skins of wine, five sheep dressed out and ready for cooking, a bushel of roasted grain, a hundred raisin cakes, and two hundred fig cakes, and she had it all loaded on some donkeys. Then she said to her young servants, "Go ahead and pave the way for me. I'm right behind you." But she said nothing to her husband Nabal.

As she was riding her donkey, descending into a ravine, David and his men were descending from the other end, so they met there on the road. David had just said, "That sure was a waste, guarding everything this man had out in the wild so that nothing he had was lost—and now he rewards me with insults. A real slap in the face! May God do his worst to me if Nabal and every cur in his misbegotten brood aren't dead meat by morning!"

As soon as Abigail saw David, she got off her donkey and fell on her knees at his feet, her face to the ground in homage, saying, "My master, let me take the blame! Let me speak to you. Listen to what I have to say. Don't dwell on what that brute Nabal did. He acts out the meaning of his name: Nabal, Fool. Foolishness oozes from him.

"I wasn't there when the young men my master sent arrived. I didn't see them."

And David said, "Blessed be God, the God of Israel. He sent you to meet me! And blessed be your good sense! Bless you for keeping me from murder and taking charge of looking out for me. A close call! As God lives, the God of Israel who kept me from hurting you, if you had not come as quickly as you did, stopping me in my tracks, by morning there would have been nothing left of Nabal but dead meat."

Then David accepted the gift she brought him and said, "Return home in peace. I've heard what you've said and I'll do what you've asked."

Ernest Gordon groans in the Death House of Chungkai, Burma. He listens to the moans of the dying and smells the stench of the dead. Pitiless jungle heat bakes his skin and parches his throat. Had he the strength, he could wrap one hand around his bony thigh. But he has neither the energy nor the interest. Diphtheria has drained both; he can't walk; he can't even feel his body. He shares a cot with flies and bedbugs and awaits a lonely death in a Japanese prisoner-of-war camp.

How harsh the war has been on him. He entered World War II in his early twenties, a robust Highlander in Scotland's Argyle and Sutherland Brigade. But then came the capture by the Japanese, months of backbreaking labor in the jungle, daily beatings, and slow starvation. Scotland seems forever away. Civility, even farther.

The Allied soldiers behave like barbarians, stealing from each other, robbing dying colleagues, fighting for food scraps. Servers shortchange rations so they can have extra for themselves. The law of the jungle has become the law of the camp.

Gordon is happy to bid it adieu. Death by disease trumps life in Chungkai. But then something wonderful happens. Two new prisoners, in whom hope still stirs, are transferred to the camp. Though also sick and frail, they heed a higher code. They share their meager meals and volunteer for extra work. They cleanse Gordon's ulcerated sores and massage his atrophied legs. They give him his first bath in six weeks. His strength slowly returns and, with it, his dignity.

Their goodness proves contagious, and Gordon contracts a case. He begins to treat the sick and share his rations. He even gives away his few belongings. Other soldiers do likewise. Over time, the tone of the camp softens and brightens. Sacrifice replaces selfishness. Soldiers hold worship services and Bible studies.

Twenty years later, when Gordon served as chaplain of Princeton University, he described the transformation with these words:

Death was still with us—no doubt about that. But we were slowly being freed from its destructive grip. . . . Selfishness, hatred . . . and pride were all anti-life. Love . . . self-sacrifice . . . and faith, on the other hand, were the essence of life . . . gifts of God to men. . . . Death no longer had the last word at Chungkai.[1]

Selfishness, hatred, and pride—you don't have to go to a POW camp to find them. A dormitory will do just fine. As will the boardroom of a corporation or the bedroom of a marriage or the backwoods of a country. The code of the jungle is alive and well. Every man for himself. Survival of the fittest.

Does the code contaminate your world? Do personal possessive pronouns dominate the language of your circle? *My career, my dreams, my stuff. I want things to go my way on my schedule.* If so, you know how savage this giant can be. Yet, every so often, a diamond glitters in the mud. A comrade shares, a soldier cares, or Abigail, stunning Abigail, stands on your trail.

She lived in the days of David and was married to Nabal, whose name means "fool" in Hebrew. He lived up to the definition.

Nabal needed the protection. He was "churlish and ill-behaved—a real Calebbite dog. . . . He is so ill-natured that one cannot speak to him" (1 Sam. 25:3, 17).[2] Nabal's world revolved around one person—Nabal. He owed nothing to anybody and laughed at the thought of sharing with anyone. Especially David.

David played a Robin Hood role in the wilderness. He and his six hundred soldiers protected the farmers and shepherds from brigands and Bedouins. Israel had no highway patrol or police force, so David and his mighty men met a definite need in the countryside. They guarded with enough effectiveness to prompt one of Nabal's shepherds to say, "Night and day they were a wall around us all the time we were herding our sheep near them" (25:16 NIV).

Trouble began to brew after the harvest. With sheep sheared and hay gathered, it was time to bake bread, roast lamb, and pour wine. Take a break from the furrows and flocks and enjoy the fruit of the labor. As we pick up the story, Nabal's men are doing just that.

David hears of the gala and thinks his men deserve an invitation. He sends ten men to Nabal with this request: "We come at a happy time, so be kind to my young men. Please give anything you can find for them and for your son David" (25:8 NCV).

Boorish Nabal scoffs at the thought:

Who is David, and who is the son of Jesse? There are many servants nowadays who break away each one from his master. Shall I then take my bread and my water and my meat that I have killed for my shearers, and give it to men when I do not know where they are from? (25:10–11 NKJV)

Nabal pretends he's never heard of David, lumping him in with runaway slaves and vagabonds. Such insolence infuriates the messengers, and they turn on their heels and hurry back to David with a full report.

David doesn't need to hear the news twice. He tells the men to form a posse. Or, more precisely, "Strap on your swords!" (25:12 MSG).

Four hundred men mount up and take off. Eyes glare. Nostrils flare. Lips snarl. Testosterone flows. David and his troops thunder down on Nabal, the scoundrel, who obliviously drinks beer and eats barbecue with his buddies. The road rumbles as David grumbles, "May God do his worst to me if Nabal and every cur in his misbegotten brood aren't dead meat by morning!" (25:22 MSG).

Then, all of a sudden, beauty appears. A daisy lifts her head in the desert; a swan lands at the meatpacking plant; a whiff of perfume floats through the men's locker room. Abigail, the wife of Nabal, stands on the trail. Whereas he is brutish and mean, she is "intelligent and good-looking" (25:3 MSG).

Brains and beauty. Abigail puts both to work. When she learns of Nabal's crude response, she springs into action. With no word to her husband, she gathers gifts and races to intercept David. As David and his men descend a ravine, she takes her position, armed with "two hundred loaves of bread, two skins of wine, five sheep dressed out and ready for cooking, a bushel of roasted grain, a hundred raisin cakes, and two hundred fig cakes, . . . all loaded on some donkeys" (25:18 MSG).

Four hundred men rein in their rides. Some gape at the food; others gawk at the female.

Abigail's no fool. She knows the importance of the moment. She stands as the final barrier between her family and sure death. Falling at David's feet, she issues a plea worthy of a paragraph in Scripture. "On me, my lord, on me let this iniquity be! And please let your maidservant speak in your ears, and hear the words of your maidservant" (25:24 NKJV).

She doesn't defend Nabal but agrees that he is a scoundrel. She begs not for justice but forgiveness, accepting blame when she deserves none. "Please forgive the trespass of your maidservant" (25:28 NKJV). She offers the gifts from her house and urges David to leave Nabal to God and avoid the dead weight of remorse.

Her words fall on David like July sun on ice. He melts.

Blessed be GOD, the God of Israel. He sent you to meet me! . . . A close call! . . . if you had not come as quickly as you did, stopping me in my tracks, by morning there would have been nothing left of Nabal but dead meat. . . . I've heard what you've said and I'll do what you've asked. (25:32–35 MSG)

David returns to camp. Abigail returns to Nabal. She finds him too drunk for conversation so waits until the next morning to describe how close David came to camp and Nabal came to death. "Right then and there he had a heart attack and fell into a coma. About ten days later GOD finished him off and he died" (25:37–38 MSG).

When David learns of Nabal's death and Abigail's sudden availability, he thanks God for the first and takes advantage of the second. Unable to shake the memory of the pretty woman in the middle of the road, he proposes, and she accepts. David gets

a new wife, Abigail a new home, and we have a great principle: beauty can overcome barbarism.

Meekness saved the day that day. Abigail's gentleness reversed a river of anger. Humility has such power. Apologies can disarm arguments. Contrition can defuse rage. Olive branches do more good than battle-axes ever will. "Soft speech can break bones" (Prov. 25:15 NLT).

Abigail teaches so much. The contagious power of kindness. The strength of a gentle heart. Her greatest lesson, however, is to take our eyes from her beauty and set them on someone else's. She lifts our thoughts from a rural trail to a Jerusalem cross. Abigail never knew Jesus. She lived a thousand years before his sacrifice. Nevertheless, her story prefigures his life.

Abigail placed herself between David and Nabal. Jesus placed himself between God and us. Abigail volunteered to be punished for Nabal's sins. Jesus allowed heaven to punish him for yours and mine. Abigail turned away the anger of David. Didn't Christ shield you from God's?

He was our "Mediator who can reconcile God and humanity—the man Christ Jesus. He gave his life to purchase freedom for everyone" (1 Tim. 2:5–6 NLT). Who is a mediator but one who stands in between? And what did Christ do but stand in between God's anger and our punishment? Christ intercepted the wrath of heaven.

Something remotely similar happened at the Chungkai camp. One evening after work detail, a Japanese guard announced that a shovel was missing. The officer kept the Allies in formation, insisting that someone had stolen it. Screaming in broken English, he demanded that the guilty man step forward. He shouldered his rifle, ready to kill one prisoner at a time until a confession was made.

A Scottish soldier broke ranks, stood stiffly at attention, and said, "I did it." The officer unleashed his anger and beat the man to death. When the guard was finally exhausted, the prisoners picked up the man's body and their tools and returned to camp. Only then were the shovels recounted. The Japanese soldier had made a mistake. No shovel was missing after all.[3]

Who does that? What kind of person would take the blame for something he didn't do?

When you find the adjective, attach it to Jesus. "God has piled all our sins, everything we've done wrong, on him, on him" (Isa. 53:6 MSG). God treated his innocent Son like the guilty human race, his Holy One like a lying scoundrel, his Abigail like a Nabal.

Christ lived the life we could not live and took the punishment we could not take to offer the hope we cannot resist. His sacrifice begs us to ask this question: If he so loved us, can we not love each other? Having been forgiven, can we not forgive? Having feasted at the table of grace, can we not share a few crumbs? "My dear, dear friends, if God loved us like this, we certainly ought to love each other" (1 John 4:11 MSG).

Do you find your Nabal world hard to stomach? Then do what David did: stop staring at Nabal. Shift your gaze to Christ. Look more at the Mediator and less at the troublemakers. "Don't let evil get the best of you; get the best of evil by doing good" (Rom. 12:21 MSG). One prisoner can change a camp. One Abigail can save a family. Be the beauty amidst your beasts and see what happens.

REFLECTION AND DISCUSSION

Describe a time you saw the good influence of one person change the atmosphere of a group or organization.

_____

_____

_____

_____

_____

_____

What specific environment could you reshape by your good influence?

_____

_____

_____

_____

_____

_____

How could you be the "beauty" that brings peace to a tense or combative situation? What would you hope to accomplish?

_____

_____

_____

_____

_____

_____

Read Proverbs 15:1. Which half of this verse did Nabal demonstrate? Which half of this verse did Abigail demonstrate? Which half of this verse do you normally demonstrate?

_____

_____

_____

_____

_____

_____

Think of a person you have injured, insulted, or alienated. Ask God to give you the grace and the humility to approach this person and ask for forgiveness. Pray that the Lord will bring peace and healing to the situation.

_____

_____

_____

_____

_____

_____

ANANIAS
AND SAUL

ANANIAS AND SAUL

BEFORE YOU BEGIN

Read Acts 9:17 NKJV

Ananias went his way and entered the house; and laying his hands on him he said, "Brother Saul, the Lord Jesus, who appeared to you on the road as you came, has sent me that you may receive your sight and be filled with the Holy Spirit."

Ananias hurries through the narrow Damascus streets.[4] His dense and bristling beard does not hide his serious face. Friends call as he passes, but he doesn't pause. He murmurs as he goes, "Saul? Saul? No way. Can't be true."

He wonders if he misheard the instructions. Wonders if he should turn around and inform his wife. Wonders if he should stop and tell someone where he is headed in case he never returns. But he doesn't. Friends would call him a fool. His wife would tell him not to go.

But he has to. He scampers through the courtyard of chickens, towering camels, and little donkeys. He steps past the shop of the tailor and doesn't respond to the greeting of the tanner. He keeps moving until he reaches the street called Straight. The inn has low arches and large rooms with mattresses. Nice by Damascus standards, the place of choice for any person of significance or power, and Saul is certainly both.

Ananias and the other Christians have been preparing for him. Some of the disciples have left the city. Others have gone into hiding. Saul's reputation as a Christian-killer preceded him. But the idea of Saul the Christ follower? That was the message of the vision. Ananias replays it one more time.

"Arise and go to the street called Straight, and inquire at the house of Judas for one called Saul of Tarsus, for behold, he is praying. And in a vision he has seen a man named Ananias coming in and putting his hand on him, so that he might receive his sight" (Acts 9:11–12 NKJV).

Ananias nearly choked on his matzo. *This isn't possible!* He reminded God of Saul's hard heart. "I have heard from many about this man, how much harm he has done to Your saints in Jerusalem" (v. 13 NKJV). Saul a Christian?

But God wasn't teasing. "Go, for he is a chosen vessel of Mine to bear My name before Gentiles, kings, and the children of Israel" (v. 15 NKJV).

Ananias rehashes the words as he walks. The name Saul doesn't couple well with *chosen vessel*. Saul the thickhead—yes. Saul the critic—okay. But Saul the "chosen vessel"? Ananias shakes his head at the thought. By now he is halfway down Straight Street and seriously considering turning around and going home. He would have, except the two guards spot him.

"What brings you here?" they shout from the second story. They stand at attention. Their faces are wintry with unrest. Ananias knows who they are—soldiers from the temple. Traveling companions of Saul. "I've been sent to help the rabbi."

They lower their spears. "We hope you can. Something has happened to him. He doesn't eat or drink. Scarcely speaks."

Ananias can't turn back now. He ascends the stone stairs. The guards step aside, and Ananias steps into the doorway. He gasps at what he sees. A gaunt man sitting cross-legged on the floor, half shadowed by a shaft of sunlight. Hollow-cheeked and dry-lipped, he rocks back and forth, groaning a prayer.

"How long has he been like this?"

"Three days."

Saul's head sits large on his shoulders. He has a beaked nose and a bushy ridge for eyebrows. The food on the plate and the water in the cup sit untouched on the floor. His eyes stare out of their sockets in the direction of an open window. A crusty film covers them. Saul doesn't even wave the flies away from his face. Ananias hesitates. If this is a setup, he is history. If not, the moment is.

No one could fault Ananias's reluctance. Saul saw Christians as couriers of a plague. He stood near the high priest at Stephen's trial. He watched over the coats of stone-throwers at the execution. He nodded in approval at Stephen's final breath. And when the Sanhedrin needed a hit man to terrorize the church, Saul stepped forward. He became the Angel of Death. He descended on the Christians in a fury "uttering threats with every breath" (Acts 9:1 NLT). He "persecuted the church of God beyond measure and tried to destroy it" (Gal. 1:13 NKJV).

Ananias knew what Saul had done to the church in Jerusalem. What he was about to learn, however, is what Jesus had done to Saul on the road to Damascus.

The trip was Saul's idea. The city had seen large numbers of conversions. When word of the revival reached Saul, he made his request: "Send me." So the fiery young Hebrew left Jerusalem on his first missionary journey, hell-bent on stopping the church. The journey to Damascus was a long one, one hundred and fifty miles. Saul likely rode horseback, careful to bypass the Gentile villages. This was a holy journey.

It was also a hot journey. The lowland between Mount Hermon and Damascus could melt silver. The sun struck like spears; the heat made waves out of the horizon. Somewhere on this thirsty trail, Jesus knocked Saul to the ground and asked him, "Saul, Saul, why are you persecuting Me?" (Acts 9:4 NKJV).

Saul jammed his fists into his eye sockets as if they were filled with sand. He rolled onto his knees and lowered his head down to the earth. "'Who are You, Lord?' Then the Lord said, 'I am Jesus, whom you are persecuting'" (v. 5 NKJV). When Saul lifted his head to look, the living centers of his eyes had vanished. He was blind. He had the vacant stare of a Roman statue.

His guards rushed to help. They led him to the Damascus inn and walked with him up the stairwell. By the time Ananias arrives, blind Saul has begun to see Jesus in a different light.

Ananias enters and sits on the stone floor. He takes the hand of the had-been terrorist and feels it tremble. He observes Saul's quivering lips. Taking note of the sword and spear resting in the corner, Ananias realizes Christ has already done the work. All that remains is for Ananias to show Saul the next step. "Brother Saul . . ." (How sweet those words must have sounded. Saul surely wept upon hearing them.)

"Brother Saul, the Lord Jesus, who appeared to you on the road as you came, has sent me that you may receive your sight and be filled with the Holy Spirit" (v. 17 NKJV).

Tears rush like a tide against the crusts on Saul's eyes. The scaly covering loosens and falls away. He blinks and sees the face of his new friend.

Within the hour he's stepping out of the waters of baptism. Within a few days he's preaching in a synagogue. The first of a thousand sermons. Saul soon becomes Paul, and Paul preaches from the hills of Athens, pens letters from the bowels of prisons, and ultimately sires a genealogy of theologians, including Aquinas, Luther, and Calvin.

God used Paul to touch the world. But he first used Ananias to touch Paul. Has God given you a similar assignment? Has God given you a Saul?

Everyone else has written off your Saul. "He's too far gone." "She's too hard . . . too addicted . . . too old . . . too cold." No one gives your Saul a prayer. But you are beginning to realize that maybe God is at work behind the scenes. Maybe it's too soon to throw in the towel . . . You begin to believe.

Don't resist these thoughts. Joseph didn't. His brothers sold him into Egyptian slavery. Yet he welcomed them into his palace.

David didn't. King Saul had a vendetta against David, but David had a soft spot for Saul. He called him "the LORD's anointed" (1 Sam. 24:10 NKJV).

Hosea didn't. His wife, Gomer, was queen of the red-light district, but Hosea kept his front door open. And she came home.

Of course, no one believed in people more than Jesus did. He saw something in Peter worth developing, in the adulterous woman worth forgiving, and in John worth harnessing. He saw something in the thief on the cross, and what he saw was worth saving. And in the life of a wild-eyed, bloodthirsty extremist, he saw an apostle of grace. He believed in Saul. And he believed in Saul through Ananias.

"Brother Saul, the Lord Jesus, who appeared to you on the road as you came, has sent me that you may receive your sight and be filled with the Holy Spirit" (Acts 9:17 NKJV).

Don't give up on your Saul. When others write him off, give him another chance. Stay strong. Call him brother. Call her sister. Tell your Saul about Jesus, and pray. And remember this: God never sends you where he hasn't already been. By the time you reach your Saul, who knows what you'll find?

My favorite Ananias-type story involves a couple of college roommates. The Ananias of the pair was a tolerant soul. He tolerated his friend's late-night drunkenness, midnight throw-ups, and all-day sleep-ins. He didn't complain when his friend disappeared for the weekend or smoked cigarettes in the car. He could have requested a roommate who went to church more or cursed less or cared about something other than impressing girls.

But he hung with his personal Saul, seeming to think that something good could happen if the guy could pull his life together. So he kept cleaning up the mess, inviting his roommate to church, and covering his back.

I don't remember a bright light or a loud voice. I've never traveled a desert road to Damascus. But I distinctly remember Jesus knocking me off my perch and flipping on the light. It took four semesters, but Steve's example and Jesus' message finally got through.

So if this book lifts your spirit, you might thank God for my Ananias, Steve Green. Even more, you might listen to that voice in your heart and look on your map for a street called Straight.

REFLECTION AND DISCUSSION

Think of a famous person who boldly declares his or her faith. How has the public reacted to this?

_____

_____

_____

_____

_____

Share a story either about yourself or someone whom you know personally who made an unexpected radical conversion to God.

_____

_____

_____

_____

"Has God given you a Saul?" Is there someone in your life whom most people have given up on and dismissed? How could you be an Ananias for that person?

_____

_____

_____

_____

What does Scripture say about reaching out to those in need? How can you be more sensitive to the Father's promptings in this area?

_____

_____

_____

_____

How would you describe your conversion? Was it sudden or gradual? What are you doing to help others experience conversion?

_____

_____

_____

_____

_____

_____

_____

_____

_____

_____

_____

_____

CORNELIUS

CORNELIUS

BEFORE YOU BEGIN
Read Acts 10:28 CEV

Peter said to them, "You know that we Jews are not allowed to have anything to do with other people. But God has shown me that he doesn't think anyone is unclean or unfit."

Molokai, a ruby on the pearl necklace of the Hawaiian Islands. Tourists travel to Molokai for its quiet charm, gentle breezes, and soft surf. But Father Damien came for a different reason. He came to help people die.

He came to Molokai because leprosy came here first. No one knows exactly how the disease reached Hawaii. The first documented case was dated around 1840. But while no one can trace the source of the disease, no one can deny its results. Disfigurement, decay, and panic.

The government responded with a civil version of Old Testament segregation. They deposited the diseased on a triangular thrust of land called Kalaupapa. Surrounded on three sides by water and on the fourth by the highest seawall in the world, it was a natural prison.

Hard to get to. Harder still to get away from.

The lepers lived a discarded existence in shanties with minimal food. Ships would draw close to shore, and sailors would dump supplies into the water, hoping the crates would float toward land. Society sent the lepers a clear message: you aren't valuable anymore.

But Father Damien's message was different. He'd already served in the islands for a decade when, in 1873, at the age of thirty-three, he wrote his provincial and offered, "I want to sacrifice myself for the poor lepers."

He immersed himself in their world, dressing sores, hugging children, burying the dead. His choir members sang through rags, and congregants received communion with stumped hands. Because they mattered to God, they mattered to him. When he referred to his congregation, he didn't say "my brothers and sisters" but "we lepers." He became one of them. Literally.

Somewhere along the way, through a touch of kindness or in the sharing of a communion wafer, the disease passed from member to priest. Damien became a leper. And on April 15, 1889, four days shy of Good Friday, he died.[5]

We've learned to treat leprosy. We don't quarantine people anymore. We've done away with such settlements. But have we done away with the attitude? Do we still see some people as inferior?

We did on our elementary school playground. All the boys in Mrs. Amburgy's first-grade class bonded together to express our male superiority. We met daily at recess and, with arms interlocked, marched around the playground, shouting, "Boys are better than girls! Boys are better than girls!" Frankly, I didn't agree, but I enjoyed the fraternity. The girls, in response, formed their own club. They paraded around the school, announcing their disdain for boys. We were a happy campus.

People are prone to pecking orders. We love the high horse. "Boys are better than girls!" The affluent over the destitute. The educated over the dropout. The old-timer over the newcomer. The Jew over the Gentile.

An impassable gulf yawned between Jews and Gentiles in the days of the early church. A Jew could not drink milk drawn by Gentiles or eat their food. Jews could not aid a Gentile mother in her hour of need. Jewish physicians could not attend to non-Jewish patients.[6]

No Jew would have anything to do with a Gentile. They were unclean.

Unless that Jew, of course, was Jesus. Suspicions of a new order began to surface because of his curious conversation with the Canaanite woman. Her daughter was dying, and her prayer was urgent. Yet her ancestry was Gentile. "I was sent only to help God's lost sheep—the people of Israel," Jesus told her. "That's true, Lord," she replied, "but even dogs are allowed to eat the scraps that fall beneath their masters' table" (Matt. 15:24, 27 NLT).

Jesus healed the woman's daughter and made his position clear. He was more concerned about bringing everyone in than shutting certain people out.

This was the tension Peter felt. His culture said, "Keep your distance from Gentiles." His Christ said, "Build bridges to Gentiles." And Peter had to make a choice. An encounter with Cornelius forced his decision.

Cornelius was an officer in the Roman army. Both Gentile and bad guy. (Think British redcoat in eighteenth-century Boston.) He ate the wrong food, hung with the wrong crowd, and swore allegiance to Caesar. He didn't quote the Torah or descend from Abraham. Toga on his body and ham in his freezer. No yarmulke on his head or beard on his face. Hardly deacon material. Uncircumcised, unkosher, unclean. Look at him.

Yet look at him again. Closely. He helped needy people and sympathized with Jewish ethics. He was kind and devout. "One who feared God with all his household, who gave alms generously to the people, and prayed to God always" (Acts 10:2 NKJV). Cornelius was even on a first-name basis with an angel. The angel told him to get in touch with Peter, who was staying at a friend's house thirty miles away in the seaside town of Joppa. Cornelius sent three men to find him.

Peter, meanwhile, was doing his best to pray with a growling stomach. "He became very hungry and wanted to eat; but while they made ready, he fell into a trance and saw heaven opened and an object like a great sheet bound at the four corners, descending to him and let down to the earth. In it were all kinds of four-footed animals of the earth, wild beasts, creeping things, and birds of the air. And a voice came to him, 'Rise, Peter; kill and eat'" (vv. 10–13 NKJV).

The sheet contained enough unkosher food to uncurl the payos of any Hasidic Jew.

Peter absolutely and resolutely refused. "Not so, Lord! For I have never eaten anything common or unclean" (v. 14 NKJV).

But God wasn't kidding about this. He three-peated the vision, leaving poor Peter in a quandary. Peter was pondering the pigs in the blanket when he heard a knock at the door. At the sound of the knock, he heard the call of God's Spirit in his heart. "Behold, three men are seeking you. Arise therefore, go down and go with them, doubting nothing; for I have sent them" (vv. 19–20 NKJV).

"Doubting nothing" can also be translated "make no distinction" or "indulge in no prejudice" or "discard all partiality." This was a huge moment for Peter.

Much to his credit, Peter invited the messengers to spend the night and headed out the next morning to meet Cornelius. When Peter arrived, Cornelius fell at his feet. Peter insisted he stand up and then confessed how difficult this decision had been. "You know that we Jews are not allowed to have anything to do with other people. But God has shown me that he doesn't think anyone is unclean or unfit" (v. 28 CEV).

Peter told Cornelius about Jesus and the gospel, and before Peter could issue an invitation, the presence of the Spirit was among them, and they were replicating Pentecost—speaking in tongues and glorifying God. Peter offered to baptize Cornelius and his friends. They accepted. They offered him a bed. Peter accepted. By the end of the visit, he was making his own ham sandwiches.

And us? We are still pondering verse 28: "God has shown me that he doesn't think anyone is unclean or unfit."

Life is so much easier without this command. As long as we can call people common or unfit, we can plant them on Kalaupapa and go our separate ways. Labels relieve us of responsibility. Pigeonholing permits us to wash our hands and leave.

Categorizing others creates distance and gives us a convenient exit strategy for avoiding involvement.

Jesus took an entirely different approach. He was all about including people, not excluding them. "The Word became flesh and blood, and moved into the neighborhood" (John 1:14 MSG). Jesus touched lepers and loved foreigners and spent so much time with partygoers that people called him a "a boozer, a friend of the misfits" (Matt. 11:19 MSG).

Racism couldn't keep him from the Samaritan woman; demons couldn't keep him from the demoniac. Jesus spent thirty-three years walking in the mess of this world. "He had equal status with God but didn't think so much of himself that he had to cling to the advantages of that status no matter what. Not at all. When the time came, he set aside the privileges of deity and took on the status of a slave, became human!" (Phil. 2:6–7 MSG).

His example sends this message: no playground displays of superiority. "Don't call any person common or unfit."

We must look within and give more of a Christlike response. Rather than see people as problems, Christ saw them as opportunities.

God calls us to change the way we look at people. Not to see them as Gentiles or Jews, insiders or outsiders, liberals or conservatives. Not to label. To label is to libel. "We have stopped evaluating others from a human point of view" (2 Cor. 5:16 NLT).

Let's view people differently; let's view them as we do ourselves. Blemished, perhaps. Unfinished, for certain. Yet once rescued and restored, we may shed light, like the two stained-glass windows in my office.

My brother found them on a junkyard heap. Some church had discarded them. Dee, a handy carpenter, reclaimed them. He repainted the chipped wood, repaired the worn frame. He sealed some of the cracks in the colored glass. The windows aren't perfect. But if suspended where the sun can pass through, they cascade multicolored light into the room.

In our lifetimes you and I are going to come across some discarded people. Tossed out. Sometimes tossed out by a church. And we get to choose. Neglect or rescue? Label them or love them? We know Jesus' choice. Just look at what he did with us.

REFLECTION AND DISCUSSION

Why did Cornelius not look the part even though he was a Christ follower?
What surface judgments do people use today to measure spirituality?

_____

_____

_____

What was the social pecking order when you were growing up? How about
today? Who is at the top, who is at the bottom, and where are you in the order?

_____

_____

_____

How could you make time for some marginalized Christians in your life?

_____

_____

_____

DAVID

DAVID

BEFORE YOU BEGIN
Read 1 Samuel 17:20-24; 45-50 NIV

Early in the morning David left the flock in the care of a shepherd, loaded up and set out, as Jesse had directed. He reached the camp as the army was going out to its battle positions, shouting the war cry. Israel and the Philistines were drawing up their lines facing each other. David left his things with the keeper of supplies, ran to the battle lines and asked his brothers how they were. As he was talking with them, Goliath, the Philistine champion from Gath, stepped out from his lines and shouted his usual defiance, and David heard it. Whenever the Israelites saw the man, they all fled from him in great fear.

David said to the Philistine, "You come against me with sword and spear and javelin, but I come against you in the name of the Lord Almighty, the God of the armies of Israel, whom you have defied. This day the Lord will deliver you into my hands, and I'll strike you down and cut off your head. This very day I will give the carcasses of the Philistine army to the birds and the wild animals, and the whole world will know that there is a God in Israel. All those gathered here will know that it is not by sword or spear that the LORD saves; for the battle is the LORD's, and he will give all of you into our hands."

As the Philistine moved closer to attack him, David ran quickly toward the battle line to meet him. Reaching into his bag and taking out a stone, he slung it and struck the Philistine on the forehead. The stone sank into his forehead, and he fell facedown on the ground.

So David triumphed over the Philistine with a sling and a stone; without a sword in his hand he struck down the Philistine and killed him.

The slender, beardless boy kneels by the brook. Mud moistens his knees. Bubbling water cools his hand. Were he to notice, he could study his handsome features in the water. Hair the color of copper. Tanned, sanguine skin and eyes that steal the breath of Hebrew maidens. He searches not for his reflection, however, but for rocks. Stones. Smooth stones. The kind that stack neatly in a shepherd's pouch, rest flush against a shepherd's leather sling. Flat rocks that balance heavy on the palm and missile with comet-crashing force into the head of a lion, a bear, or, in this case, a giant.

Goliath stares down from the hillside. Only disbelief keeps him from laughing. He and his Philistine herd have rendered their half of the valley into a forest of spears. Goliath towers above them all: nine feet, nine inches tall in his stocking feet, wearing 125 pounds of armor, and snarling like the main contender at the World Wrestling Federation championship night. He wears a size-20 collar, a 10 1/2 hat, and a 56-inch belt. His biceps burst, thigh muscles ripple, and boasts belch through the canyon. "This day I defy the ranks of Israel! Give me a man and let us fight each other" (1 Sam. 17:10 NIV). *Who will go mano a mano conmigo? Give me your best shot.*

No Hebrew volunteers. Until today. Until David.

David just showed up this morning. He clocked out of sheep watching to deliver bread and cheese to his brothers on the battlefront. That's where David hears Goliath defying God, and that's when David makes his decision. Then he takes his staff in his hand, and he chooses for himself five smooth stones from the brook and puts them in a shepherd's bag, in a pouch that he has, and his sling is in his hand. And he draws near to the Philistine (17:40).[7]

Goliath scoffs at the kid, nicknames him Twiggy. "Am I a dog, that you come to me with sticks?" (17:43 NASB). Skinny, scrawny David. Bulky, brutish Goliath. What odds do you give David against his giant?

Better odds, perhaps, than you give yourself against yours.

Your Goliath doesn't carry sword or shield; he brandishes blades of unemployment, abandonment, sexual abuse, or depression. Your giant doesn't parade up and down the hills of Elah; he prances through your office, your bedroom, your classroom. He brings bills you can't pay, grades you can't make, people you can't please, a career you can't escape, a past you can't shake, and a future you can't face.

You know well the roar of Goliath.

David faced one who fog horned his challenges morning and night. "For forty days, twice a day, morning and evening, the Philistine giant strutted in front of the Israelite army" (17:16 NLT). Yours does the same. First thought of the morning, last worry of the night—your Goliath dominates your day and infiltrates your joy.

How long has he stalked you? Goliath's family was an ancient foe of the Israelites. Joshua drove them out of the promised land three hundred years earlier. He destroyed everyone except the residents of three cities: Gaza, Gath, and Ashdod. Gath bred giants like Yosemite grows sequoias.

Saul's soldiers saw Goliath and mumbled, "Not again. My dad fought his dad. My granddad fought his granddad."

You've groaned similar words. "I'm becoming a workaholic, just like my father." "Divorce streaks through our family tree like oak wilt." "My mom couldn't keep a friend either. Is this ever going to stop?"

Goliath: the long-standing bully of the valley. He awaits you in the morning, torments you at night. He stalked your ancestors and now looms over you. He blocks the sun and leaves you standing in the shadow of a doubt. "When Saul and his troops heard the Philistine's challenge, they were terrified and lost all hope" (v. 11 MSG).

But what am I telling you? You know Goliath. You recognize his walk and wince at his talk. You've seen your Godzilla. The question is, is he all you see? You know his voice—but is it all you hear? David saw and heard more. Read the first words he spoke, not just in the battle, but in the Bible: "David asked the men standing near him, 'What will be done for the man who kills this Philistine and removes this disgrace from Israel? Who is this uncircumcised Philistine that he should defy the armies of the living God?'" (v. 26 NIV).

David shows up discussing God. The soldiers mentioned nothing about him, the brothers never spoke his name, but David takes one step onto the stage and raises the subject of the living God. He does the same with King Saul: no chitchat about the battle or questions about the odds. Just a God-birthed announcement: "The LORD, who delivered me from the paw of the lion and from the paw of the bear, He will deliver me from the hand of this Philistine" (v. 37 NKJV).

He continues the theme with Goliath. When the giant mocks David, the shepherd boy replies:

> "You come against me with sword and spear and javelin, but I come against you in the name of the LORD Almighty, the God of the armies of Israel, whom you have defied. This day the LORD will deliver you into my hands, and I'll strike you down and cut off your head. Today I will give the carcasses of the Philistine army to the birds of the air and the beasts of the earth, and the whole world will know that there is a God in Israel. All those gathered here will know that it is not by sword or spear that the LORD saves; for the battle is the LORD's, and he will give all of you into our hands." (vv. 45–47 NIV)

No one else discusses God. David discusses no one else but God. A subplot appears in the story. More than "David versus Goliath," this is "God-focus versus giant-focus."

David sees what others don't and refuses to see what others do. He sees the giant, mind you; he just sees God more so. Look carefully at David's battle cry: "You come to me with a sword, with a spear, and with a javelin. But I come to you in the name of the LORD of hosts, the God of the armies of Israel" (17:45 NKJV).

Note the plural noun—armies of Israel. Armies? The common observer sees only one army of Israel. Not David. He sees the Allies on D-day: platoons of angels and infantries of saints, the weapons of the wind and the forces of the earth. God could pellet the enemy with hail as he did for Moses, collapse walls as he did for Joshua, stir thunder as he did for Samuel.[8]

David sees the armies of God. And because he does, David hurries and runs toward the army to meet the Philistine (v. 48).

David's brothers cover their eyes, both in fear and embarrassment. Saul sighs as the young Hebrew races to certain death. Goliath throws back his head in laughter, just enough to shift his helmet and expose a square inch of forehead flesh. David spots the target and seizes the moment. The sound of the swirling sling is the only sound in the valley. The stone torpedoes through the air and into the skull; Goliath's eyes cross and legs buckle. He crumples to the ground and dies. David runs over and yanks Goliath's sword from its sheath, shish kebabs the Philistine, and cuts off his head.

You might say that David knew how to get a head of his giant.

When was the last time you did the same? How long since you ran toward your challenge? We tend to retreat, duck behind a desk of work, or crawl into a nightclub of distraction or a bed of forbidden love. For a moment, a day, or a year, we feel safe, insulated, anesthetized, but then the work runs out, the liquor wears off, or the lover leaves, and we hear Goliath again.

Try a different tack. Rush your giant with a God-saturated soul. Giant of divorce, you aren't entering my home! Giant of depression? It may take a lifetime, but you won't conquer me. Giant of alcohol, bigotry, child abuse, insecurity . . . you're going down. How long since you loaded your sling and took a swing at your giant?

Too long, you say? Then David is your model. God called him "a man after my own heart" (Acts 13:22 NIV). He gave the appellation to no one else. Not Abraham or Moses or Joseph. He called Paul an apostle, John his beloved, but neither was tagged a man after God's own heart.

One might read David's story and wonder what God saw in him. The fellow fell as often as he stood, stumbled as often as he conquered. He stared down Goliath, yet ogled at Bathsheba; defied God-mockers in the valley, yet joined them in the wilderness. He could lead armies but couldn't manage a family. Raging David. Weeping David. Bloodthirsty. God-hungry. Eight wives. One God.

A man after God's own heart? That God saw him as such gives hope to us all.

David's life has little to offer the unstained saint. Straight-A souls find David's story disappointing. The rest of us find it reassuring. We ride the same roller coaster.

In David's good moments, no one was better. In his bad moments, could one be worse? The heart God loved was a checkered one.

We need David's story. Giants lurk in our neighborhoods. Rejection. Failure. Revenge. Remorse.

Giants. We must face them. Yet we need not face them alone. Focus first, and most, on God. The times David did, giants fell. The days he didn't, David did.

Test this theory with an open Bible. Read 1 Samuel 17 and list the observations David made regarding Goliath.

I find only two. One statement to Saul about Goliath (v. 36). And one to Goliath's face: "Who is this uncircumcised Philistine that he should defy the armies of the living God?" (v. 26 NIV).

That's it. Two Goliath-related comments and no questions. No inquiries about Goliath's skill, age, social standing, or IQ. David asks nothing about the weight of the spear, the size of the shield, or the meaning of the skull and crossbones tattooed on the giant's bicep. David gives no thought to the diplodocus on the hill.

But he gives much thought to God. Read David's words again, this time underlining his references to his Lord.

"The armies of the living God" (v. 26).

"The armies of the living God" (v. 36).

"The LORD of hosts, the God of the armies of Israel" (v. 45 NKJV).

"The LORD will deliver you into my hand . . . that all the earth may know that there is a God in Israel" (v. 46 NKJV).

"The LORD does not save with sword and spear; for the battle is the LORD's, and He will give you into our hands" (v. 47 NKJV).

I count nine references. God-thoughts outnumber Goliath-thoughts nine to two. Do you ponder God's grace four times as much as you ponder your guilt? Is your list of blessings four times as long as your list of complaints? Is your mental file of hope four times as thick as your mental file of dread? Are you four times as likely to describe the strength of God as you are the demands of your day?

No? Then David is your man.

Some note the absence of miracles in his story. No Red Sea openings, chariots flaming, or dead Lazaruses walking. No miracles.

But there is one. David is one. A rough-edged walking wonder of God who neon lights this truth:

Focus on giants—you stumble.

Focus on God—your giants tumble.

Lift your eyes, giant slayer. The God who made a miracle out of David stands ready to make one out of you.

REFLECTION AND DISCUSSION

Read 1 Samuel 17:1–54. What reason does David give for his confidence in a fight against Goliath (vv. 34–37)? What do verses 45–47 reveal about the man after God's own heart?

_____

_____

_____

_____

_____

_____

What Goliaths have you confronted in the past? How does your Goliath block your vision of God and make it harder to hear from the Lord?

_____

_____

_____

When you focus on your giants, what kind of stumbles do you tend to take? When you focus on God, what kind of tumbles do your giants tend to take?

_____

_____

_____

What Goliath is staring you in the face right now, taunting you and defying God to rescue you? Set aside time in which you focus on God—on his power and his wisdom and his glory—and in which you concentrate your prayers for help on this problem.

_____

_____

_____

ESTHER

ESTHER

BEFORE YOU BEGIN

Read Esther 4:13–16; 7:2–3 NKJV

Mordecai told them to answer Esther: "Do not think in your heart that you will escape in the king's palace any more than all the other Jews. For if you remain completely silent at this time, relief and deliverance will arise for the Jews from another place, but you and your father's house will perish. Yet who knows whether you have come to the kingdom for such a time as this?"

Then Esther told them to reply to Mordecai: "Go, gather all the Jews who are present in Shushan, and fast for me; neither eat nor drink for three days, night or day. My maids and I will fast likewise. And so I will go to the king, which is against the law; and if I perish, I perish!"

And on the second day, at the banquet of wine, the king again said to Esther, "What is your petition, Queen Esther? It shall be granted you. And what is your request, up to half the kingdom? It shall be done!"

Then Queen Esther answered and said, "If I have found favor in your sight, O king, and if it pleases the king, let my life be given me at my petition, and my people at my request."

I will never forget the time our family went desk shopping. I needed a new one for the office, and we'd promised Andrea and Sara desks for their rooms. Sara was especially enthused. When she comes home from school, guess what she does? She plays school! I never did that as a kid. I tried to forget the classroom activities, not rehearse them. Denalyn assures me not to worry, that this is one of those attention-span differences between genders. So off to the furniture store we went.

When Denalyn buys furniture, she prefers one of two extremes—so antique it's fragile or so new it's unpainted. This time we opted for the latter and entered a store of in-the-buff furniture.

Andrea and Sara succeeded quickly in making their selections, and I set out to do the same. Somewhere in the process Sara learned we weren't taking the desks home that day, and this news disturbed her deeply. I explained that the piece had to be painted and they would deliver the desk in about four weeks. I might as well have said four millennia.

Her eyes filled with tears, "But, Daddy, I wanted to take it home today."

Much to her credit she didn't stomp her feet and demand her way. She did, however, set out on an urgent course to change her father's mind. Every time I turned a corner, she was waiting on me.

"Daddy, don't you think we could paint it ourselves?"

"Daddy, I just want to draw some pictures on my new desk."

"Daddy, please let's take it home today."

After a bit she disappeared, only to return, arms open wide and bubbling with a discovery. "Guess what, Daddy. It'll fit in the back of the car!"

You and I know that a seven-year-old has no clue what will or won't fit in a vehicle, but the fact that she had measured the trunk with her arms softened my heart. The clincher, though, was the name she called me: "Daddy, can't we please take it home?"

The Lucado family took a desk home that day.

I heard Sara's request for the same reason God hears ours. Her desire was for her own good. What dad wouldn't want his child to spend more time writing and drawing? Sara wanted what I wanted for her, she only wanted it sooner. When we agree with what God wants, he hears us as well (see 1 John 5:14).

Sara's request was heartfelt. God, too, is moved by our sincerity. The "earnest prayer of a righteous man has great power" (James 5:16 TLB).

But most of all, I was moved to respond because Sara called me "Daddy." Because she is my child, I heard her request. Because we are his children, God hears ours. The King of creation gives special heed to the voices of his family. He is not only willing to hear us, he loves to hear us. He even tells us what to ask him.

"Thy kingdom come."

We're often content to ask for less. We enter the throne room of God with a satchel full of requests—promotions desired, pay raises wanted, transmission repairs needed, and tuitions due. We'd typically say our prayers as casually as we'd order a burger at the drive-through: "I'll have one solved problem and two blessings, cut the hassles, please."

But such complacency seems inappropriate in the chapel of worship. Here we are before the King of kings. The pay raise is still needed and the promotion is still desired, but is that where we start? Jesus tells us how to begin. "When you pray, pray like this. 'Our Father who is in heaven, hallowed be thy name. Thy kingdom come'" (Matt. 6:9, paraphrase).

When you say, "Thy kingdom come," you are inviting the Messiah himself to walk into your world. "Come, my King! Take your throne in our land. Be present in my heart. Be present in my office. Come into my marriage. Be Lord of my family, my fears, and my doubts." This is no feeble request; it's a bold appeal for God to occupy every corner of your life.

Who are you to ask such a thing? Who are you to ask God to take control of your world? You are his child, for heaven's sake! And so you ask boldly. "So let us come boldly to the very throne of God and stay there to receive his mercy and to find grace to help us in our times of need" (Heb. 4:16 TLB).

A wonderful illustration of this kind of boldness is in the story of Hadassah. Though her language and culture are an atlas apart from ours, she can tell you about the power of a prayer to a king. There are a couple of differences, though. Her request was not to her father, but to her husband, the king. Her prayer wasn't for a desk, but for the delivery of her people. And because she entered the throne room, because she opened her heart to the king, he changed his plans and millions of people in 127 different countries were saved.

Oh, how I'd love for you to meet Hadassah. But since she lived in the fifth century BC such an encounter is not likely. We'll have to be content with reading about her in the book that bears her name—her other name—the book of Esther.

Let's review the central characters.

Xerxes was the king of Persia. He was an absolute monarch over the land from India to Ethiopia. Let Xerxes raise an eyebrow and the destiny of the world would change. In this respect he symbolized the power of God, for our King guides the river of life, and he doesn't even raise an eyebrow.

Haman was the right-hand man of Xerxes. Read every word about the man and you'll find nothing good about him. He was an insatiable egotist who wanted the worship of every person in the kingdom. Perturbed by a peculiar minority called the Jews, he decided to exterminate them. He convinced Xerxes that the world would be better with a holocaust and set a date for the genocide of all Abraham's children.

Haman is a servant of hell and a picture of the devil himself, who has no higher aim than to have every knee bow as he passes. Satan also has no other plan than to persecute the promised people of God. He comes to "steal and kill and destroy" (John 10:10 NIV). "He is filled with anger, because he knows he does not have much time" (Rev. 12:12 NCV). Since the lie in the garden, he has sought to derail God's plan. In this case Satan hopes to destroy the Jews, thereby destroying the lineage of Jesus. For Haman, the massacre is a matter of expediency. For Satan, it is a matter of survival. He will do whatever it takes to impede the presence of Jesus in the world.

That's why he doesn't want you to pray as Jesus taught, "Thy kingdom come."

Esther, Mordecai's adopted daughter, became queen by winning a Miss Persia contest. In one day she went from obscurity to royalty, and in more ways than one she reminds you of you. Both of you are residents of the palace: Esther, the bride of Xerxes and you, the bride of Christ. Both of you have access to the throne of the king, and you both have a counselor to guide and teach you. Your counselor is the Holy Spirit. Esther's counselor was Mordecai.

It was Mordecai who urged Esther to keep her Jewish nationality a secret. It was also Mordecai who persuaded Esther to talk to Xerxes about the impending massacre.

You may wonder why she would need any encouragement. Mordecai must have wondered the same thing. Listen to the message he got from Esther:

> "No man or woman may go to the king in the inner courtyard without being called. There is only one law about this: Anyone who enters must be put to death unless the king holds out his gold scepter. Then that person may live. And I have not been called to go to the king for thirty days." (Est. 4:11 NCV)

As strange as it may sound to us, not even the queen could approach the king without an invitation. To enter his throne room uninvited was to risk a visit to the gallows. But Mordecai convinces her to take the risk. If you wonder why I see Mordecai as a picture of the Holy Spirit, watch how he encourages her to do what is right. "Just because you live in the king's palace, don't think that out of all the Jewish people you alone will escape. If you keep quiet at this time, someone else will help and save the Jewish people, but you and your father's family will all die. And who knows, you may have been chosen queen for such a time as this" (4:13–14 NCV).

Watch how Esther responds. "Esther put on her royal robes and stood in the inner courtyard of the king's palace, facing the king's hall . . . When the king saw Queen Esther standing in the courtyard, he was pleased. He held out to her the gold scepter that was in his hand, so Esther went forward and touched the end of it" (5:1–2 NCV).

What follows is the rapid collapse of Satan's deck of cards. Haman schemes to string up Mordecai, the only man who won't grovel at his feet. Esther plans to throw a couple of banquets for Xerxes and Haman. At the end of the second banquet Xerxes begs Esther to ask for something. Esther looks sort of sheepishly at the floor and says, "Well, now that you mention it, there is one small favor I've been wanting to ask." And she proceeds to inform the king about the raging anti-Semite who was hell-bent on killing her friends like rats, which meant that Xerxes was about to lose his bride if he didn't act soon, and you don't want that, do you honey?

Xerxes demands the name of the murderer, and Haman looks for the exits. Esther spills the beans, and Xerxes loses his cool. He storms out the door only to return and find Haman at the feet of Esther. Haman is begging for mercy, but the king thinks he's making a move on the queen. And before Haman has a chance to explain, he's headed to the same gallows he'd built for Mordecai.

Haman gets Mordecai's rope. Mordecai gets Haman's job. Esther gets a good night's sleep. The Jews live to see another day. And we get a dramatic reminder of what happens when we approach our King.

Like Esther, we have been plucked out of obscurity and given a place in the palace.

Like Esther, we have royal robes; she was dressed in cloth, we are dressed in righteousness.

Like Esther, we have the privilege of making our request.

That's what Sara did. Her request wasn't as dramatic as Esther's, but it changed her father's plans. By the way, the living parable of Sara and her desk didn't stop at the store.

On the way home she realized that my desk was still at the store. "I guess you didn't beg, did you, Daddy?" (We have not because we ask not.)

When we unloaded her desk she invited me to christen it with her by drawing a picture. I made a sign that read, "Sara's desk." She made a sign that read, "I love my Daddy." (Worship is the right response to answered prayer.)

My favorite part of the story is what happened the next day. I shared this account in my Sunday sermon. A couple from our church dropped by and picked the desk up, telling us they would paint it. When they returned it a couple of days later, it was covered with angels. And I was reminded that when we pray for God's kingdom to come, it comes! All the hosts of heaven rush to our aid.

REFLECTION AND DISCUSSION

Consider the phrase "thy kingdom come." When you think of God's coming kingdom, what comes to mind? Why do you think we should pray that God's kingdom would come?

_____

_____

_____

_____

_____

Read Esther 3–9. What part did Esther play in this drama? What part did Mordecai play? What was the role of the king? From the text's point of view, who is the central character?

_____

_____

_____

_____

_____

If God's kingdom were to come into your workplace, what would happen? In your marriage? In your family?

_____

_____

_____

_____

_____

_____

_____

_____

_____

_____

_____

_____

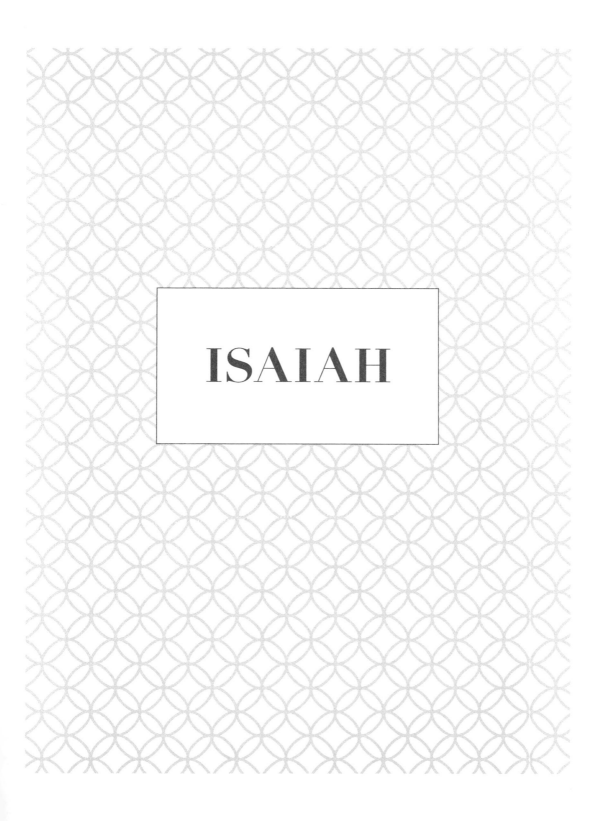

ISAIAH

ISAIAH

BEFORE YOU BEGIN

Read Isaiah 6:2–5 NASB 1995

Seraphim stood above Him, each having six wings: with two he covered his face, and with two he covered his feet, and with two he flew. And one called out to another and said, "Holy, Holy, Holy, is the LORD of hosts, The whole earth is full of His glory." And the foundations of the thresholds trembled at the voice of him who called out, while the temple was filling with smoke. Then I said, "Woe is me, for I am ruined! Because I am a man of unclean lips, And I live among a people of unclean lips; For my eyes have seen the King, the LORD of hosts."

John Hanning Speke stands on the river edge and stares at the wall of water. He has dedicated the better part of 1858 to getting here. For weeks he and his party slashed through African brush and forded deep rivers. Natives bearing iron-headed spears pursued them. Crocodiles and sterns kept an eye on them. But finally, after miles of jungle marching and grass plodding, they found the falls.

Only a Britisher could so clearly understate the sight. "We were well rewarded," he wrote in his journal.

The roar of the waters, the thousands of passenger fish leaping at the falls with all their might, the Wasoga and Waganda fishermen coming out in boats and taking post on all rocks with rod and hook, hippotami and crocodiles lying sleepily on the water made in all as interesting a picture as one would want to see.[9]

Speke could not leave. He sketched the sight over and over. He dedicated an entire day to simply staring at the majesty of the falls at the upper Nile. Not hard to understand why.

Fourteen years later, halfway around the globe, Frederick Dellenbaugh was equally impressed. He was only eighteen when he joined Major Powell on his pioneering river voyage through the Grand Canyon. Led by the one-armed Powell, the explorers floated on leaky boats and faced high waters. It's a wonder they survived. It's every bit as much a wonder what they saw. Dellenbaugh described the scene:

> My back being towards the fall I could not see it . . . Nearer and nearer came the angry tumult; the Major shouted "Back water!" there was a sudden dropping away of all support; then the mighty wavers [sic] smote us. The boat rose to them well, but we were flying at twenty-five miles an hour and at every leap the breakers rolled over us. "Bail!" shouted the Major,—"Bail for your lives!" and we dropped the oars to bail, though bailing was almost useless. . . . The boat rolled and pitched like a ship in a tornado. . . . canopies of foam pour[ed] over gigantic black boulders, first on one side, then on the other. . . . If you will take a watch and count by it ninety seconds, you will probably have about the time we were in this chaos, though it seemed much longer to me. Then we were through.[10]

Young Dellenbaugh knew rapids. Rivers and raging water were not new to him. The sudden immensity, stark intensity—something stole the oarsman's breath. He knew rapids. But none like this.

Speke, speechless. Dellenbaugh, drenched and awestruck.

And Isaiah, face-first on the temple floor. Arms crossed above his head, muffled voice crying for mercy. Like the explorers, he's just seen the unseen. But unlike the explorers, he's seen more than creation—he's seen the Creator. He's seen God.

Seven and one-half centuries before Christ, Isaiah was ancient Israel's version of a Senate chaplain or court priest. His family, aristocratic. His Hebrew, impeccable. Polished, professional, and successful. But the day he saw God only one response seemed appropriate: "Woe is me, for I am ruined." What caused such a confession? What stirred such a reply? The answer is found in the thrice-repeated words of the seraphim: "Holy, holy, holy."

> Seraphim stood above Him, each having six wings: with two he covered his face, and with two he covered his feet, and with two he flew. And one called out to another and said, "Holy, Holy, Holy, is the LORD of hosts, The whole earth is full of His glory."
>
> And the foundations of the thresholds trembled at the voice of him who called out, while the temple was filling with smoke. Then I said, "Woe is me, for I am ruined! Because I am a man of unclean lips, And I live among a people of unclean lips; For my eyes have seen the King, the LORD of hosts." (Isa. 6:2–5 NASB 1995)

On the one occasion seraphim appear in Scripture, they endlessly trilogize the same word.

"Holy, holy, holy is the LORD Almighty" (NIV). Repetition, in Hebrew, performs the work of our highlighter. A tool of emphasis. God, proclaims the six-winged angels, is not holy. He is not holy, holy. He is holy, holy, holy.

What other attribute receives such enforcement? No verse describes God as "wise, wise, wise" or "strong, strong, strong." Only as "holy, holy, holy." God's holiness commands headline attention. The adjective qualifies his name more than all other combined.[11] The first and final songs of the Bible magnify the holiness of God. Having crossed the Red Sea, Moses and the Israelites sang, "Who among the gods is like you, O LORD? Who is like you—majestic in holiness, awesome in glory, working wonders?" (Ex. 15:11 NIV). In Revelation those who had been victorious over the beast sang, "Who will not fear you, Lord, and bring glory to your name? For you alone are holy" (15:4 NIV).

The Hebrew word for *holy* is *qadosh*, which means "cut off" or "separate." Holiness, then, speaks of the "otherness" of God. His total uniqueness. Everything about God is different from the world he has made.

What you are to a paper airplane, God is to you. Take a sheet of paper and make one. Contrast yourself with your creation. Dare it to race you around the block. Who is faster? Invite the airplane to a game of one-on-one basketball. Will you not dominate the court?

And well you should. The thing has no brain waves, no pulse. It exists only because you formed it and flies only when someone throws it. Multiply the contrasts between you and the paper airplane by infinity, and you will begin to catch a glimpse of the disparity between God and us.

To what can we compare God? "Who in the skies is comparable to the LORD? Who among the sons of the mighty is like the LORD?"(Ps. 89:6 NASB). "To whom then will you liken God? Or what likeness will you compare with Him?" (Isa. 40:18 NASB). Even God asks, "To whom will you compare me? Who is my equal?" (Isa. 40:25 NLT).

As if his question needed an answer, he gives one:

I alone am God! I am God, and there is no one else like me. Only I can tell you the future before it even happens. Everything I plan will come to pass, for I do whatever I wish. I will call a swift bird of prey from the east—a leader from a distant land who will come and do my bidding. I have said I would do it, and I will do it. (Isa. 46:9–11 NLT)

Any pursuit of God's counterpart is in vain. Any search for godlike person or position on earth is futile. No one and nothing compares with him. No one advises him. No one helps him. It is he who "executes judgment, putting down one and lifting up another" (Ps. 75:7 ESV).

You and I may have power. But God is power. We may be a lightning bug, but he is lightning itself. "Wisdom and power are his" (Dan. 2:20 NIV).

Consider the universe around us. Unlike the potter who takes something and reshapes it, God took nothing and created something.

God even created the darkness. "I create the light and make the darkness" (Isa. 45:7 NLT). John proclaimed, "You created all things, and they exist because you created what you pleased" (Rev. 4:11 NLT).

Trace the universe back to God's power, and follow his power upstream to his wisdom. God's omniscience governs his omnipotence. Infinite knowledge rules infinite strength. "He is wise in heart, and mighty in strength" (Job 9:4 KJV). "He is mighty in strength and wisdom" (Job 36:5 KJV).

His power is not capricious or careless. Quite the contrary, his wisdom manages and equals his strength. Paul announced, "Oh, the depth of the riches of the wisdom and knowledge of God! How unsearchable his judgments, and his paths beyond tracing out" (Rom. 11:33 NIV).

His knowledge about you is as complete as his knowledge about the universe. "Even before a word is on my tongue, O LORD, you know it altogether. . . . Your eyes saw my unformed substance; in your book were written, every one of them, the days that were formed for me, when as yet there was none of them" (Ps. 139:4, 16 ESV).

The veils that block your vision and mine do not block God's. Unspoken words are as if uttered. Unrevealed thoughts are as if proclaimed. He knows the future, the past, the hidden, and the untold. Nothing is concealed from God. He is all-powerful, all-knowing, and all-present.

King David marveled, "Where can I go from Your Spirit? Or where can I flee from Your presence?" (Ps. 139:7 NASB). God reminds us, "I am everywhere—both near and far, in heaven and on earth" (Jer. 23:23–24 CEV).

See the "holy otherness" of God? In Isaiah's encounter, those who see him most clearly regard him most highly. He is so holy that sinless seraphim cannot bear to look at him!

They cover their faces with their wings. They also, oddly, cover their feet. Why? In Hebrew the word *feet* and the word for *genitalia* are the same.[12] Forgive the thought, but the confession of the angels is that they are absolutely impotent in the presence of God.

Isaiah could relate. When he sees the holiness of God, Isaiah does not boast or swagger. He takes no notes, plans no sermon series, launches no seminar tours. Instead, he falls on his face and begs for mercy. "Woe is me, for I am ruined! Because I am a man of unclean lips, and I live among people of unclean lips; for my eyes have seen the King, the LORD of hosts" (Isa. 6:5 NASB).

The God-given vision was not about Isaiah but about God and his glory. Isaiah gets the point. "It's not about me. It's all about him." He finds humility, not through seeking it, but through seeking him. One glimpse and the prophet claims citizenship among the infected and diseased—the "unclean," a term used to describe those with leprosy. God's holiness silences human boasting.

And God's mercy makes us holy. Look what happens next.

Then one of the seraphim flew to me with a burning coal in his hand, which he had taken from the altar with tongs. He touched my mouth with it and said, "Behold, this has touched your lips; and your iniquity is taken away and your sin is forgiven." (vv. 6–7 NASB 1995)

Isaiah makes no request. He asks for no grace. Indeed, he likely assumed mercy was impossible. But God, who is quick to pardon and full of mercy, purges Isaiah of his sin and redirects his life.

God solicits a spokesman. "Whom shall I send, and who will go for Us?" (v. 8 NASB 1995)

Isaiah's heart and hand shoot skyward. "Here am I. Send me!" (v. 8 NASB 1995). A glimpse of God's holiness and Isaiah had to speak. As if he'd found the source of the river, ridden the rage of the canyon. As if he'd seen what Moses had seen—God himself. Albeit a glimpse, but a God-glimpse nonetheless.

And he was different as a result. Holy different.

REFLECTION AND DISCUSSION

What does "holiness" mean to you? How would you describe it to someone who knows nothing about the Bible?

_____

_____

_____

_____

How does God's holiness silence human boasting?

_____

_____

_____

_____

_____

When was the last time you experienced God's quick pardon and fullness of mercy? Describe what happened. How did you recognize God's forgiveness?

_____

_____

_____

_____

_____

Read Isaiah 6:1–8. How does Isaiah react to this revelation of God's glory
(v. 5)? How do you think you would have reacted? Explain.

_____

_____

_____

_____

_____

_____

What resulted from Isaiah's cleansing (v. 8)? How do you think God wants to
use Isaiah's experience in your own life?

_____

_____

_____

_____

_____

JACOB

JACOB

BEFORE YOU BEGIN

Read Genesis 32:22–30 NIV

That night Jacob got up and took his two wives, his two female servants and his eleven sons and crossed the ford of the Jabbok. After he had sent them across the stream, he sent over all his possessions. So Jacob was left alone, and a man wrestled with him till daybreak. When the man saw that he could not overpower him, he touched the socket of Jacob's hip so that his hip was wrenched as he wrestled with the man. Then the man said, "Let me go, for it is daybreak."

But Jacob replied, "I will not let you go unless you bless me."

The man asked him, "What is your name?"

"Jacob," he answered.

Then the man said, "Your name will no longer be Jacob, but Israel, because you have struggled with God and with humans and have overcome."

Jacob said, "Please tell me your name."

But he replied, "Why do you ask my name?" Then he blessed him there.

So Jacob called the place Peniel, saying, "It is because I saw God face to face, and yet my life was spared."

He was the riverboat gambler of the patriarchs. A master of sleight of hand and fancy footwork. He had gained a seamy reputation for getting what he wanted by hook or crook—or both.

Twice he dealt hidden cards to his dull-witted brother Esau in order to climb the family tree. He once pulled the wool over the eyes of his own father, a trick especially dirty since his father's eyes were rather dim and this trick ensured him a gift he would never have received otherwise.

He later conned his father-in-law out of his best livestock and, when no one was looking, he took the kids and the cattle and skedaddled.

Yes, Jacob had a salty reputation, deservedly so. For him the ends always justified the means. His cleverness was outranked only by his audacity. His conscience was calloused just enough to let him sleep and his feet were just fast enough to keep him one step ahead of the consequences.

That is, until he reached a river called Jabbok (Genesis 32). At Jabbok his own cunning caught up with him.

Jacob was camped near the river Jabbok when word reached him that big, hairy Esau was coming to see him. It had been twenty years since Jacob had tricked his brother. More than enough time, Jacob realized, for Esau to stir up a boiling pot of revenge. Jacob was in trouble. He was finally forced to face up to himself and to God.

To Jacob's credit, he didn't run away from the problem. One must wonder why. Whatever the motivation, it was enough to cause him to come out of the shadows, cross Jabbok Creek alone, and face the facts.

The word *Jabbok* in Hebrew means "wrestle," and wrestle is what Jacob did. He wrestled with his past: all the white lies, scheming, and scandalizing. He wrestled with his situation: a spider trapped in his own web of deceit and craftiness. But more than anything, he wrestled with God.

He wrestled with the same God who had descended the ladder at Bethel to assure Jacob he wasn't alone. He met the same God who had earlier guaranteed Jacob that he would never break his promise. He confronted the same God who had reminded Jacob that the land prepared for him was still his.

Jacob wrestled with God the entire night. On the banks of Jabbok, he rolled in the mud of his mistakes. He met God face-to-face, sick of his past and in desperate need of a fresh start. And because Jacob wanted it so badly, God honored his determination. God gave him a new name and a new promise. But he also gave him a wrenched hip as a reminder of that mysterious night at the river.

Jacob wasn't the only man in the Bible to wrestle with self and God because of past antics. David did after his rendezvous with Bathsheba. Samson wrestled, blind and bald after Delilah's seduction. Elijah was at his own Jabbok when he heard the "still small voice" (1 Kings 19:12 NKJV). Peter wrestled with his guilt with echoes of a crowing cock still ringing in his ears.

And I imagine that most of us have spent some time on the riverbanks as well. Our scandalous deeds have a way of finding us. All of us at one time or another come face-to-face with our past. And it's always an awkward encounter. When our sins catch up with us we can do one of two things: run or wrestle.

Many choose to run. They brush it off with a shrug of rationalization. "I was a victim of circumstances." Or, "It was his fault." Or, "There are many who do worse things." The problem with this escape is that it's no escape at all. It's only a shallow camouflage. No matter how many layers of makeup you put over a black eye, underneath it is still black. And down deep it still hurts.

Jacob finally figured that out. As a result, his example is one worthy of imitation. The best way to deal with our past is to hitch up our pants, roll up our sleeves, and face it head-on.

We, too, should cross the creek alone and struggle with God over ourselves. We, too, should stand eyeball to eyeball with him and be reminded that left alone we fail. We, too, should unmask our stained hearts and grimy souls and be honest with the one who knows our most secret sins.

The result could be refreshing. We know it was for Jacob. After his encounter with God, Jacob was a new man. He crossed the river in the dawn of a new day and faced Esau with newfound courage.

Each step he took, however, was a painful one. His stiff hip was a reminder of the lesson he had learned at Jabbok: shady dealings bring pain. Mark it down: play today and tomorrow you'll pay.

And for you who wonder if you've played too long to change, take courage from Jacob's legacy. No man is too bad for God. To transform a riverboat gambler into a man of faith would be no easy task. But for God, it was all in a night's work.

REFLECTION AND DISCUSSION

What happens when we try to ignore the past?

_____

_____

_____

_____

_____

What does Max mean by "The best way to deal with our past is to hitch up our pants, roll up our sleeves, and face it head-on"? How is that different from dwelling on the past?

_____

_____

_____

_____

How can we wrestle with God in dealing with our past? In what way might we also carry a limp?

_____

_____

_____

_____

_____

_____

Have you ever worried that your past would prevent God from accepting you? What helped you change your thinking?

_____

_____

_____

_____

_____

_____

JAIRUS

JAIRUS

BEFORE YOU BEGIN
Read Mark 5:21-24, 35-43 NIV

When Jesus had again crossed over by boat to the other side of the lake, a large crowd gathered around him while he was by the lake. Then one of the synagogue leaders, named Jairus, came, and when he saw Jesus, he fell at his feet. He pleaded earnestly with him, "My little daughter is dying. Please come and put your hands on her so that she will be healed and live." So Jesus went with him.

A large crowd followed and pressed around him.

While Jesus was still speaking, some people came from the house of Jairus, the synagogue leader. "Your daughter is dead," they said. "Why bother the teacher anymore?"

Overhearing what they said, Jesus told him, "Don't be afraid; just believe."

He did not let anyone follow him except Peter, James and John the brother of James. When they came to the home of the synagogue leader, Jesus saw a commotion, with people crying and wailing loudly. He went in and said to them, "Why all this commotion and wailing? The child is not dead but asleep." But they laughed at him.

After he put them all out, he took the child's father and mother and the disciples who were with him, and went in where the child was. He took her by the hand and said to her, *"Talitha koum!"* (which means "Little girl, I say to you, get up!"). Immediately the girl stood up and began to walk around (she was twelve years old). At this they were completely astonished. He gave strict orders not to let anyone know about this, and told them to give her something to eat.

When my daughters were young, we tried an experiment.

I asked Jenna, then eight years old, to go to one side of the den. I had Andrea, six, stand on the other. Three-year-old Sara and I sat on the couch in the middle and watched. Jenna's job was to close her eyes and walk. Andrea's job was to be Jenna's eyes and talk her safely across the room.

With phrases like, "Take two baby steps to the left" and, "Take four giant steps straight ahead," Andrea successfully navigated her sister through a treacherous maze of chairs, a vacuum cleaner, and a laundry basket.

Then Jenna took her turn. She guided Andrea past her mom's favorite lamp and shouted just in time to keep her from colliding into the wall when she thought her right foot was her left foot.

After several treks through the darkness, they stopped and we processed.

"I didn't like it," Jenna complained. "It's scary going where you can't see."

"I was afraid I was going to fall," Andrea agreed. "I kept taking little steps to be safe."

I can relate, can't you? We grown-ups don't like the dark either. But we walk in it. We, like Jenna, often complain about how scary it is to walk where we can't see. And we, like Andrea, often take timid steps so we won't fall.

We've reason to be cautious: We are blind. Blind to the future.

It's one limitation we all share. The wealthy are just as blind as the poor. The educated are just as sightless as the unschooled. And the famous know as little about the future as the unknown.

None of us knows how our children will turn out. None of us knows the day we will die. No one knows whom he or she will marry or even if marriage lies before him or her. We are universally, absolutely, unalterably blind.

We are all Jenna with her eyes shut, groping through a dark room, listening for a familiar voice—but with one difference. Her surroundings are familiar and friendly. Ours can be hostile and fatal. Her worst fear is a stubbed toe. Our worst fear is more threatening: cancer, divorce, loneliness, death.

And try as we might to walk as straight as we can, chances are a toe is going to get stubbed and we are going to get hurt.

Just ask Jairus. He is a man who has tried to walk as straight as he can. But Jairus is a man whose path has taken a sudden turn into a cave—a dark cave. And he doesn't want to enter it alone.

Jairus is the leader of the synagogue. That may not mean much to you and me, but in the days of Christ the leader of the synagogue was the most important man in the community. The synagogue was the center of religion, education, leadership, and social activity. The leader of the synagogue was the senior religious leader, the highest-ranking professor, the mayor, and the best-known citizen all in one.

Jairus has it all. Job security. A guaranteed welcome at the coffee shop. A pension plan. Golf every Thursday and an annual all-expenses-paid trip to the national convention.

Who could ask for more? Yet Jairus does. In fact, he would trade the whole package of perks and privileges for just one assurance—that his daughter will live.

The Jairus we see in this story is not the clear-sighted, black-frocked, nicely groomed civic leader. He is instead a blind man begging for a gift. He fell at Jesus' feet, "saying again and again, 'My daughter is dying. Please come and put your hands on her so she will be healed and will live'" (Mark 5:23 NIV).

He doesn't barter with Jesus. He just pleads.

There are times in life when everything you have to offer is nothing compared to what you are asking to receive. Jairus is at such a point. What could a man offer in exchange for his child's life? So, there are no games. No haggling. No masquerades. The situation is starkly simple: Jairus is blind to the future and Jesus knows the future. So Jairus asks for his help.

And Jesus, who loves the honest heart, goes to give it.

And God, who knows what it is like to lose a child, empowers his Son.

But before Jesus and Jairus get very far, they are interrupted by emissaries from Jairus's house.

"Your daughter is dead. There is no need to bother the teacher anymore" (v. 35 NIV).

Get ready. Hang on to your hat. Here's where the story gets moving. Jesus goes from being led to leading, from being convinced by Jairus to convincing Jairus. From being admired to being laughed at, from helping out the people to casting out the people.

Here is where Jesus takes control.

"But Jesus paid no attention to what they said . . ." (v. 36 NRSV).

I love that line! It describes the critical principle for seeing the unseen: Ignore what people say. Block them out. Turn them off. Close your ears. And, if you must, walk away.

Ignore the ones who say it's too late to start over.

Disregard those who say you'll never amount to anything.

Turn a deaf ear toward those who say that you aren't smart enough, fast enough, tall enough, or big enough—ignore them.

Faith sometimes begins by stuffing your ears with cotton.

Jesus turns immediately to Jairus and pleads: "Don't be afraid; just believe" (v. 36 NIV).

Jesus compels Jairus to see the unseen. When Jesus says, "Just believe," he is imploring, "Don't limit your possibilities to the visible. Don't listen only for the audible. Don't be controlled by the logical. Believe there is more to life than meets the eye!"

"Trust me," Jesus is pleading. "Don't be afraid; just trust."

As Paul wrote: "We set our eyes not on what we see but on what we cannot see. What we see will last only a short time, but what we cannot see will last forever" (2 Cor. 4:18 NCV).

Jesus is asking Jairus to see the unseen. To make a choice. Either to live by the facts or to see by faith. When tragedy strikes we, too, are left to choose what we see. We can see either the hurt or the Healer.

The choice is ours.

Jairus made his choice. He opted for faith and Jesus . . . and faith in Jesus led him to his daughter.

At the house Jesus and Jairus encounter a group of mourners. Jesus is troubled by their wailing. It bothers him that they express such anxiety over death. "Why are you crying and making so much noise? The child is not dead, only asleep" (v. 39 NKJV).

That's not a rhetorical question. It's an honest one. From his perspective, the girl is not dead—she is only asleep. From God's viewpoint, death is not permanent. It is a necessary step for passing from this world to the next. It's not an end; it's a beginning.

As a young boy I had two great loves—playing and eating. Summers were made for afternoons on the baseball diamond and meals at Mom's dinner table. Mom had a rule, however. Dirty, sweaty boys could never eat at the table. Her first words to us as we came home were always, "Go clean up and take off those clothes if you want to eat."

Now, no boy is fond of bathing and dressing, but I never once complained and defied my mom by saying, "I'd rather stink than eat!" In my economy a bath and a clean shirt were a small price to pay for a good meal.

And from God's perspective death is a small price to pay for the privilege of sitting at his table. "Flesh and blood cannot have a part in the kingdom of God. . . . This body that can be destroyed must clothe itself with something that can never be destroyed. And this body that dies must clothe itself with something that can never die" (1 Cor. 15:50, 53 NCV).

God is even more insistent than my mom was. In order to sit at his table, a change of clothing must occur. And we must die in order for our body to be exchanged for a new one. So, from God's viewpoint, death is not to be dreaded; it is to be welcomed.

And when he sees people crying and mourning over death, he wants to know, "Why are you crying?" (v. 39 NCV).

When we see death, we see disaster. When Jesus sees death, he sees deliverance.

That's too much for the people to take. "They laughed at him" (v. 40 NCV). (The next time people mock you, you might remember they mocked him too.)

Now look closely because you aren't going to believe what Jesus does next. He throws the mourners out! That's what the text says: "after throwing them out of the house . . ." (v. 40 NCV). He doesn't just ask them to leave. He throws them out. He picks them up by collar and belt and sets them sailing. Jesus' response is decisive and strong. In the original text, the word used here is the same word used to describe what Jesus did to the money changers in the temple. It's the same verb used thirty-eight times to describe what Jesus did to the demons.

Why? Why such force? Why such intolerance?

Perhaps the answer is found by going back to my family's living room experience. After Jenna and Andrea had taken turns guiding each other through the den, I decided to add a diabolical twist. On the last trip, I snuck up behind Jenna, who was walking with her eyes shut, and began whispering, "Don't listen to her. Listen to me. I'll take care of you."

Jenna stopped. She analyzed the situation and made her choice between the two voices. "Be quiet, Daddy," she giggled and then continued in Andrea's direction.

Undeterred, I grabbed the lid of a pan, held it next to her ear, and banged it with a spoon. She jumped and stopped, startled by the noise. Andrea, seeing that her pilgrim was frightened, did a great thing. She ran across the room and threw her arms around her sister and said, "Don't worry, I'm right here."

She wasn't about to let the noise distract Jenna from the journey.

And God isn't going to let the noise distract you from yours. He's still busy casting out the critics and silencing the voices that could deter you.

Some of his work you have seen. Most of it you haven't.

Only when you get home will you know how many times he has protected you from luring voices. Only eternity will reveal the time he:

Interfered with the transfer, protecting you from involvement in unethical business.

Fogged in the airport, distancing you from a shady opportunity.

Flattened your tire, preventing you from checking into the hotel and meeting a seductive man.

And only heaven will show the times he protected you by:

Giving you a mate who loves God more than you do.

Opening the door for a new business so you could attend the same church.

Having the right voice with the right message on the right radio station the day you needed his encouragement.

Mark it down: God knows you and I are blind. He knows living by faith and not by sight doesn't come naturally. And I think that's one reason he raised Jairus's daughter from the dead. Not for her sake—she was better off in heaven. But for our sake—to teach us that heaven sees when we trust.

One final thought from the seeing-with-your-eyes-closed experiment. I asked Jenna how she could hear Andrea's voice guiding her across the room when I was trying to distract her by whispering in her ear.

Her answer? "I just concentrated and listened as hard as I could."

REFLECTION AND DISCUSSION

What was Max trying to teach his young daughters through this "faith experiment"? What did you learn from his experiment?

_____

_____

_____

_____

_____

_____

_____

_____

Do you ever wish you could see into the future? What would be the benefits of doing so? The drawbacks? If you could acquire the ability to see your whole future, would you do so? Explain.

_____

_____

_____

_____

_____

Max claims that a critical principle for seeing the unseen is to ignore what people say. What does he mean? What sort of people do you ignore? What kinds of advice do you refuse to heed? Couldn't Max's advice be dangerous in some circumstances? In what kind of circumstances?

_____

_____

_____

_____

_____

Why did Jesus throw the people out of Jairus's home?

_____

_____

_____

_____

_____

_____

_____

_____

Read 2 Corinthians 4:16–18. How permanent is the world we see? How permanent is the world we do not see? How do we "set our eyes" on Jesus?

_____

_____

_____

_____

_____

_____

_____

JESUS'
BROTHERS

JESUS' BROTHERS

BEFORE YOU BEGIN
Read Mark 3:35 NIV

"Whoever does God's will is my brother and sister and mother."

Give me a word picture to describe a relative in your life who really bugs you."

I was asking the question of a half-dozen friends sitting around a lunch table. They all gave me one of those *what-in-the-world?* expressions. So I explained.

"I keep meeting people who can't deal with somebody in their family. Either their mother-in-law is a witch or their uncle is a bum or they have a father who treats them like they were never born."

Now their heads nodded. We were connecting. And the word pictures started coming.

"I've got a description," one volunteered. "A parasite on my neck. My wife has this brother who never works and always expects us to provide."

"A cactus wearing a silk shirt," said another. "It's my mother. She looks nice.

Everyone thinks she's the greatest, but get close to her and she is prickly, dry, and . . . thirsty for life."

"A marble column," was the way another described an aunt. Dignified, noble, but high and hard.

"Tar baby in Br'er Rabbit," someone responded. Everyone understood the reference except me. I didn't remember the story of Br'er Rabbit. I asked for the short version. Wily Fox played a trick on Br'er Rabbit. The fox made a doll out of tar and stuck it on the side of the road. When Rabbit saw the tar baby, he thought it was a person and stopped to visit.

It was a one-sided conversation. The tar baby's silence bothered the rabbit. He couldn't stand to be next to someone and not communicate with him. So in his frustration he hit the tar baby and stuck to it. He hit the tar baby again with the other hand and, you guessed it, the other hand got stuck.

"That's how we are with difficult relatives," my fable-using friend explained. "We're stuck to someone we can't communicate with."

Stuck is right. It's not as if they are neighbors you can move away from or employees you can fire. They are family. And you can choose your friends, but you can't . . . well, you know. Odds are, you probably know very well.

You've probably got a tar baby in your life, someone you can't talk to and can't walk away from. A mother who whines, an uncle who slurps his soup, a dad who is still waiting for you to get a real job, or a mother-in-law who wonders why her daughter married you.

Tar-baby relationships—stuck together but falling apart.

It's like a crammed elevator. People thrust together by chance on a short journey, saying as little as possible. The only difference is you'll eventually get off the elevator and never see these folks again—not so with difficult relatives. Family reunions, Christmas, Thanksgiving, weddings, funerals—they'll be there.

And you'll be there sorting through the tough questions. Why does life get so relatively difficult? If we expect anyone to be sensitive to our needs, it is our family members. When we hurt physically, we want our family to respond. When we struggle emotionally, we want our family to know.

But sometimes they act like they don't know. Sometimes they act like they don't care. What can you do when those closest to you keep their distance? When you can get along with others, but you and your kin can't?

Does Jesus have anything to say about dealing with difficult relatives? Is there an example of Jesus bringing peace to a painful family? Yes, there is. His own.

It may surprise you to know that Jesus had a difficult family. It may surprise you to know that Jesus had a family at all! You may not be aware that Jesus had brothers and sisters. He did. Quoting Jesus' hometown critics, Mark wrote, "[Jesus] is just the carpenter, the son of Mary and the brother of James, Joseph, Judas, and Simon. And his sisters are here with us" (Mark 6:3 NCV).

And it may surprise you to know that his family was less than perfect. If your family doesn't appreciate you, take heart, neither did Jesus'. "A prophet is honored everywhere except in his hometown and with his own people and in his own home" (v. 4 NCV).

I wonder what he meant when he said those last five words. He went to the synagogue where he was asked to speak. The people were proud that this hometown boy had done well—until they heard what he said. He referred to himself as the Messiah, the one to fulfill prophecy.

Their response? "Isn't this Joseph's son?" Translation? This is no Messiah! He's just like us!

One minute he was a hero, the next a heretic. Look what happens next. "They got up, forced Jesus out of town, and took him to the edge of the cliff on which the town was built. They planned to throw him off the edge, but Jesus walked through the crowd and went on his way" (Luke 4:29–30 NCV).

What an ugly moment! Jesus' neighborhood friends tried to kill him. But even uglier than what we see is what we don't see. Notice what is missing from this verse. Note what words should be there, but aren't. "They planned to throw him over the cliff, but Jesus' brothers came and stood up for him."

We'd like to read that, but we can't because it doesn't say that. That's not what happened. When Jesus was in trouble, his brothers were invisible.

They weren't always invisible, however. There was a time when they spoke. There was a time when they were seen with him in public. Not because they were proud of him but because they were ashamed of him. "His family . . . went to get him because they thought he was out of his mind" (Mark 3:21 NCV).

Jesus' siblings thought their brother was a lunatic. They weren't proud—they were embarrassed!

Hurtful words spoken by those closest to Jesus.

Here are some more:

So Jesus' brothers said to him, "You should leave here and go to Judea so your followers there can see the miracles you do. Anyone who wants to be well known does not hide what he does. If you are doing these things, show yourself to the world." (John 7:3–5 NCV)

Listen to the sarcasm in those words! They drip with ridicule. How does Jesus put up with these guys? How can you believe in yourself when those who know you best don't? How can you move forward when your family wants to pull you back? When you and your family have two different agendas, what do you do?

Jesus gives us some answers.

It's worth noting that he didn't try to control his family's behavior, nor did he let their behavior control his. He didn't demand that they agree with him. He didn't sulk when they insulted him. He didn't make it his mission to try to please them.

Each of us has a fantasy that our next of kin will be our dearest friends. Jesus didn't have that expectation. Look how he defined his family: "My true brother and sister and mother are those who do what God wants" (Mark 3:35 NCV).

When Jesus' brothers didn't share his convictions, he didn't try to force them. He recognized that his spiritual family could provide what his physical family didn't. If Jesus himself couldn't force his family to share his convictions, what makes you think you can force yours?

We can't control the way our family responds to us. When it comes to the behavior of others toward us, our hands are tied. We have to move beyond the naive expectation that if we do good, people will treat us right. The fact is they may and they may not—we cannot control how people respond to us.

If your father is a jerk, you could be the world's best daughter and he still won't tell you so. If your aunt doesn't like your career, you could change jobs a dozen times and still never satisfy her. If your sister is always complaining about what you got and she didn't, you could give her everything and she still may not change.

If you think you can control people's behavior toward you, you are held in bondage by their opinions. If you think you can control their opinion and their opinion isn't positive, then guess who you have to blame? Yourself.

It's a game with unfair rules and fatal finishes. Jesus didn't play it, nor should you.

We don't know if Joseph affirmed his son Jesus in his ministry—but we know God did: "This is my Son, whom I love, and I am very pleased with him" (Matt. 3:17).

I can't assure you that your family will ever give you the blessing you seek, but I know God will. Let God give you what your family doesn't. If your earthly father doesn't affirm you, then let your heavenly Father take his place.

How do you do that? By emotionally accepting God as your Father. You see, it's one thing to accept him as Lord, another to recognize him as Savior—but it's another matter entirely to accept him as Father.

To recognize God as Lord is to acknowledge that he is sovereign and supreme in the universe. To accept him as Savior is to accept his gift of salvation offered on the cross. To regard him as Father is to go a step further. Ideally, a father is the one in your life who provides and protects. That is exactly what God has done.

He has provided for your needs (Matt. 6:25–34). He has protected you from harm (Ps. 139:5). He has adopted you (Eph. 1:5). And he has given you his name (1 John 3:1).

God has proven himself as a faithful Father. Now it falls to us to be trusting children. Let God give you what your family doesn't. Let him fill the void others have left. Rely upon him for your affirmation and encouragement. Look at Paul's words: "You are God's child, and God will give you the blessing he promised, because you are his child" (Gal. 4:7 NCV).

Having your family's approval is desirable but not necessary for happiness and not always possible. Jesus did not let the difficult dynamic of his family overshadow his call from God. And because he didn't, this chapter has a happy ending.

What happened to Jesus' family?

Mine with me a golden nugget hidden in a vein of the book of Acts. "Then [the disciples] went back to Jerusalem from the Mount of Olives. . . . They all continued praying together with some women, including Mary the mother of Jesus, and Jesus' brothers" (Acts 1:12, 14).

What a change! The ones who mocked him now worship him. The ones who pitied him now pray for him. What if Jesus had disowned them? Or worse still, what if he'd suffocated his family with his demand for change?

He didn't. He instead gave them space, time, and grace. And because he did, they changed. How much did they change? One brother became an apostle (Gal. 1:19) and others became missionaries (1 Cor. 9:5).

So don't lose heart. God still changes families. A tar baby today might be your dearest friend tomorrow.

REFLECTION AND DISCUSSION

Do you have any "tar-baby relatives"? If so, what makes it hard to communicate with them?

_____

_____

_____

_____

_____

How does it make you feel to know that Jesus had a difficult family?

_____

_____

_____

_____

_____

_____

Go back through the chapter and list the many ways Jesus' family dishonored him. How did Jesus respond to these insults? What can we learn from these incidents?

_____

_____

_____

_____

_____

_____

Max writes, "It's worth noting that [Jesus] didn't try to control his family's behavior, nor did he let their behavior control his." In what ways is this an excellent principle for us?

_____

_____

_____

_____

_____

How did the members of Jesus' family finally change in their appraisal of him? How can this give us hope?

_____

_____

_____

_____

_____

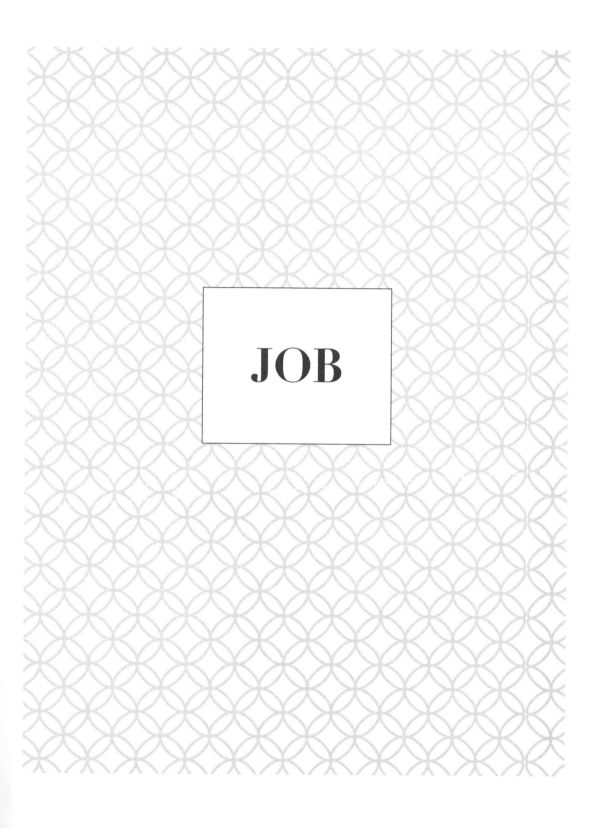

JOB

JOB

BEFORE YOU BEGIN
Read Job 1:1-3; 2:6-8; 40:1-4 NIV

In the land of Uz there lived a man whose name was Job. This man was blame-
less and upright; he feared God and shunned evil. He had seven sons and three
daughters, and he owned seven thousand sheep, three thousand camels, five
hundred yoke of oxen and five hundred donkeys, and had a large number of
servants. He was the greatest man among all the people of the East.

The LORD said to Satan, "Very well, then, he is in your hands; but you must
spare his life."

So Satan went out from the presence of the LORD and afflicted Job with
painful sores from the soles of his feet to the crown of his head. Then Job
took a piece of broken pottery and scraped himself with it as he sat among
the ashes.

The LORD said to Job:
"Will the one who contends with the Almighty correct him?
Let him who accuses God answer him!"

Then Job answered the LORD:

"I am unworthy—how can I reply to you?
I put my hand over my mouth.

When I lived in Brazil I took my mom and her friend to see Iguazu Falls, the largest waterfalls in the world. Some weeks earlier I'd become an expert on the cataracts by reading an article in a *National Geographic* magazine. Surely, I thought, my guests would appreciate their good fortune in having me as a guide.

To reach the lookout point, tourists must walk a winding trail that leads them through a forest. I took advantage of the hike to give an Iguazu nature report to my mom and her friend. After some minutes, however, I caught myself speaking louder and louder. A sound in the distance forced me to raise my voice. With each turn in the trail, my volume increased. Finally, I was shouting above a roar, which was proving to be quite irritating.

Only after reaching the clearing did I realize that the noise we heard was the waterfalls. My words were drowned out by the force and fury of what I was trying to describe. I could no longer be heard.

There are times when to speak is to violate the moment . . . when silence represents the highest respect. The word for such times is *reverence*. The prayer for such times is "Hallowed be thy name." Only you and God are here, and you can surmise who occupies the throne.

Don't worry about having the right words; worry more about having the right heart. It's not eloquence he seeks, just honesty.

This was a lesson Job learned. If he had a fault, it was his tongue. He talked too much.

Not that anyone could blame him. Calamity had pounced on the man like a lioness on a herd of gazelles, and by the time the rampage passed, there was hardly a wall standing or a loved one living. Enemies had slaughtered Job's cattle, and lightning had destroyed his sheep. Strong winds had left his partying kids buried in wreckage.

And that was just the first day. Job hadn't even had time to call anyone before he saw the leprosy on his hands and the boils on his skin. His wife, compassionate soul that she was, told him to "curse God and die" (2:9 NIV). His four friends came with the bedside manner of drill sergeants, telling him that God is fair and pain is the result of evil, and as sure as two-plus-two equals four, Job must have some criminal record in his past to suffer so.

Each had his own interpretation of God and each spoke long and loud about who God is and why God did what he did. They weren't the only ones talking about God. When his accusers paused, Job gave his response. Back and forth they went . . .

Job cried out . . . (3:1).

Then Eliphaz the Temanite answered . . . (4:1).

Then Job answered . . . (6:1).

Then Bildad the Shuhite answered . . . (8:1).

Then Job answered . . . (9:1).

Then Zophath the Naamathite answered . . . (11:1).

This verbal ping-pong continues for twenty-three chapters. Finally Job has enough of this "answering." No more discussion-group chit chat. It's time for the keynote address. He grips the microphone with one hand and the pulpit with the other and launches forth. For six chapters Job gives his opinions on God. This time the chapter headings read: "And Job continued," "And Job continued," "And Job continued." He defines God, explains God, and reviews God. One gets the impression that Job knows more about God than God does!

We are thirty-seven chapters into the book before God clears his throat to speak. Chapter 38 begins with these words: "Then the LORD answered Job."

"I will ask you questions and you must answer me. Where were you when I made the earth's foundation? Tell me if you understand. Who marked off how big it should be? Surely you know! Who stretched a ruler across it? What were the earth's foundations set on, or who put its cornerstone in place while the morning stars sang together and all the angels shouted with joy?" (38:3–6 NCV)

God floods the sky with queries, and Job cannot help but get the point: Only God defines God. For the first time, Job is quiet. Silenced by a torrent of questions.

Have you ever gone to where the sea begins or walked the valleys under the sea? . . .
Have you ever gone to the storehouse for snow or seen the storehouses for hail . . . ?
Are you the one who gives the horse his strength or puts the flowing mane on its neck?
Do you make the horse jump like a locust? . . . Is it through your wisdom that the hawk
flies and spreads its wings toward the south? (38:16, 22; 39:19–20, 26 NCV)

Job barely has time to shake his head at one question before he is asked another. The Father's implication is clear: "As soon as you are able to handle these simple matters of storing stars and stretching the neck of the ostrich, then we'll have a talk about pain and suffering. But until then, we can do without your commentary."

Job understands the message and replies, "I am not worthy; I cannot answer you anything, so I will put my hand over my mouth" (40:4 NCV).

Notice the change. Before he heard God, Job couldn't speak enough. After he heard God, he couldn't speak at all.

Silence was the only proper response. There was a time in the life of Thomas à Kempis when he, too, covered his mouth. He had written profusely about the character of God. But one day God confronted him with such holy grace that, from that moment on, all à Kempis's words "seemed like straw." He put down his pen and never wrote another line. He put his hand over his mouth.

The word for such moments is *reverence*: "Hallowed be thy name."

This phrase is a petition, not a proclamation. A request, not an announcement. Hallowed be your name. Do whatever it takes to be holy in my life. Take your rightful place on the throne. Exalt yourself. Magnify yourself. Glorify yourself. You be Lord, and I'll be quiet.

The word *hallowed* comes from the word *holy*, and the word *holy* means "to separate." The ancestry of the term can be traced back to an ancient word that means "to cut." To be holy, then, is to be a cut above the norm, superior, extraordinary. The Holy One dwells on a different level from the rest of us. What frightens us does not frighten him. What troubles us does not trouble him.

I'm more a landlubber than a sailor, but I've puttered around in a bass boat enough to know the secret for finding land in a storm . . . You don't aim at another boat. You certainly don't stare at the waves. You set your sights on an object unaffected by the wind—a light on the shore—and go straight toward it. The light is unaffected by the storm.

When you set your sights on our God, you focus on one "a cut above" any storm life may bring.

Like Job, you find peace in the pain. Like Job, you cover your mouth and sit still. "Be still and know that I am God" (Ps. 46:10 NCV). This verse contains a command with a promise.

The command? Be still. Cover your mouth. Bend your knees. The promise? You will know that I am God. The vessel of faith journeys on soft waters. Belief rides on the wings of waiting.

In the midst of your daily storms, make it a point to be still and set your sights on him. Let God be God. Let him bathe you in his glory so that both your breath and your troubles are sucked from your soul. Be still. Be quiet. Be open and willing. Then you will know that God is God, and you can't help but confess, "Hallowed be thy name."

REFLECTION AND DISCUSSION

How does one "hallow" God's name? From the opposite viewpoint, how does one profane it? In the last week, did you do more of one than the other? Explain.

_____

_____

_____

_____

Read Job 38:3–18. What is the point of all God's questions? What lesson does he want Job to learn? What do you learn about God in this passage?

_____

_____

_____

_____

_____

_____

Read Job 40:4–5; 42:1–6. What did Job finally learn about God? How did it change his attitude toward his circumstances?

_____

_____

_____

_____

_____

_____

If you had been in Job's shoes, do you think you would have reacted much as he did? Why or why not?

_____

_____

_____

_____

_____

_____

_____

In times of trouble, do you ever demand answers of God? If he were to respond to your questions, what do you think he'd say?

_____

_____

_____

_____

_____

_____

JOHN

JOHN

BEFORE YOU BEGIN

Read John 20:2-8 NIV

She came running to Simon Peter and the other disciple, the one Jesus loved, and said, "They have taken the Lord out of the tomb, and we don't know where they have put him!"

So Peter and the other disciple started for the tomb. Both were running, but the other disciple outran Peter and reached the tomb first. He bent over and looked in at the strips of linen lying there but did not go in. Then Simon Peter came along behind him and went straight into the tomb. He saw the strips of linen lying there, as well as the cloth that had been wrapped around Jesus' head. The cloth was still lying in its place, separate from the linen. Finally the other disciple, who had reached the tomb first, also went inside. He saw and believed.

What do you say we have a chat about graveclothes? Sound like fun? Sound like a cheery topic? Hardly. Make a list of depressing subjects, and burial garments is somewhere between IRS audits and long-term dental care.

No one likes graveclothes. No one discusses graveclothes. Have you ever spiced up dinner table chat with the question, "What are you planning to wear in your casket?" Have you ever seen a store specializing in burial garments?

The apostle John, however, was an exception. Ask him, and he'll tell you how he came to see burial garments as a symbol of triumph. He didn't always see them that way. A tangible reminder of the death of his best friend, Jesus, they used to seem like a symbol of tragedy. But on the first Easter Sunday, God took the clothing of death and made it a symbol of life.

Could he do the same for you? We all face tragedy. What's more, we've all received the symbols of tragedy.

Could God use such things for something good? How far can we go with verses like Romans 8:28? "In everything God works for the good of those who love him" (ESV). Does "everything" include tumors and tests and tempers and terminations? John would answer yes. John would tell you that God can turn any tragedy into a triumph, if only you will wait and watch.

To prove his point, he would tell you about one Friday in particular.

Later, Joseph from Arimathea asked Pilate if he could take the body of Jesus. Pilate gave his permission, so Joseph came and took Jesus' body away. Nicodemus, who earlier had come to Jesus at night, went with Joseph. He brought about seventy-five pounds of myrrh and aloes. [The amount is worth noting, for such a quantity of burial ointments was typically used only for kings.] These two men took Jesus' body and wrapped it with the spices in pieces of linen cloth, which is how they bury the dead. (John 19:38–40, paraphrase)

Reluctant during Christ's life but courageous at his death, Joseph and Nicodemus came to serve Jesus. They came to bury him. They ascended the hill bearing the burial clothing.

Could there have been a greater tragedy for John than a dead Jesus? John didn't know on that Friday what you and I now know. He didn't know that Friday's tragedy would be Sunday's triumph. John would later confess that he "did not yet understand from the Scriptures that Jesus must rise from the dead" (John 20:9 NCV).

That's why what he did on Saturday is so important. We don't know anything about this day; we have no passage to read, no knowledge to share. All we know is this: When Sunday came, John was still present. When Mary Magdalene came looking for him, she found him.

You'd think John would have left. Who was to say that the men who crucified Christ wouldn't come after him? Why didn't John get out of town?

Perhaps the answer was pragmatic; perhaps he was taking care of Jesus' mother. Or perhaps he didn't have anywhere else to go. Could be he didn't have any money or energy or direction . . . or all of the above. Or maybe he lingered because he loved Jesus.

To others, Jesus was a miracle worker. To others, Jesus was a master teacher. To others, Jesus was the hope of Israel. But to John, he was all of these and more. To John, Jesus was a friend.

You don't abandon a friend—not even when that friend is dead. John stayed close to Jesus.

He had a habit of doing this. He was close to Jesus in the upper room. He was close to Jesus in the Garden of Gethsemane. He was at the foot of the cross at the crucifixion, and he was a quick walk from the tomb at the burial.

Did he understand Jesus? No. Was he glad Jesus did what he did? No. But did he leave Jesus? No.

What about you? When you're in John's position, what do you do? When it's Saturday in your life, how do you react? When you are somewhere between yesterday's tragedy and tomorrow's triumph, what do you do? Do you leave God—or do you linger near him?

John chose to linger. And because he lingered on Saturday, he was around on Sunday to see the miracle.

Mary said, "They have taken the Lord out of the tomb, and we don't know where they have put him" (John 20:2 NIV).

So Peter and the other follower started for the tomb. They were both running, but the other follower ran faster than Peter and reached the tomb first. He bent down and looked in and saw the strips of linen cloth lying there, but he did not go in. Then following him, Simon Peter arrived and went into the tomb and saw the strips of linen lying there. He also saw the cloth that had been around Jesus' head, which was folded up and laid in a different place from the strips of linen. Then the other follower, who had reached the tomb first, also went in. He saw and believed. (John 20:2–8 NCV)

Very early on Sunday morning Peter and John were given the news: "Jesus' body is missing!" Mary was urgent, both with her announcement and her opinion. She thought Jesus' enemies had taken his body away. Instantly the two disciples hurried to the sepulcher, John outrunning Peter and arriving first. What he saw so stunned him he froze at the entrance.

What did he see? "Strips of linen cloth." He saw "the cloth that had been around Jesus' head . . . folded up and laid in a different place from the strips of linen." He saw "cloth lying."

The original Greek provides helpful insight here. John employs a term that means "rolled up,"[13] "still in their folds."[14] These burial wraps had not been ripped off and thrown down. They were still in their original state! The linens were undisturbed. The graveclothes were still rolled and folded.

How could this be? This was John's question, and this question led to John's discovery. "He saw and believed" (John 20:8 NIV).

Through the rags of death, John saw the power of life. Should we be surprised that he takes the wrappings of death and makes them the picture of life?

Which takes us back to the question. Could God do something similar in your life? Could he take what today is a token of tragedy and turn it into a symbol of triumph? You simply need to do what John did. Don't leave. Hang around.

"God works for the good of those who love him" (Rom. 8:28 NCV). That's how John felt about Jesus. He loved him. He didn't understand him or always agree with him, but he loved him.

In the first part of that verse, the Bible says that "in everything God works for the good of those who love him." Before we close this chapter, do this simple exercise. Remove the word *everything*, and replace it with the symbol of your tragedy. For the apostle John, the verse would read: "In burial clothing God works for the good of those who love him." For some it would read: "In scars God works for the good of those who love him."

How would Romans 8:28 read in your life? In hospital stays God works for the good. In divorce papers God works for the good. In a prison term God works for the good.

If God can change John's life through a tragedy, could it be he will use a tragedy to change yours?

REFLECTION AND DISCUSSION

"When it's Saturday in your life, how do you react?" What does Max mean by "Saturday in your life?" After tragedy strikes, do you leave God or linger near him? Explain.

_____

_____

_____

_____

_____

_____

Read John 19:38–40; 20:3–9 (NIV). What did Peter and "the other disciple" find when they entered the empty tomb on the day of Jesus' resurrection? Why did what they saw cause John to believe?

_____

_____

_____

_____

_____

Read Romans 8:28. What does this verse say we "know"?

_____

_____

_____

_____

_____

Follow through on Max's suggestion: "Do this simple exercise. Remove the word *everything* [in Romans 8:28], and replace it with the symbol of your tragedy." How does this change your interpretation of this verse?

_____

_____

_____

_____

_____

On your own or with someone else, think of several stories in the Bible in which God took what appeared to be a clear defeat for his people and turned it into a triumph. In what area of your life could you use such a triumph right now? Enlist a friend to pray with you that God would engineer just such a reversal on your behalf.

_____

_____

_____

_____

JOSEPH

JOSEPH

BEFORE YOU BEGIN

Read Matthew 1:18–25 NIV

This is how the birth of Jesus the Messiah came about: His mother Mary was pledged to be married to Joseph, but before they came together, she was found to be pregnant through the Holy Spirit. Because Joseph her husband was faithful to the law, and yet did not want to expose her to public disgrace, he had in mind to divorce her quietly.

But after he had considered this, an angel of the Lord appeared to him in a dream and said, "Joseph son of David, do not be afraid to take Mary home as your wife, because what is conceived in her is from the Holy Spirit. She will give birth to a son, and you are to give him the name Jesus, because he will save his people from their sins."

All this took place to fulfill what the Lord had said through the prophet: "The virgin will conceive and give birth to a son, and they will call him Immanuel" (which means "God with us").

When Joseph woke up, he did what the angel of the Lord had commanded him and took Mary home as his wife. But he did not consummate their marriage until she gave birth to a son. And he gave him the name Jesus.

The white space between Bible verses is fertile soil for questions. One can hardly read Scripture without whispering, "I wonder . . ."

"I wonder if Eve ever ate any more fruit."

"I wonder if Noah slept well during storms."

"I wonder if Jonah liked fish or if Jeremiah had friends."

"Did Moses avoid bushes? Did Jesus tell jokes? Did Peter ever try water walking again?"

"Would any woman have married Paul had he asked?"

The Bible is a fence full of knotholes through which we can peek but not see the whole picture.

You'll find them in every chapter about every person. But nothing stirs so many questions as does the birth of Christ. Characters appear and disappear before we can ask them anything. The innkeeper too busy to welcome God—did he ever learn who he turned away? The shepherds—did they ever hum the song the angels sang? The wise men who followed the star—what was it like to worship a toddler? And Joseph, especially Joseph. I've got questions for Joseph.

Did you and Jesus arm wrestle? Did he ever let you win?

Did you ever look up from your prayers and see Jesus listening?

How do you say "Jesus" in Egyptian?

What ever happened to the wise men?

What ever happened to you?

We don't know what happened to Joseph. His role in Act I is so crucial that we expect to see him the rest of the drama—but with the exception of a short scene with twelve-year-old Jesus in Jerusalem, he never reappears. The rest of his life is left to speculation, and we are left with our questions.

But of all my questions, my first would be about Bethlehem. I'd like to know about the night in the stable. I can picture Joseph there. Moonlit pastures. Stars twinkle above. Bethlehem sparkles in the distance. There he is, pacing outside the stable.

What was he thinking while Jesus was being born? What was on his mind while Mary was giving birth? He'd done all he could do—heated the water, prepared a place for Mary to lie. He'd made Mary as comfortable as she could be in a barn and then he stepped out. She'd asked to be alone, and Joseph had never felt more so.

In that eternity between his wife's dismissal and Jesus' arrival, what was he thinking? He walked into the night and looked into the stars. Did he pray?

For some reason, I don't see him silent; I see Joseph animated, pacing. Head shaking one minute, fist shaking the next. This isn't what he had in mind. I wonder what he said . . .

This isn't the way I planned it, God. Not at all. My child being born in a stable? This isn't the way I thought it would be. A cave with sheep and donkeys, hay, and straw? My wife giving birth with only the stars to hear her pain?

This isn't at all what I imagined. No, I imagined family. I imagined grandmothers. I imagined neighbors clustered outside the door and friends standing at my side. I imagined the house erupting with the first cry of the infant. Slaps on the back. Loud laughter. Jubilation.

That's how I thought it would be.

The midwife would hand me my child and all the people would applaud. Mary would rest and we would celebrate. All of Nazareth would celebrate.

But now. Now look. Nazareth is five days' journey away. And here we are in a . . . in a sheep pasture. Who will celebrate with us? The sheep? The shepherds? The stars?

This doesn't seem right. What kind of husband am I? I provide no midwife to aid my wife. No bed to rest her back. Her pillow is a blanket from my donkey. My house for her is a shed of hay and straw.

The smell is bad, the animals are loud. Why, I even smell like a shepherd myself.

Did I miss something? Did I, God?

When you sent the angel and spoke of the son being born—this isn't what I pictured. I envisioned Jerusalem, the temple, the priests, and the people gathered to watch. A pageant perhaps. A parade. A banquet at least. I mean, this is the Messiah!

Or, if not born in Jerusalem, how about Nazareth? Wouldn't Nazareth have been better? At least there I have my house and my business. Out here, what do I have? A weary mule, a stack of firewood, and a pot of warm water. This is not the way I wanted it to be! This is not the way I wanted my son.

Oh my, I did it again. I did it again, didn't I, Father? I don't mean to do that; it's just that I forget. He's not my son . . . he's yours.

The child is yours. The plan is yours. The idea is yours. And forgive me for asking but . . . is this how God enters the world? The coming of the angel, I've accepted. The questions people asked about the pregnancy, I can tolerate. The trip to Bethlehem, fine. But why a birth in a stable, God?

Any minute now Mary will give birth. Not to a child, but to the Messiah. Not to an infant, but to God. That's what the angel said. That's what Mary believes. And, God, my God, that's what I want to believe. But surely you can understand; it's not easy. It seems so . . . so . . . so . . . bizarre.

I'm unaccustomed to such strangeness, God. I'm a carpenter. I make things fit. I square off the edges. I follow the plumb line. I measure twice before I cut once. Surprises are not the friend of a builder. I like to know the plan. I like to see the plan before I begin.

But this time I'm not the builder, am I? This time I'm a tool. A hammer in your grip. A nail between your fingers. A chisel in your hands. This project is yours, not mine.

I guess it's foolish of me to question you. Forgive my struggling. Trust doesn't come easy to me, God. But you never said it would be easy, did you?

One final thing, Father. The angel you sent, any chance you could send another? If not an angel, maybe a person? I don't know anyone around here and some company would be nice. Maybe the innkeeper or a traveler? Even a shepherd would do.

I wonder. Did Joseph ever pray such a prayer? Perhaps he did. Perhaps he didn't. But you probably have.

You've stood where Joseph stood. Caught between what God says and what makes sense. You've done what he told you to do only to wonder if it was him speaking in the first place. You've stared into a sky blackened with doubt. And you've asked what Joseph asked.

You've asked if you're still on the right road. You've asked if you were supposed to turn left when you turned right. And you've asked if there is a plan behind this scheme. Things haven't turned out like you thought they would.

Each of us knows what it's like to search the night for light. Not outside a stable, but perhaps outside an emergency room. On the gravel of a roadside. On the manicured grass of a cemetery. We've asked our questions. We've questioned God's plan. And we've wondered why God does what he does.

The Bethlehem sky is not the first to hear the pleadings of a confused pilgrim.

If you are asking what Joseph asked, let me urge you to do what Joseph did. Obey. That's what he did. He obeyed. He obeyed when the angel called. He obeyed when Mary explained. He obeyed when God sent.

He was obedient to God.

He was obedient when the sky was bright.

He was obedient when the sky was dark.

He didn't let his confusion disrupt his obedience. He didn't know everything. But he did what he knew. He shut down his business, packed up his family, and went to another country. Why? Because that's what God said to do.

What about you? Just like Joseph, you can't see the whole picture. Just like Joseph your task is to see that Jesus is brought into your part of your world. And just like Joseph you have a choice: to obey or disobey. Because Joseph obeyed, God used him to change the world.

Can he do the same with you?

God still looks for Josephs today. Men and women who believe that God is not through with this world. Common people who serve an uncommon God.

Will you be that kind of person? Will you serve . . . even when you don't understand?

No, the Bethlehem sky is not the first to hear the pleadings of an honest heart, nor the last. And perhaps God didn't answer every question for Joseph. But he answered the most important one. "Are you still with me, God?" And through the first cries of the God-child the answer came.

"Yes. Yes, Joseph. I'm with you."

REFLECTION AND DISCUSSION

What is the connection between our obedience and divine guidance?

_____

_____

_____

_____

_____

Has a situation in the past caused you to question God's action or apparent inaction?

_____

_____

_____

_____

_____

When you question God's handling of your life or circumstances, how is your attitude changed?

_____

_____

_____

_____

_____

_____

_____

Read Hebrews 3:12–19. What advice is given in verse 13 to help us obey God? Note the close connection between obedience and belief in verses 18 and 19. How would you describe this connection in your own life?

_____

_____

_____

_____

_____

JOSIAH

JOSIAH

BEFORE YOU BEGIN
Read 2 Chronicles 34:4-5, 7 NIV

Under his direction the altars of the Baals were torn down; he cut to pieces the incense altars that were above them, and smashed the Asherah poles and the idols. These he broke to pieces and scattered over the graves of those who had sacrificed to them. He burned the bones of the priests on their altars, and so he purged Judah and Jerusalem.

. . . he tore down the altars and the Asherah poles and crushed the idols to powder and cut to pieces all the incense altars throughout Israel. Then he went back to Jerusalem.

Stefan can tell you about family trees. He makes his living from them. He inherited a German forest that has been in his family for four hundred years. The trees he harvests were planted 180 years ago by his great-grandfather. The trees he plants won't be ready for market until his great-grandchildren are born.

He's part of a chain. "Every generation must make a choice," he told me. "They can either pillage or plant. They can rape the landscape and get rich, or they can care for the landscape, harvest only what is theirs, and leave an investment for their children."[15]

Stefan harvests seeds sown by men he never knew. Stefan sows seeds to be harvested by descendants he'll never see. Dependent upon the past, responsible for the future: he's part of a chain.

Like us. Children of the past are we. Parents of the future. Heirs. Benefactors. Recipients of the work done by those before. Born into a forest we didn't seed.

Which leads me to ask, how's your forest?

As you stand on the land bequeathed by your ancestors, how does it look? How do you feel?

Pride at legacy left? Perhaps. Some inherit nourished soil. Deeply rooted trees of conviction. Row after row of truth and heritage. Could be that you stand in the forest of your fathers with pride. If so, give thanks, for many don't.

Many aren't proud of their family trees. Poverty. Shame. Abuse. Such are the forests found by some of you. The land was pillaged. Harvest was taken, but no seed was sown.

Perhaps you were reared in a home of bigotry and so you are intolerant of minorities. Perhaps you were reared in a home of greed, hence your desires for possessions are insatiable.

Perhaps your childhood memories bring more hurt than inspiration. The voices of your past cursed you, belittled you, ignored you. At the time, you thought such treatment was typical. Now you see it isn't. And now you find yourself trying to explain your past.

I came across a story of a man who must have had such thoughts. His heritage was tragic. His grandfather was a murderer and a mystic who sacrificed his own children in ritual abuse. His dad was a punk who ravaged houses of worship and made a mockery of believers. He was killed at the age of twenty-four . . . by his friends.

The men were typical of their era. What do you do when your grandfather followed black magic, your father was a scoundrel, and your nation is corrupt? Follow suit? Some assumed he would. Branded him as a delinquent before he was born, a chip off the old rotten block. You can almost hear the people moan as he passes, "Gonna be just like his dad."

But they were wrong. He wasn't. He reversed the trend and defied the odds. His achievements were so remarkable, we still tell his story twenty-six hundred years later.

The story of King Josiah. The world has seen wiser kings; the world has seen wealthier kings; the world has seen more powerful kings. But history has never seen a more courageous king than young Josiah.

Born some six hundred years before Jesus, Josiah inherited a fragile throne and a tarnished crown. The temple was in disarray, the Law was lost, and the people worshiped whatever god they desired. But by the end of Josiah's thirty-one-year reign, the temple had been rebuilt, the idols destroyed, and the law of God was once again elevated to a place of prominence and power. The forest had been reclaimed.

Josiah's grandfather, King Manasseh, was remembered as the king who filled "Jerusalem from one end to the other with [the people's] blood" (2 Kings 21:16 NCV). His father, King Amon, died at the hands of his own officers. "He did what God said was wrong," reads his epitaph.

The citizens formed a posse and killed the assassins, and eight-year-old Josiah ascended the throne. Early in his reign Josiah made a brave choice. "He lived as his ancestor David had lived, and he did not stop doing what was right" (2 Kings 22:2 NCV).

He flipped through his family scrapbook until he found an ancestor worthy of emulation. Josiah skipped his dad's life and bypassed his grandpa's. He leapfrogged back in time until he found David and resolved, "I'm going to be like him."

The principle? We can't choose our parents, but we can choose our mentors. And since Josiah chose David (who had chosen God), things began to happen.

> The people tore down the altars for the Baal gods as Josiah directed. Then Josiah cut down the incense altars that were above them. He broke up the Asherah idols and . . . beat them into powder. . . . He burned the bones of their priests on their own altars. . . . Josiah broke down the altars. . . . He cut down all the incense altars in all of Israel. (2 Chron. 34:4–5, 7 NCV)

Not what you call a public relations tour. But, then again, Josiah was not out to make friends. He was out to make a statement: "What my fathers taught, I don't teach. What they embraced, I reject."

And he wasn't finished. Four years later, at the age of twenty-six, he turned his attention to the temple. It was in shambles. The people had allowed it to fall into disrepair. But Josiah was determined. Something had happened that fueled his passion to restore the temple. A baton had been passed. A torch had been received.

Early in his reign he'd resolved to serve the God of his ancestor David. Now he chose to serve the God of someone else. Note 2 Chronicles 34:8: "In Josiah's eighteenth year as king, he made Judah and the Temple pure again. He sent Shaphan . . . to repair the Temple of the LORD, the God of Josiah" (NCV).

God was his God. David's faith was Josiah's faith. He had found the God of David and made him his own. As the temple was being rebuilt, one of the workers happened upon a scroll. On the scroll were the words of God given to Moses nearly a thousand years earlier.

When Josiah heard the words, he was shocked. He wept that his people had drifted so far from God that his Word was not a part of their lives. He sent word to a prophetess and asked her, "What will become of our people?"

She told Josiah that since he had repented when he heard the words, his nation would be spared the anger of God (2 Chron. 34:27). Incredible. An entire generation received grace because of the integrity of one man.

Could it be that God placed him on earth for that reason? Could it be that God has placed you on earth for the same?

Maybe your past isn't much to brag about. Maybe you've seen raw evil. And now you, like Josiah, have to make a choice. Do you rise above the past and make a difference? Or do you remain controlled by the past and make excuses?

Many choose the latter. Many choose the convalescent homes of the heart. Healthy bodies. Sharp minds. But retired dreams. Back and forth they rock in the chair of regret, repeating the terms of surrender. Lean closely and you will hear them: "If only." The white flag of the heart.

"If only . . ."

"If only I'd been born somewhere else . . ."

"If only I'd been treated fairly . . ."

"If only I'd had kinder parents, more money, greater opportunities . . ."

Maybe you've used those words. Maybe you have every right to use them. Perhaps you, like Josiah, were hearing the ten count before you even got into the ring. For you to find an ancestor worth imitating, you, like Josiah, have to flip way back in your family album.

If such is the case, let me show you where to turn. Pick up your Bible. Go to John's gospel and read Jesus' words: "Human life comes from human parents, but spiritual life comes from the Spirit" (John 3:6 NCV).

Think about that. Spiritual life comes from the Spirit! Your parents may have given you genes, but God gives you grace. Your parents may be responsible for your body, but God has taken charge of your soul. You may get your looks from your mother, but you get eternity from your Father, your heavenly Father.

By the way, he's not blind to your problems. In fact, God is willing to give you what your family didn't. Didn't have a good father? He'll be your Father.

"You are a son. And, if you are a son, then you are certainly an heir" (Gal. 4:7 PHILLIPS).

Didn't have a good role model? Try God. You are God's children whom he loves, so try to be like him (Eph. 5:1 NCV).

Never had a parent who wiped away your tears? Think again. God has noted each one. "You have seen me tossing and turning through the night. You have collected all my tears and preserved them in your bottle! You have recorded every one in your book" (Ps. 56:8 TLB).

God has not left you adrift on a sea of heredity. Just like Josiah, you cannot control the way your forefathers responded to God. But you can control the way you respond to him. The past does not have to be your prison. You have a voice in your destiny. You have a say in your life. You have a choice in the path you take.

Choose well and someday—generations from now—your grandchildren and great-grandchildren will thank God for the seeds you sowed.

REFLECTION AND DISCUSSION

Think about your ancestry. Were your parents and grandparents positive role models? If yes, in what ways? If no, why?

_____

_____

_____

_____

Choose one word to describe how you feel about your past: Grateful? Angry? Discouraged? Proud? Depressed? Blessed? Explain.

_____

_____

_____

_____

How do we sometimes allow ourselves to be controlled by the past? Have you ever slipped into this mode? Explain.

_____

_____

_____

_____

_____

_____

"Spiritual life comes from the Spirit! Your parents may have given you genes, but God gives you grace." How does this principle change your outlook on your family history?

_____

_____

_____

_____

_____

_____

_____

"We can't choose our parents, but we can choose our mentors." What mentors have you chosen? Why did you choose them? How have your mentors broadened your understanding of God and guided you on a positive path?

_____

_____

_____

_____

_____

What sort of spiritual heritage do you have now? Describe it.

_____

_____

_____

_____

_____

_____

LAZARUS

LAZARUS

BEFORE YOU BEGIN
Read John 11:1-3, 17-19, 20-23, 33-35, 38-44 NIV

Now a man named Lazarus was sick. He was from Bethany, the village of Mary and her sister Martha. (This Mary, whose brother Lazarus now lay sick, was the same one who poured perfume on the Lord and wiped his feet with her hair.) So the sisters sent word to Jesus, "Lord, the one you love is sick."

On his arrival, Jesus found that Lazarus had already been in the tomb for four days. Now Bethany was less than two miles from Jerusalem, and many Jews had come to Martha and Mary to comfort them in the loss of their brother.

When Martha heard that Jesus was coming, she went out to meet him, but Mary stayed at home.

"Lord," Martha said to Jesus, "if you had been here, my brother would not have died. But I know that even now God will give you whatever you ask."

Jesus said to her, "Your brother will rise again."

When Jesus saw her weeping, and the Jews who had come along with her also weeping, he was deeply moved in spirit and troubled. "Where have you laid him?" he asked.

"Come and see, Lord," they replied.

Jesus wept.

Jesus, once more deeply moved, came to the tomb. It was a cave with a stone laid across the entrance. "Take away the stone," he said.

"But, Lord," said Martha, the sister of the dead man, "by this time there is a bad odor, for he has been there four days."

Then Jesus said, "Did I not tell you that if you believe, you will see the glory of God?"

So they took away the stone. Then Jesus looked up and said, "Father, I thank you that you have heard me. I knew that you always hear me, but I said this for the benefit of the people standing here, that they may believe that you sent me."

When he had said this, Jesus called in a loud voice, "Lazarus, come out!" The dead man came out, his hands and feet wrapped with strips of linen, and a cloth around his face.

Jesus said to them, "Take off the grave clothes and let him go."

John doesn't tell us everything Jesus did. But he tells us those acts that will lead us to faith. John selects seven miracles. He begins softly with the quiet miracle of water to wine and then crescendos to the public resurrection of Lazarus. Seven miracles are offered, and seven witnesses are examined, each one building on the testimony of the previous.

Let's see if we can feel their full impact. Pretend you are in a courtroom, a nearly empty courtroom. Present are four people: a judge, a lawyer, an orphan, and a would-be guardian. The judge is God, Jesus is the one who seeks to be the guardian, and you are the orphan. You have no name, no inheritance, no home. The lawyer is proposing that you be placed in Jesus' care.

Who is the lawyer? A Galilean fisherman by the name of John.

He has presented the court with six witnesses. It is time for the seventh. But before calling him to the stand, the lawyer reviews the case. "We started this case with the wedding in Cana." He paces as he speaks, measuring each word. "They had no wine, none at all. But when Jesus spoke, water became wine. The best wine. Delicious wine. You heard the testimony of the wedding attendants. They saw it happen."

He pauses, then moves on. "Then we heard the words of the foreign official. His son was nearly dead."

You nod. You remember the man's testimony. Articulate, he had spoken of how he had called every doctor and tried every treatment, but nothing had helped his son. Just when he was about to give up hope, someone told him about a healer in Galilee.

Through his thickened accent the dignitary had explained, "I had no other choice. I went to him out of desperation. Look! Look what the teacher did for my son." The boy had stood, and you had stared. It was hard to believe such a healthy youngster had ever been near death.

You listen intently as John continues, "And, your honor, don't forget the crippled man near the pool. For thirty-eight years he had not walked. But then Jesus came and, well, the court saw him. Remember? We saw him walk into this room. We heard his story.

"And, as if that was not enough, we also heard the testimony of the boy with the lunch. He was part of a crowd of thousands who had followed Jesus in order to hear him teach and to see him heal. Just when the little boy was about to open his lunch basket to eat, he was asked to bring it to Jesus. One minute it held a lunch; the next it held a feast."

John pauses again, letting the silence of the courtroom speak. No one can deny these testimonies. The judge listens. The lawyer listens. And you, the orphan, say nothing.

"Then there was the storm. Peter described it to us. The boat bouncing on the waves. Thunder. Lightning. Storms like that can kill. I know. I used to make a living on a boat! Peter's testimony about what happened was true. I was there. The Master walked on the water. And the moment he stepped into the boat, we were safe."

John pauses again. Sunlight squared by a window makes a box on the floor. John steps into the box. "Then, yesterday, you met a man who had never seen light. His world was dark. He was blind. Blind from birth."

John pauses and dramatically states what the man born blind had said: "Jesus healed my eyes."

Six testimonies have been given. Six miracles have been verified. John gestures toward the table where sit the articles of evidence: The water jugs that held the wine. The signed affidavit of the doctor who'd treated the sick son. The cot of the cripple, the basket of the boy. Peter had brought a broken oar to show the strength of the storm. And the blind man had left his cup and cane. He didn't need to beg anymore.

"And now," John says, turning to the judge, "we have one final witness to call and one more piece of evidence to submit."

He goes to his table and returns with a white linen sheet. You lean forward, unsure of what he is holding. "This is a burial shroud," he explains. Placing the clothing on the table he requests, "Your honor permitting, I call our final witness to the chair, Lazarus of Bethany."

Heavy courtroom doors open, and a tall man enters. He strides down the aisle and pauses before Jesus long enough to place a hand on his shoulder and say, "Thank you." You can hear the tenderness in his voice. Lazarus then turns and takes his seat in the witness chair.

"State your name for the court."

"Lazarus."

"Have you heard of a man called Jesus of Nazareth?"

"Who hasn't?"

"How do you know him?"

"He is my friend. We, my sisters and I, have a house in Bethany. When he comes to Jerusalem, he often stays with us. My sisters, Mary and Martha, have become believers in him as well."

"Believers?"

"Believers that he is the Messiah. The Son of God."

"Why do you believe that?"

Lazarus smiles. "How could I not believe? I was dead. I had been dead for four days. I was in the tomb. I was prayed for and buried. I was dead. But Jesus called me out of the grave."

"Tell us what happened."

"Well, I've always been sickly. That's why I've stayed with my sisters, you know. They care for me. My heart never has been the strongest, so I have to be careful. Martha, the oldest sister, she's, well, she's like a mother to me. It was Martha who called Jesus when my heart failed."

"Is that when you died?"

"No, but almost. I lingered for a few days. But I knew I was near the edge. The doctors would just come in and shake their heads and walk out. I had one sandal in the grave."

"Is that when Jesus came?"

"No, we kept hoping he would. Martha would sit by the bed at night, and she would whisper over and over and over, 'Be strong, Lazarus. Jesus will be here any minute.' We just knew he would come. I mean, he had healed all those strangers; surely he would heal me. I was his friend."

"What delayed him?"

"For the longest time we didn't know. I thought he might be in prison or something. I kept waiting and waiting. Every day I got weaker. My vision faded, and I couldn't see. I drifted in and out. Every time someone entered my room, I thought it might be him. But it never was. He never came."

"Were you angry?"

"More confused than angry. I just didn't understand."

"Then what happened?"

"Well, I woke up one night. My chest was so tight I could hardly breathe. I must have sat up because Martha and Mary came to my bed. They took my hand. I heard them calling my name, but then I began to fall. It was like a dream, I was falling, spinning wildly in midair. Their voices grew fainter and fainter and then nothing. The spinning stopped, the falling stopped. And the hurting stopped. I was at peace."

"At peace?"

"Like I was asleep. Resting. Tranquil. I was dead."

"Then what happened?"

"Well, Martha can tell the details. The funeral was planned. The family came. Friends traveled from Jerusalem. They buried me."

"Did Jesus come to the funeral?"

"No."

"He still wasn't there?"

"No, when he heard I was buried, he waited an extra four days."

"Why?"

Lazarus stopped and looked at Jesus. "To make his point."

John smiled knowingly.

"What happened next?"

"I heard his voice."

"Whose voice?"

"The voice of Jesus."

"But I thought you were dead."

"I was."

"I, uh, thought you were in a grave."

"I was."

"How does a dead man in a grave hear the voice of a man?"

"He doesn't. The dead hear only the voice of God. I heard the voice of God."

"What did he say?"

"He didn't say it; he shouted it."

"What did he shout?"

"'Lazarus, come out!'"

"And you heard him?"

"As if he were in the tomb with me. My eyes opened; my fingers moved. I lifted my head. I was alive again. I heard the stone being rolled away. The light poured in. It took a minute for my eyes to adjust."

"What did you see?"

"A circle of faces looking in at me."

"Then what did you do?"

"I stood up. Jesus gave me his hand and pulled me out. He told the people to get me some real clothes, and they did."

"So you died, were in the tomb four days, then Jesus called you back to life? Were there any witnesses to this?"

Lazarus chuckles. "Only a hundred or so."

"That's all, Lazarus, thank you. You may step down."

John returns to the judge. "You have heard the testimonies. I now leave the decision in your hands." With that he returns to the table and takes his seat. The guardian stands. He doesn't identify himself. He doesn't need to. All recognize him. He is Jesus Christ.

Jesus' voice fills the courtroom. "I represent an orphan who is the sum of all you have seen. Like the party that had no wine, this one has no cause for celebration. Like the dignitary's son, this child is spiritually ill. Like the cripple and the beggar, he can't walk and is blind. He is starving, but earth has no food to fill him. He faces storms as severe as the one on Galilee, but earth has no compass to guide him. And most of all, he is dead. Just like Lazarus. Dead. Spiritually dead."

"I will do for him what I did for them. I'll give him joy, strength, healing, sight, safety, nourishment, new life. All are his. If you will permit."

The judge speaks his answer. "You are my Son, whom I love, and I am very pleased with you" (Luke 3:22 NCV). God looks at you. "I will permit it," he says, "on one condition. That the orphan request it."

John has presented the witnesses and they have told their stories.

The Master has offered to do for you what he did for them. He will bring wine to your table, sight to your eyes, strength for your step and, most of all, power over your grave. He will do for you what he did for them.

The Judge has given his blessing. The rest is up to you. Now the choice is yours.

REFLECTION AND DISCUSSION

"'The dead hear only the voice of God . . . ,' said Lazarus . . . 'I heard the voice of God.'" If a man is dead, how can he hear anything? How did Lazarus know it was the voice of God he heard? In what way do "dead men" still hear the voice of God today?

_____

_____

_____

_____

"Jesus said . . . 'I'll give him joy, strength, healing, sight, safety, nourishment, new life.'" Does Jesus still give us these gifts today? If so, how?

_____

_____

_____

_____

Which of the gifts listed means the most to you? Explain your choice.

_____

_____

_____

_____

_____

_____

Read John 20:30-31. What was the purpose of writing down Jesus'
miracles? Have they had this intended effect on you? Why or why not?

_____

_____

_____

_____

_____

_____

Read Ephesians 2:1–5. How could we be described in our pre-Christian days, according to verses 1–3? How was our status changed as described in verses 4–5? What prompted this change in status?

_____

_____

_____

_____

_____

_____

_____

_____

_____

_____

_____

MARY AND MARTHA

MARY AND MARTHA

BEFORE YOU BEGIN
Read John 12:2–3 NIV

Here a dinner was given in Jesus' honor. Martha served, while Lazarus was among those reclining at the table with him. Then Mary took about a pint of pure nard, an expensive perfume; she poured it on Jesus' feet and wiped his feet with her hair. And the house was filled with the fragrance of the perfume.

Two of my teenage years were spent carrying a tuba in my high school marching band. My mom wanted me to learn to read music, and the choir was full while the band was a tuba-tooter short, so I signed up. Not necessarily what you would describe as a call from God, but it wasn't a wasted experience either.

Now, what I saw years ago in the band, I see today in the church. We need each other. Not all of us play the same instrument. Some believers are lofty, and others are solid. Some keep the pace while others lead the band. Not all of us make the same sound. Some are soft, and others are loud. And not all of us have the same ability.

Some perform rousing solos. Others need to be in the background playing backup. But each of us has a place.

Some play the drums (like Martha). Some play the flute (like Mary). And others sound the trumpet (like Lazarus).

Mary, Martha, and Lazarus were like family to Jesus. After the Lord raised Lazarus from the dead, they decided to give a dinner for Jesus. They decided to honor him by having a party on his behalf (John 12:2).

All three worked together with one purpose. But each one fulfilled that purpose in his or her unique manner. Martha served; she always kept everyone in step. Mary worshiped; she anointed her Lord with an extravagant gift, and its aroma filled the air. Lazarus had a story to tell, and he was ready to tell it.

Three people, each one with a different skill, a different ability. But each one of equal value. Think about it. Could their family have done without one of the three?

Every church needs a Martha. Change that. Every church needs a hundred Marthas. Sleeves rolled up and ready, they keep the pace for the church. Because of Marthas, the church budget gets balanced, the church babies get bounced, and the church building gets built. You don't appreciate Marthas until a Martha is missing, and then all the Marys and Lazaruses are scrambling around looking for the keys and the thermostats and the projectors.

Marthas are the Energizer bunnies of the church. They keep going and going and going. They store strength like a camel stores water. Since they don't seek the spotlight, they don't live off the applause. That's not to say they don't need it. They just aren't addicted to it.

Marthas have a mission. In fact, if Marthas have a weakness, it is their tendency to elevate the mission over the Master. Remember when Martha did that? A younger Martha invites a younger Jesus to come for dinner. Jesus accepts and brings his disciples.

The scene Luke describes has Mary seated and Martha fuming. Martha is angry because Mary is, horror of horrors, sitting at the feet of Jesus. I mean, who has time to sit and listen when there is bread to be baked, tables to be set, and souls to be saved? So Martha complained, "Lord, don't you care that my sister has left me alone to do all the work? Tell her to help me" (Luke 10:40 NCV).

"Martha, Martha, you are worried and upset about many things. Only one thing is important. Mary has chosen the better thing, and it will never be taken away from her" (Luke 10:41–42 NCV). Apparently Martha got the point, for later we find her serving again.

> Here a dinner was given in Jesus' honor. Martha served, while Lazarus was among those reclining at the table with him. Then Mary took about a pint of pure nard, an expensive perfume; she poured it on Jesus' feet and wiped his feet with her hair. And the house was filled with the fragrance of the perfume. (John 12:2–3 NIV)

Is Mary in the kitchen? No, she is playing her flute for Jesus. She is worshiping, for that is what she loves to do. But this time Martha doesn't object. She has learned that there is a place for praise and worship, and that is what Mary is doing. And what is Mary's part in the dinner? She brings a pint of very expensive perfume and pours it on Jesus' feet, then wipes his feet with her hair. The smell of the perfume fills the house, just like the sound of praise can fill a church.

An earlier Martha would have objected. Such an act was too lavish, too extravagant, too generous. But this mature Martha has learned that just as there is a place in the kingdom of God for sacrificial service, there is also a place for extravagant praise.

Marys are gifted with praise. They don't just sing; they worship. They don't simply attend church; they go to offer praise. They don't just talk about Christ; they radiate Christ.

Marys have one foot in heaven and the other on a cloud. It's not easy for them to come to earth, but sometimes they need to. Sometimes they need to be reminded that there are bills to be paid and classes to be taught. But don't remind them too harshly. Flutes are fragile. Marys are precious souls with tender hearts. If they have found a place at the foot of Jesus, don't ask them to leave. Much better to ask them to pray for you.

That's what I do. When I find a Mary, I'm quick to ask, "How do I get on your prayer list?"

Every church desperately needs some Marys. We need them because we tend to

forget how much God loves worship. Marys don't forget. They know that God wants to be known as a father. They know that a father likes nothing more than to have his children sit as his feet and spend time with him.

Marys need to remember that service is worship. Marthas need to remember that worship is service. And Lazarus? He needs to remember that not everyone can play the trumpet.

You see, as far as we know, Lazarus did nothing at the dinner. He saved his actions for outside the house. Carefully read John 12:9–11:

> A large crowd of Jews heard that Jesus was in Bethany. So they went there to see not only Jesus, but Lazarus, whom Jesus raised from the dead. So the leading priests made plans to kill Lazarus, too. Because of Lazarus many Jews were leaving them and believing in Jesus. (NCV)

Because of Lazarus many Jews were "believing in Jesus." Lazarus has been given a trumpet. He has a testimony to give—and what a testimony he has!

God gave Martha a bass drum of service. God gave Mary a flute for praise. And God gave Lazarus a trumpet. And he stood on center stage and played it.

God still gives trumpets. God still calls people from the pits. God still gives pinch-me-I'm-dreaming, too-good-to-be-true testimonies. But not everyone has a dramatic testimony. Who wants a band full of trumpets?

If God has called you to be a Martha, then serve! Remind the rest of us that there is evangelism in feeding the poor and there is worship in nursing the sick.

If God has called you to be a Mary, then worship! Remind the rest of us that we don't have to be busy to be holy. Urge us with your example to put down our clipboards and megaphones and be quiet in worship.

If God has called you to be a Lazarus, then testify. Remind the rest of us that we, too, have a story to tell. We, too, have neighbors who are lost. We, too, have died and been resurrected.

Each of us has our place at the table.

Except one. There was one at Martha's house who didn't find his place. Though he

had been near Jesus longer than any of the others, he was furthest away in his faith. His name was Judas. He was a thief. When Mary poured the perfume, he feigned spirituality. "The perfume could have been sold and given to the poor," he said. But Jesus knew Judas's heart, and Jesus defended Mary's worship. Years later, John, too, knew Judas's heart, and John explained that Judas was a thief (John 12:6). And all these years he had been dipping his hand in the treasury. The reason he wanted the perfume to be sold and the money put in the treasury was so that he could get his hands on it.

What a sad ending to a beautiful story. But what an appropriate ending. For in every church there are those like Judas who take, take, take, and never give in return. There are those like Martha who take time to serve. There are those like Mary who take time to worship. And there are those like Lazarus who take time to testify. We need fewer like Judas and more like Martha, Mary, and Lazarus.

REFLECTION AND DISCUSSION

"Marys need to remember that service is worship. Marthas need to remember that worship is service. And Lazarus? He needs to remember that not everyone can play the trumpet." How can service be worship? How can worship be service?

_____

_____

_____

_____

Are you more like Martha or Mary? Explain.

_____

_____

_____

_____

Are you satisfied with how you're fitting in with God's band? Why or why not?

_____

_____

_____

_____

Read Romans 12:4–8. What does this passage teach us about unity?
What does it teach us about diversity? What does it teach us about the
relationship of the two?

_____

_____

_____

_____

MARY MAGDALENE

MARY MAGDALENE

BEFORE YOU BEGIN
Read Isaiah 40:28–29 NLT

Have you never heard?
  Have you never understood?
The Lord is the everlasting God,
  the Creator of all the earth.
He never grows weak or weary.
  No one can measure the depths of his understanding.
He gives power to the weak
  and strength to the powerless.

Anyone can give pep talks. Self-help manuals might get you through a bad mood or a tough patch. But what about an abusive childhood or a debilitating accident or years of chronic pain or public ridicule? Does God have a word for the dark nights of the soul?

He does. The promise begins with this phrase: "Weeping may last through the night" (Ps. 30:5 NLT).

Of course, you knew that much. You didn't need to read the verse to know its truth. Weeping can last through the night. Just ask the widow in the cemetery or the mother in the emergency room. The man who lost his job can tell you. So can the teenager who lost her way. Weeping may last through the night, and the next night, and the next. This is not new news to you.

But this may be: "Joy comes with the morning" (Ps. 30:5 NLT). Despair will not rule the day. Sorrow will not last forever. The clouds may eclipse the sun, but they cannot eliminate it. Night might delay the dawn, but it cannot defeat it. Morning comes. Not as quickly as we want. Not as dramatically as we desire. But morning comes, and with it comes joy.

Do you need this promise? Have you wept a river? Have you forsaken hope? Do you wonder if a morning will ever bring this night to an end? Mary Magdalene did.

In the forest of the New Testament, she is the weeping willow. She is the one upon whom tragedy cast its coldest winter. Before she knew Jesus, she had seven demons (Luke 8:2). She was a prisoner of seven afflictions. What might this list include? Depression? Loneliness? Shame? Fear? Perhaps she was a recluse or a prostitute. Maybe she'd been abused, abandoned. The number seven is sometimes used in the Bible to describe completeness. It could be that Mary Magdalene was completely consumed with troubles.

But then something happened. Jesus stepped into her world. He spoke and the demons fled. For the first time in a long time, the oppressive forces were gone. Banished. Evicted. Mary Magdalene could sleep well, eat enough, and smile again. The face in the mirror wasn't anguished.

Jesus restored life to her life.

She reciprocated. She was among the female followers who "were contributing from their own resources to support Jesus and his disciples" (Luke 8:3 NLT). Wherever Jesus went, Mary Magdalene followed. She heard him teach. She saw him perform miracles. She helped pay expenses. She may have even prepared his meals. She was always near Christ.

Even at his crucifixion. She stood "near the cross" (John 19:25 NLT).

When they pounded the nails in his hands, she heard the hammer. When they pierced his side with a spear, she saw the blood. When they lowered his body from the cross, she was there to help prepare it for burial.

On Friday Mary Magdalene watched Jesus die. On Saturday she observed a sad Sabbath.

When Sunday came, Mary Magdalene went to the tomb to finish the work she had begun on Friday. "Early on the first day of the week, Mary Magdalene went to the tomb while it was still dark" (John 20:1 NCV). She knew nothing of the empty tomb. She came with no other motive than to wash the remaining clots of blood from his beard and say goodbye.

It was a dark morning.

When she arrived at the tomb, the bad news became worse. Mary Magdalene "saw that the stone had been taken away" (v. 1 NKJV). Assuming that grave robbers had taken the body, she hurried back down the trail until she found Peter and John. "They have taken the Lord from the tomb," she told them (v. 2 NASB).

Peter and John ran to the grave site. John was faster, but Peter was bolder. He stepped inside. John followed him. Peter saw the empty slab and stared. But John saw the empty slab and believed. The evidence all came together for him: the resurrection prophecies, the removed stone, the linen wrappings, the head cloth folded and placed. John did the math. No one took Jesus' body. No one robbed the grave. Jesus rose from the dead. John looked and believed. Easter had its first celebrant.

Peter and John hurried to tell the others. We expect the camera lens of the gospel to follow them. After all, they were apostles, future authors of epistles. They compose two-thirds of the inner circle. We expect John to describe what the apostles did next. He doesn't. He tells the story of the one who remained behind.

"But Mary stood outside by the tomb weeping" (v. 11 NKJV).

Her face was awash with tears. Her shoulders heaved with sobs. She felt all alone. It was just Mary Magdalene, her despair, and a vacant tomb. "As she wept she stooped down and looked into the tomb. And she saw two angels in white sitting, one at the head and the other at the feet, where the body of Jesus had lain. Then they said to her, 'Woman, why are you weeping?'" (vv. 11–13 NKJV).

Mary Magdalene mistook the angels for men. It's easy to imagine why. It was still dark outside, even darker in the tomb. Her eyes were tear filled. She had no reason to think angels would be in the tomb. Bone diggers? Maybe. Caretakers? Possibly. But her Sunday was too dark to expect the presence of angels. "They have taken away my Lord, and I do not know where they have laid Him" (v. 13 NKJV).

Mary's world had officially hit rock bottom. Her Master murdered. His body buried in a borrowed grave. His tomb robbed. His body stolen. Now two strangers were sitting on the slab where his body had been laid. Sorrow intermingled with anger.

Have you ever had a moment like this? A moment in which bad news became worse? In which sadness wrapped around you like a fog? In which you came looking for God yet couldn't find him?

Maybe Mary Magdalene's story is your story. If so, you're going to love what happened next. In the midst of Mary's darkest moment, the Son came out.

Now when she had said this, she turned around and saw Jesus standing there, and did not know that it was Jesus. Jesus said to her, "Woman, why are you weeping? Whom are you seeking?"

She, supposing Him to be the gardener, said to Him, "Sir, if You have carried Him away, tell me where You have laid Him, and I will take Him away." (vv. 14–15 NKJV)

She didn't recognize her Lord. So Jesus did something about it. He called her by name. "Jesus said to her, 'Mary!'" (v. 16 NKJV).

Maybe it was the way he said it. The inflection. The tone. The Galilean accent. Maybe it was the memory associated with it, the moment she first heard someone say her name unladen with perversion or an agenda.

"Mary."

When she heard him call her by name, she knew the source. "She turned and said to Him, 'Rabboni!' (which is to say, Teacher)" (v. 16 NKJV). In a second. In a pivot of the neck. In the amount of time it took her to rotate her head from this way to that, her world went from a dead Jesus to a living one. Weeping may last through the night, but joy . . .

She took hold of him. We know this to be true because of the next words Jesus said: "Don't hold on to me, because I have not yet gone up to the Father" (v. 17 NCV).

Maybe she fell at his feet and held his ankles. Maybe she threw her arms around his shoulders and held him close. We don't know how she held him. We just know she did.

And Jesus let her do so. Even if the gesture lasted for only a moment, Jesus allowed it. How wonderful that the resurrected Lord was not too holy, too otherly, too divine, too supernatural to be touched.

This moment serves a sacred role in the Easter story. It, at once, reminds us that Jesus is the conquering King and the Good Shepherd. He has power over death. But he also has a soft spot for the Mary Magdalenes of the world. The regal hero is relentlessly tender.

I wish I could paint this scene. Capture it in oil on canvas and frame it. The brilliant golden sunrise. The open tomb. Angels watching from a distance. The white-robed Messiah. The joy-filled Mary. Her hands extended to him. His eyes upon her. If you are an artist and paint it, please include the reflection of the sunrise in the tears of Mary. And, by all means, paint a broad smile on the face of Jesus.

Then "Mary Magdalene came and told the disciples that she had seen the Lord, and that He had spoken these things to her" (v. 18 NKJV). To her! Of all the people to whom he could have spoken, Jesus went first to her. He'd just ripped the gates of hell off their hinges. He'd just yanked the fangs out of Satan's mouth. He'd just turned BC into AD, for heaven's sake! Jesus was the undisputed King of the universe. Ten thousand angels stood in rapt attention ready to serve. And what was his first act? To whom did he go? To Mary, the weeping, heartbroken woman who once had seven demons.

Why? Why her? As far as we know, she didn't become a missionary. No epistle bears her name. No New Testament story describes her work. Why did Jesus create this moment for Mary Magdalene? Perhaps to send this message to all the heavyhearted people: "Weeping may last through the night, but joy comes with the morning" (Ps. 30:5 NLT).

Joy comes.

Joy comes because Jesus comes. And if we don't recognize his face, he will call our names. "See, I have engraved you on the palms of my hands" (Isa. 49:16 NIV).

Your name is not buried in some heavenly file. God needs no name tag to jog his memory about you. Your name is tattooed, engraved, on his hand. He has more thoughts about you than the Pacific coast has grains of sand.

You are everything to God.

Do you find this hard to believe? You think I'm talking to someone else? Someone who is holier, better, nicer? Someone who didn't screw up his marriage or mess up her career? Someone who didn't get hooked on pills or porn or popularity?

I'm not. I'm talking directly to you.

I'm saying the greatest news in the world is not that God made the world but that God loves the world. He loves you. You did not earn this love. His love for you will not end if you lose your temper. His love for you will not fade if you lose your way. His love for you will not diminish if your discipline does.

You have never lived one unloved day.

Someone told you that God loves good people. Wrong. There are no good people.

Someone told you that God loves you if you love him first. Wrong. He loves people who have never thought of him.

Someone told you that God is ticked off, cranky, and vindictive. Wrong. We tend to be ticked off, cranky, and vindictive. But God?

> GOD is sheer mercy and grace;
> > not easily angered, he's rich in love.
> He doesn't endlessly nag and scold,
> > nor hold grudges forever.
> He doesn't treat us as our sins deserve,
> > nor pay us back in full for our wrongs.
> As high as heaven is over the earth,
> > so strong is his love to those who fear him.
> And as far as sunrise is from sunset,
> > he has separated us from our sins.
> As parents feel for their children,
> > GOD feels for those who fear him.
> > (Ps. 103:8–13 MSG)

158

God loves you, and because he does, you can be assured joy will come.

Expect it as you would the morning sunrise or the evening twilight. It came to Mary Magdalene. And it will come to you, my friend.

Do what People of the Promise do. Keep coming to Jesus. Even though the trail is dark. Even though the sun seems to sleep. Even though everyone else is silent, walk to Jesus. Mary Magdalene did this. No, she didn't comprehend the promise of Jesus. She came looking for a dead Jesus, not a living one. But at least she came. And because she came to him, he came to her.

And you? You'll be tempted to give up and walk away. But don't. Even when you don't feel like it, keep walking the trail to the empty tomb. Open your Bible. Meditate on Scripture. Sing hymns. Talk to other believers. Place yourself in a position to be found by Jesus, and listen carefully. That gardener very well might be your Redeemer.

Weeping comes. It comes to all of us. Heartaches leave us with tear-streaked faces and heavy hearts. Weeping comes. But so does joy. Darkness comes, but so does the morning. Sadness comes, but so does hope. Sorrow may have the night, but it cannot have our lives.

REFLECTION AND DISCUSSION

Why is it significant that Mary Magdalene was one of the first people to witness the risen Christ?

_____

_____

_____

_____

What lessons can you learn from Mary's story about the way God likes to surprise us and get us out of our comfort zones?

_____

_____

_____

_____

_____

_____

What "stones" has God moved in your life? How did this bring you closer to him? How has the movement impacted your life?

_____

_____

_____

_____

_____

_____

MARY, MOTHER OF JESUS

MARY, MOTHER OF JESUS

BEFORE YOU BEGIN

Read Luke 1:38 NIV

"I am the Lord's servant," Mary answered. "May your word to me be fulfilled." Then the angel left her.

The pint-size Joseph scurries across the church stage, wearing sandals, a robe, and his best attempt at an anxious face. He raps on the door his dad built for the children's Christmas play, then shifts from one foot to the other, partly because he's supposed to act nervous. Mostly because he is exactly that.

The innkeeper answers. He, too, wears a tow sack of a robe and a towel turned turban. An elastic band secures a false beard to his face. He looks at Joseph and chokes back a giggle. Just a couple of hours ago the two boys were building a front-lawn snowman. Their moms had to tell them twice to get dressed for the Christmas Eve service.

Here they stand. The innkeeper crosses his arms; Joseph waves his. He describes a donkey ride from Nazareth, five days on the open road, a census here in Bethlehem, and, most of all, a wife. He turns and points in the direction of a pillow-stuffed nine-year-old girl.

She waddles onto center stage with one hand on the small of her back and the other mopping her brow. She limps with her best portrayal of pregnant pain, though, if pressed, she would have no clue about the process of childbirth.

She plays up the part. Groan. Sigh. "Joseph, I need help!" The crowd chuckles. Joseph looks at the innkeeper. The innkeeper looks at Mary.

And we all know what happens next. Joseph urges. The innkeeper shakes his head. His hotel is packed. Guests occupy every corner. There is no room at the inn.

The innkeeper huffs and turns. Joseph and Mary exit. The choir sings "Away in a Manger" as stagehands wheel out a pile of hay, a feed trough, and some plastic sheep. The audience smiles and claps and sings along. They love the song, the kids, and they cherish the story. But most of all, they cling to the hope. The Christmas hope that God indwells the everydayness of our world.

The story drips with normalcy. This isn't Queen Mary or King Joseph. The couple doesn't caravan into Bethlehem with camels, servants, purple banners, and dancers. Mary and Joseph have no tax exemption or political connection. They have the clout of a migrant worker and the net worth of a minimum wage earner.

They are, well, normal. Normal has calluses like Joseph, stretch marks like Mary. Normal stays up late with laundry and wakes up early for work. Normal drives the carpool wearing a bathrobe and slippers. Normal is Norm and Norma, not Prince and Princess.

Norm sings off-key. Norma works in a cubicle and struggles to find time to pray. Both have stood where Joseph stood and have heard what Mary heard. Not from the innkeeper in Bethlehem, but from the coach in middle school or the hunk in high school or the foreman at the plant. "We don't have room for you . . . time for you . . . a space for you . . . a job for you . . . interest in you. Besides, look at you. You are too slow . . . fat . . . inexperienced . . . late . . . young . . . old . . . pigeon-toed . . . cross-eyed . . . hackneyed. You are too . . . ordinary."

But then comes the Christmas story—Norm and Norma from Normal, Ohio, plodding into Bethlehem in the middle of the night. No one notices them. No one looks twice in their direction. The innkeeper won't even clean out a corner in the attic.

The splendor of the first Christmas is the lack thereof. Step into the stable, and cradle in your arms the infant Jesus, still moist from the womb, just wrapped in the rags. Run a finger across his chubby cheek, and listen as one who knew him well puts lyrics to the event:

"In the beginning was the Word" (John 1:1 NIV).

The words "In the beginning" take us to the beginning. "In the beginning God created the heavens and the earth" (Gen. 1:1 NIV). The baby Mary held was connected to the dawn of time. He saw the first ray of sunlight and heard the first crash of a wave. The baby was born, but the Word never was.

"All things were made through him" (1 Cor. 8:6 NCV). Not by him, but through him. Jesus didn't fashion the world out of raw material he found. He created all things out of nothing.

Jesus: the Genesis Word, "the firstborn over all creation" (Col. 1:15 NIV). He is the "one Lord, Jesus Christ, through whom God made everything and through whom we live" (1 Cor. 8:6 NLT).

And then, what no theologian conceived, what no rabbi dared to dream, God did. "The Word became flesh" (John 1:14 NIV). The Artist became oil on his own palette. The Potter melted into the mud on his own wheel. God became an embryo in the belly of a village girl. Christ in Mary. God in Christ.

Astounding, this thought of heaven's fetus floating within the womb. Jesus was an ordinary baby. There is nothing in the story to imply that he levitated over the manger or walked out of the stable. Just the opposite. He "dwelt among us" (John 1:14 NKJV). John's word for *dwelt* traces its origin to tabernacle or tent. Jesus did not separate himself from his creation; he pitched his tent in the neighborhood.

The Word of God entered the world with the cry of a baby. His family had no cash or connections or strings to pull. Jesus, the Maker of the universe, the one who invented time and created breath, was born into a family too humble to swing a bed for a pregnant mom-to-be.

God writes his story with people like Joseph and Mary.

Ordinary folks. Ordinary place. But a conduit of extraordinary grace. And in God's story, ordinary matters.

REFLECTION AND DISCUSSION

Max says, "The Christmas hope [is] that God indwells the everydayness of our world." What splendors affect your normal every day? Nothing is too big, small, or monotonous.

_____

_____

_____

_____

_____

Why do you think God chooses ordinary people like Joseph and Mary? What does this say about God's nature and his attention to each of his children?

_____

_____

_____

_____

When Christ dwells in us, our ordinary identity becomes extraordinary. List some of the ordinary things that make you special and one-of-a-kind.

MATTHEW

MATTHEW

BEFORE YOU BEGIN
Read Matthew 9:9 NLT

As Jesus was walking along, he saw a man named Matthew sitting at his tax collector's booth. "Follow me and be my disciple," Jesus said to him. So Matthew got up and followed him.

The surprise in this invitation is the one invited—a tax collector. Combine the greed of an embezzling executive with the presumption of a hokey television evangelist. Throw in the audacity of an ambulance-chasing lawyer and the cowardice of a drive-by sniper. Stir in a pinch of a pimp's morality, and finish it off with the drug peddler's code of ethics—and what do you have?

A first-century tax collector.

According to the Jews, these guys ranked barely above plankton on the food chain. Caesar permitted these Jewish citizens to tax almost anything—your boat, the fish you caught, your house, your crops. If Caesar got his due, they could keep the rest.

Matthew was a public tax collector. Private tax collectors hired other people to do the dirty work. Public publicans, like Matthew, just pulled their stretch limos into the poor side of town and set up shop. As crooked as corkscrews.

His given name was Levi, a priestly name (Mark 2:14; Luke 5:27–28). Did his parents aspire for him to enter the priesthood? If so, he was a flop in the family circle.

You can bet he was shunned. The neighborhood cookouts? Never invited. High school reunions? Somehow his name was left off the list. The guy was avoided like streptococcus A. Everybody kept his distance from Matthew.

Everyone except Jesus. "'Follow me and be my disciple,' Jesus said to him. So Matthew got up and followed him" (Matt. 9:9 NLT).

Matthew must have been ripe. Jesus hardly had to tug. Within a punctuation mark, Matthew's shady friends and Jesus' green followers are swapping email addresses. "Then Levi gave a big dinner for Jesus at his house. Many tax collectors and other people were eating there, too" (Luke 5:29 NCV).

What do you suppose led up to that party? Let's try to imagine. I can see Matthew going back to his office and packing up. He removes the Quisling of the Year Award from the wall and boxes up the Shady Business School certificate. His coworkers start asking questions.

"What's up, Matt? Headed on a cruise?"

"Hey, Matthew, the Missus kick you out?"

Matthew doesn't know what to say. He mumbles something about a job change. But as he reaches the door, he pauses. Holding his box full of office supplies, he looks back.

He feels a lump in his throat. Oh, these guys aren't much. Parents warn their kids about this sort. Salty language. Mardi Gras morals. They keep the phone number of the bookie on speed dial. But a friend is a friend. Yet what can he do? Invite them to meet Jesus? Yeah, right. They like preachers the way sheep like butchers. What if he snuck little Torah tracts in their desks? Nah, they don't read.

So, not knowing what else to do, he shrugs his shoulders and gives them a nod. "These stupid allergies," he says, rubbing the mist from one eye.

Later that day the same thing happens. He goes to the bar to settle his account. The décor is blue-collar chic: a seedy, smoky place with a Budweiser chandelier over the pool table and a jukebox in the corner. Not the country club, but for Matthew, it's his home on the way home. And when he tells the owner he's moving on, the bartender responds, "Whoa, Matt. What's comin' down?"

Matthew mumbles an excuse about a transfer but leaves with an empty feeling in his gut.

Later on, he meets up with Jesus at a diner and shares his problem. "It's my buddies—you know, the guys at the office. And the fellows at the bar."

"What about them?" Jesus asks.

"Well, we kinda run together, you know. I'm gonna miss 'em. Take Josh for instance—as slick as a can of Quaker State, but he visits orphans on Sunday. And Bruno at the gym? Can crunch you like a roach, but I've never had a better friend. He's posted bail for me three times."

Jesus motions for him to go on. "What's the problem?"

"Well, I'm gonna miss those guys. I mean, I've got nothing against Peter and James and John, Jesus . . . but they're Sunday morning, and I'm Saturday night. I've got my own circle, ya know?"

Jesus starts to smile and shake his head. "Matthew, Matthew, you think I came to quarantine you? Following me doesn't mean forgetting your friends. Just the opposite. I want to meet them."

"Are you serious?"

"Is the high priest a Jew?"

"But, Jesus, these guys . . . half of them are on parole. Josh hasn't worn socks since his bar mitzvah . . ."

"I'm not talking about a religious service, Matthew. Let me ask you—what do you like to do? Bowl? Play Monopoly? How's your golf game?"

Matthew's eyes brighten. "You ought to see me cook. I get on steaks like a whale on Jonah."

"Perfect." Jesus smiles. "Then throw a little going away party. A hang-up-the-clipboard bash. Get the gang together."

Matthew's all over it. Calling the caterer, his housekeeper, his secretary. "Get the word out, Thelma. Drinks and dinner at my house tonight. Tell the guys to come and bring a date."

And so Jesus ends up at Matthew's house, a classy split-level with a view of the Sea of Galilee. Parked out front is everything from BMWs to Harleys to limos. And the crowd inside tells you this is anything but a clergy conference.

Earrings on the guys and tattoos on the girls. Moussified hair. Music that rumbles teeth roots. And buzzing around in the middle of the group is Matthew, making more connections than an electrician. He hooks up Peter with the tax collector bass club and Martha with the kitchen staff. Simon the Zealot meets a high school debate partner. And Jesus? Beaming. What could be better? Sinners and saints in the same room, and no one's trying to determine who is which. But an hour or so into the evening the door opens, and an icy breeze blows in. "The Pharisees and the men who taught the law for the Pharisees began to complain to Jesus' followers, 'Why do you eat and drink with tax collectors and sinners?'" (Luke 5:30 NCV).

Enter the religious police and their thin-lipped piety. Big black books under arms. Cheerful as Siberian prison guards. Clerical collars so tight that veins bulge. They like to grill too. But not steaks.

Matthew is the first to feel the heat. "Some religious fellow you are," one says, practically pulling an eyebrow muscle. "Look at the people you hang out with."

Matthew doesn't know whether to get mad or get out. Before he has time to choose, Jesus intervenes, explaining that Matthew is right where he needs to be. "Healthy people don't need a doctor—sick people do. I have come to call not those who think they are righteous, but those who know they are sinners and need to repent" (vv. 31–32 NLT).

Quite a story. Matthew goes from double dealer to disciple. He throws a party that makes the religious right uptight, but Christ proud. The good guys look good, and the bad guys hit the road. Some story indeed.

What do we do with it?

That depends on which side of the tax collector's table you find yourself. You and I are Matthew. Don't look at me that way. There's enough hustler in the best of us to qualify for Matthew's table. Maybe you've never taken taxes, but you've taken liberty with the truth, taken credit that wasn't yours, taken advantage of the weak. You and me? Matthew.

If you're still at the table, you receive an invitation. "Follow me." So what if you've got a rube reputation? So did Matthew. You may end up writing your own gospel.

If you've left the table, you receive a clarification. You don't have to be weird to follow Jesus. You don't have to stop liking your friends to follow him. Just the opposite. A few introductions would be nice. Do you know how to grill a steak?

REFLECTION AND DISCUSSION

What's good about having saints and sinners in the same room?

_____

_____

_____

_____

_____

What's good about not trying to figure out who belongs to which group?

_____

_____

_____

_____

_____

Why did Matthew's party make the pious people uptight?

_____

_____

_____

_____

_____

_____

What parallel situations do you see today? Do you generally respond to them like Christ or like the religious leaders? Why?

_____

_____

_____

_____

_____

_____

MEPHIBOSHETH

MEPHIBOSHETH

BEFORE YOU BEGIN
Read 2 Samuel 4:4, 9:3–11 NIV

(Jonathan son of Saul had a son who was lame in both feet. He was five years old when the news about Saul and Jonathan came from Jezreel. His nurse picked him up and fled, but as she hurried to leave, he fell and became disabled. His name was Mephibosheth.)

The king asked, "Is there no one still alive from the house of Saul to whom I can show God's kindness?"

Ziba answered the king, "There is still a son of Jonathan; he is lame in both feet."

"Where is he?" the king asked.

Ziba answered, "He is at the house of Makir son of Ammiel in Lo Debar."

So King David had him brought from Lo Debar, from the house of Makir son of Ammiel.

When Mephibosheth son of Jonathan, the son of Saul, came to David, he bowed down to pay him honor.

David said, "Mephibosheth!"

"At your service," he replied.

"Don't be afraid," David said to him, "for I will surely show you kindness for the sake of your father Jonathan. I will restore to you all the land that belonged to your grandfather Saul, and you will always eat at my table."

Mephibosheth bowed down and said, "What is your servant, that you should notice a dead dog like me?"

Then the king summoned Ziba, Saul's steward, and said to him, "I have given your master's grandson everything that belonged to Saul and his family. You and your sons and your servants are to farm the land for him and bring in the crops, so that your master's grandson may be provided for. And Mephibosheth, grandson of your master, will always eat at my table." (Now Ziba had fifteen sons and twenty servants.)

Then Ziba said to the king, "Your servant will do whatever my lord the king commands his servant to do." So Mephibosheth ate at David's table like one of the king's sons.

God, too, has made a covenant to adopt his people. His covenant is not invalidated by our rebellion. It's one thing to love us when we are strong, obedient, and willing. But when we ransack his house and steal what is his? This is the test of love.

And God passes the test. "God shows his great love for us in this way: Christ died for us while we were still sinners" (Rom. 5:8 NCV). God didn't look at our frazzled lives and say, "I'll die for you when you deserve it." Nor did David look at Mephibosheth and say, "I'll rescue you when you've learned to walk."

Mephibosheth was the son of Jonathan and the grandson of Saul, who was the first king of Israel. Jonathan and Saul were killed in battle, leaving the throne to be occupied by David.

David had no intention of following this tradition, but the family of Saul didn't know that. So they hurried to escape. Of special concern to them was five-year-old

Mephibosheth, for upon the deaths of his father and grandfather, he was the presumptive heir to the throne. If David was intent on murdering Saul's heirs, this boy would be first on his list. So the family got out of Dodge. But in the haste of the moment, Mephibosheth slipped from the arms of his nurse, permanently damaging both feet. For the rest of his life, he would be a cripple.

For nearly two decades the young prince lived in a distant land, unable to walk to the king, too fearful to talk to the king. He was unable to help himself.

Meanwhile, David's kingdom flourished. Under his leadership, Israel grew to ten times its original size. He knew no defeat on the battlefield nor insurrection in his court. Israel was at peace. The people were thankful. And David, the shepherd made king, did not forget his promise to Jonathan.

Jonathan "loved David as much as he loved himself" (1 Sam. 20:17 NCV). Their legendary friendship met its ultimate test the day David learned that Saul was trying to kill him. Jonathan pledged to save David and asked his friend one favor in return: "You must never stop showing your kindness to my family, even when the LORD has destroyed all your enemies from the earth. So Jonathan made an agreement with David" (1 Sam. 20:15–16 NCV).

Don't you know this was a tender memory for David? Can't you imagine him reflecting on this moment years later? Perhaps such a moment of reflection prompted him to turn to his servants and ask, "Is anyone still left in Saul's family? I want to show kindness to that person for Jonathan's sake!" (2 Sam. 9:1 NCV).

Those who are prone to extend grace tend to ask such questions. Can't I do something for somebody? Can't I be kind to someone because others have been kind to me? David isn't seeking to do good to be applauded by people. He is driven by the singular thought that he, too, was once weak. And in his weakness, he was helped. David, while hiding from Saul, qualified for Paul's epitaph, "when we were unable to help ourselves" (Rom. 5:6 NCV).

David was delivered; now he desires to do the same. A servant named Ziba knows of a descendant. "'Jonathan has a son still living who is crippled in both feet.' The king asked Ziba, 'Where is this son?' Ziba answered, 'He is at the house of Makir son of Ammiel in Lo Debar'" (2 Sam. 9:3–4 NCV).

Just one sentence and David knew he had more than he bargained for. The boy was "crippled in both feet." Who would have blamed David for asking Ziba, "Are there any other options? Any healthy family members?"

Who would have faulted him for the following thoughts, reasoning that a cripple would not fit well into the castle crowd?

Only the elite walk these floors; this kid can't even walk! And what service could he provide? No wealth, no education, no training. And who knows what he looks like? All these years he's been living in . . . what was it again? Lo Debar? Even the name means "barren place." Surely there is someone I can help who isn't so needy.

But such words were never recorded. David's only response was, "Where is this son?" (v. 4 NCV).

This son. One wonders how long it had been since Mephibosheth was referred to as a son. In all previous references he was called a cripple. Many of you know what it's like to carry a stigma. Each time your name is mentioned, your calamity follows.

Like a pesky sibling, your past follows you wherever you go. Isn't there anyone who sees you for who you are and not what you did? Yes. There is one who does. Your King. When God speaks of you, he doesn't mention your plight, pain, or problem; he lets you share his glory. He calls you his child.

Mephibosheth carried his stigma for twenty years. When people mentioned his name, they mentioned his problem. But when the king mentioned his name, he called him "son." And one word from the palace offsets a thousand voices in the streets.

David's couriers journeyed to Mephibosheth's door, carried him to a chariot, and escorted him to the palace. He was taken before the king, where he bowed face-down on the floor and confessed, "I am your servant" (2 Sam. 9:6 NCV). His fear is understandable. Though he may have been told that David was kind, what assurance did he have? Though the emissaries surely told him that David meant no harm, he was afraid. David's first words to him were, "Don't be afraid" (v.7 NCV).

By the way, your king has been known to say the same. Are you aware that the most repeated command from the lips of Jesus was "Fear not"? Are you aware that the command from heaven not to be afraid appears in every book of the Bible?

Mephibosheth had been called, found, and rescued, but he still needed assurance.

Don't we all? Don't we, like the trembling guest, need assurance that we are bowing before a gracious king? Paul says we have that assurance. The apostle points to the cross as our guarantee of God's love. "God shows his great love for us in this way: Christ died for us while we were still sinners" (Rom. 5:8 NCV). God proved his love for us by sacrificing his Son.

Just as David kept his promise to Jonathan, so God keeps his promise to us. The name Mephibosheth means "he who scatters shame." And that is exactly what David intended to do for the young prince.

In swift succession David returned to Mephibosheth all his land, crops, and servants and then insisted that the cripple eat at the king's table. Not just once but four times!

"I will give you back all the land of your grandfather Saul, and you will always eat at my table."

"Mephibosheth . . . will always eat at my table."

"So Mephibosheth ate at David's table as if he were one of the king's sons."

"Mephibosheth lived in Jerusalem, because he always ate at the king's table. And he was crippled in both feet" (2 Sam. 9:7, 10, 11, 13 NCV).

And I ask you, do you see our story in his?

Children of royalty, crippled by the fall, permanently marred by sin. Living parenthetical lives in the chronicles of earth only to be remembered by the king. Driven not by our beauty but by his promise, he calls us to himself and invites us to take a permanent place at his table. Though we often limp more than we walk, we take our place next to the other sinners-made-saints and we share in God's glory.

Like Mephibosheth, we are sons of the King.

"God didn't look at our frazzled lives and say, 'I'll die for you when you deserve it.'" Had God said such a thing, how would that affect you right now? Has anyone ever deserved for God to die for them? Explain.

_____

_____

_____

_____

_____

Do you see your story in Mephibosheth's? Explain.

_____

_____

_____

_____

_____

Is there a Mephibosheth in your life? If so, what have you learned from knowing that person?

_____

_____

_____

_____

_____

_____

Read Matthew 5:6. What group of people does Jesus describe in this verse? What promise does he give to them?

_____

_____

_____

_____

_____

Do you believe you are included in this group? Explain.

_____

_____

_____

_____

_____

_____

_____

_____

_____

_____

_____

_____

_____

MOSES

MOSES

Moses was tending the flock of Jethro his father-in-law, the priest of Midian, and he led the flock to the far side of the wilderness and came to Horeb, the mountain of God. There the angel of the LORD appeared to him in flames of fire from within a bush. Moses saw that though the bush was on fire it did not burn up. So Moses thought, "I will go over and see this strange sight— why the bush does not burn up."

When the LORD saw that he had gone over to look, God called to him from within the bush, "Moses! Moses!"

And Moses said, "Here I am."

"Do not come any closer," God said. "Take off your sandals, for the place where you are standing is holy ground." Then he said, "I am the God of your father, the God of Abraham, the God of Isaac and the God of Jacob." At this, Moses hid his face, because he was afraid to look at God.

[God said,] "And now the cry of the Israelites has reached me, and I have seen the way the Egyptians are oppressing them. So now, go. I am sending you to Pharaoh to bring my people the Israelites out of Egypt."

The hallway is silent except for the wheels of the mop bucket and the shuffle of the old man's feet. Both sound tired.

Both know these floors. How many nights has Hank cleaned them? Always careful to get in the corners. Always careful to set up his yellow caution sign warning of wet floors. Always chuckling as he does. "Be careful everyone," he laughs to himself, knowing no one is near. Not at 3:00 a.m.

Hank's health isn't what it used to be. Gout keeps him awake. Arthritis makes him limp. His glasses are so thick his eyeballs look twice their size. Shoulders stoop. But he does his work. Slopping soapy water on linoleum. Scrubbing the heel marks left by the well-heeled lawyers. He'll be finished an hour before quitting time. Always finishes early. Has for twenty years.

When finished he'll put away his bucket and take a seat outside the office of the senior partner and wait. Never leaves early. Could. No one would know. But he doesn't. He broke the rules once. Never again.

Sometimes, if the door is open, he'll enter the office. Not for long. Just to look. The suite is larger than his apartment. He once had such an office.

Back when Hank was Henry. Back when the custodian was an executive. Long ago. Before the night shift. Before the mop bucket. Before the maintenance uniform. Before the scandal.

Hank doesn't think about it much now. Got in trouble, got fired, and got out. That's it. Not many people know about it. It's his secret.

Hank's story, by the way, is true. I changed the name and a detail or two. I gave him a different job and put him in a different century. But the story is factual. You've heard it. You know it. When I give you his real name, you'll remember.

But more than a true story, it's a common story. It's a story of a derailed dream. It's a story of high hopes colliding with harsh realities.

Happens to all dreamers. And since all have dreamed, it happens to us all.

In Hank's case, it was a mistake he could never forget. A grave mistake. Hank killed someone. He came upon a criminal beating up an innocent man, and Hank lost control. He killed the mugger. When word got out, Hank got out.

Hank would rather hide than go to jail. The executive became a fugitive.

True story. Common story. Most stories aren't as extreme as Hank's. Few spend their lives running from the law. Many, however, live with regrets.

"I could have gone to college on a golf scholarship," a fellow told me on the golf course. "Had an offer right out of school. But I joined a rock-and-roll band. Ended up never going. Now I'm stuck fixing garage doors."

"Now I'm stuck." Epitaph of a derailed dream.

Pick up a high school yearbook and read the "What I want to do" sentence under each picture. You'll get dizzy breathing the thin air of mountaintop visions.

Yet, take the yearbook to a twentieth-year reunion and read the next chapter. Some dreams have come true, but many haven't. Not that all should, mind you. I hope the little guy who dreamed of being a sumo wrestler came to his senses. And I hope he didn't lose his passion in the process. Changing direction in life is not tragic. Losing passion in life is.

Something happens to us along the way. Convictions to change the world downgrade to commitments to pay the bills. Rather than make a difference, we make a salary. Rather than look forward, we look back. Rather than look outward, we look inward. And we don't like what we see.

Hank didn't. Hank saw a man who'd settled for the mediocre. Trained in the finest institutions of the world, yet working the night shift in a minimum wage job so he wouldn't be seen in the day.

But all that changed when he heard the voice from the mop bucket. At first, he thought the voice was a joke. Some of the fellows on the third floor play these kinds of tricks.

"Henry, Henry," the voice called. Hank turned. No one called him Henry anymore. "Henry, Henry."

He turned toward the pail. It was glowing. Bright red. Hot red. He could feel the heat ten feet away. He stepped closer and looked in. The water wasn't boiling.

"This is strange," Hank mumbled to himself as he took another step to get a closer look. But the voice stopped him. "Don't come any closer. Take off your shoes. You are on holy tile." Suddenly Hank knew who was speaking. "God?"

I'm not making this up. I know you think I am. Sounds crazy. Almost irreverent. God speaking from a hot mop bucket to a janitor named Hank? Would it be believable if I said God was speaking from a burning bush to a shepherd named Moses?

Maybe that one's easier to handle—because you've heard it before. But just because it's Moses and a bush rather than Hank and a bucket, it's no less spectacular.

It sure shocked the sandals off Moses. We wonder what amazed the old fellow more: that God spoke in a bush or that God spoke at all.

Moses, like Hank, had made a mistake. You remember his story. Adopted nobility. An Israelite reared in an Egyptian palace. His countrymen were slaves, but Moses was privileged. Ate at the royal table. Educated in the finest schools.

But his most influential teacher had no degree. She was his mother. A Jewess who was hired to be his nanny. "Moses," you can almost hear her whisper to her young son, "God has put you here on purpose. Someday you will set your people free. Never forget, Moses. Never forget."

Moses didn't. The flame of justice grew hotter until it blazed. Moses saw an Egyptian beating a Hebrew slave. Just like Hank killed the mugger, Moses killed the Egyptian.

The next day Moses saw the Hebrew. You'd think the slave would say thanks. He didn't. Rather than express gratitude, he expressed anger. "Will you kill me too?" he asked (see Ex. 2:14).

Moses knew he was in trouble. He fled Egypt and hid in the wilderness. Call it a career shift. He went from dining with heads of state to counting heads of sheep.

And so it happened that a bright, promising Hebrew began herding sheep in the hills. Moses thought the move was permanent. There is no indication he ever intended to go back to Egypt. In fact, there is every indication he wanted to stay with his sheep. Standing barefoot before the bush, he confessed, "I am not a great man! How can I go to the king and lead the Israelites out of Egypt?" (Ex. 3:11 NCV).

I'm glad Moses asked that question. It's a good one. Why Moses? Or, more specifically, why eighty-year-old Moses? The forty-year-old version was more appealing. The

Moses we saw in Egypt was brash and confident. But the Moses we find four decades later is reluctant and weather beaten.

Had you or I looked at Moses back in Egypt, we would have said, "This man is ready for battle." Educated in the finest system in the world. Trained by the ablest soldiers. Instant access to the inner circle of the Pharaoh. Moses spoke their language and knew their habits. He was the perfect man for the job.

Moses at forty we like. But Moses at eighty? No way. Too old. Too tired. Smells like a shepherd. What impact would he have on Pharaoh? He's the wrong man for the job.

And Moses would have agreed. "Tried that once before," he would say. "Those people don't want to be helped. Just leave me here to tend my sheep. They're easier to lead."

Moses wouldn't have gone. You wouldn't have sent him. I wouldn't have sent him.

But God did. How do you figure? Benched at forty and suited up at eighty. Why? What does he know now that he didn't know then? What did he learn in the desert that he didn't learn in Egypt?

The ways of the desert, for one. Forty-year-old Moses was a city boy. Octogenarian Moses knows the name of every snake and the location of every watering hole. If he's going to lead thousands of Hebrews into the wilderness, he better know the basics of Desert Life 101.

Family dynamics, for another. If he's going to be traveling with families for forty years, it might help to understand how they work. He marries a woman of faith, the daughter of a Midianite priest, and establishes his own family.

But more than the ways of the desert and the people, Moses needed to learn something about himself.

Apparently, he has learned it. God says Moses is ready. And to convince him, God speaks through a bush. "School's out," God tells him. "Now it's time to get to work." Poor Moses. He didn't even know he was enrolled.

But he was. And, guess what? So are you. The voice from the bush is the voice that whispers to you. It reminds you that God is not finished with you yet. Oh, you may think he is. You may think you've peaked. You may think he's got someone else to do the job.

If so, think again.

"God began doing a good work in you, and I am sure he will continue it until it is finished when Jesus Christ comes again" (Phil. 1:6 NCV).

He may speak through a bush, a mop bucket, or stranger still, he may speak through this book.

REFLECTION AND DISCUSSION

Have your convictions changed as you've grown older? If so, in what way? Have your evolving convictions brought you closer to understanding God? Explain.

_____

_____

_____

_____

_____

Would you have given Moses the job of bringing Israel out of slavery? Explain.

_____

_____

_____

_____

_____

_____

What do you think God saw in Moses? What do you think he might see in you?

_____

_____

_____

_____

What do you think God may still be calling you to do?

_____

_____

_____

_____

Read Philippians 1:6. What promise is given in this verse? How can it change the way you live? Does it affect the way you live personally? Explain.

_____

_____

_____

_____

_____

_____

_____

_____

_____

_____

_____

_____

_____

NICODEMUS

NICODEMUS

BEFORE YOU BEGIN

Read John 3:1-21 NIV

There was a Pharisee, a man named Nicodemus who was a member of the Jewish ruling council. He came to Jesus at night and said, "Rabbi, we know that you are a teacher who has come from God. For no one could perform the signs you are doing if God were not with him."

Jesus replied, "Very truly I tell you, no one can see the kingdom of God unless they are born again."

"How can someone be born when they are old?" Nicodemus asked. "Surely they cannot enter a second time into their mother's womb to be born!"

Jesus answered, "Very truly I tell you, no one can enter the kingdom of God unless they are born of water and the Spirit. Flesh gives birth to flesh, but the Spirit gives birth to spirit. You should not be surprised at my saying, 'You must be born again.' The wind blows wherever it pleases. You hear its sound, but you cannot tell where it comes from or where it is going. So it is with everyone born of the Spirit."

"How can this be?" Nicodemus asked.

"You are Israel's teacher," said Jesus, "and do you not understand these things? Very truly I tell you, we speak of what we know, and we testify to what we have seen, but still you people do not accept our testimony. I have spoken to you of earthly things and you do not believe; how then will you believe if I speak of heavenly things? No one has ever gone into heaven except the one who came from heaven—the Son of Man. Just as Moses lifted up the snake in the wilderness, so the Son of Man must be lifted up, that everyone who believes may have eternal life in him."

For God so loved the world that he gave his one and only Son, that whoever believes in him shall not perish but have eternal life. For God did not send his Son into the world to condemn the world, but to save the world through him. Whoever believes in him is not condemned, but whoever does not believe stands condemned already because they have not believed in the name of God's one and only Son. This is the verdict: Light has come into the world, but people loved darkness instead of light because their deeds were evil. Everyone who does evil hates the light, and will not come into the light for fear that their deeds will be exposed. But whoever lives by the truth comes into the light, so that it may be seen plainly that what they have done has been done in the sight of God.

It's a fact of the farm. The most fertile ground remains barren if no seed is sown.

Apparently, Nicodemus didn't know that. He thought the soil could bear fruit with no seeds. He was big on the farmer's part but forgetful of the seed's part. He was a legalist. And that is how a legalist thinks. A legalist prepares the soil but forgets the seed.

Nicodemus came about his legalism honestly. He was a Pharisee.

Pharisees taught that faith was an outside job. What you wore, how you acted, the title you carried, the sound of your prayers, the amount of your gifts—all these were the Pharisees' measure of spirituality.

Had they been farmers, they would have had the most attractive acreage in the region—painted silos and sparkling equipment. The fences would have been white-washed and clean. The soil overturned and watered.

The Pharisees had only one problem. For all their discussion about the right techniques, they harvested little fruit. In fact, one untrained Galilean had borne more fruit in a few short months than all the Pharisees had in a generation. This made them jealous. Angry. Condescending. And they dealt with him by ignoring his results and insulting his methods.

That is, all the Pharisees except Nicodemus. He was curious. No, more than curious, he was stirred, stirred by the way people listened to Jesus. They listened as if he were the only one with truth. As if he were a prophet.

Nicodemus was stirred by what he saw Jesus do. Like the time Jesus stormed into the temple and overturned the tables of the money changers. Nicodemus once knew such passion. But that was a long time ago—before the titles, before the robes, before the rules.

Nicodemus is drawn to the carpenter, but he can't be seen with him. Nicodemus is on the high court. He can't approach Jesus in the day. So Nicodemus goes to meet him at night and begins with courtesies. "'Teacher, we know you are a teacher sent from God, because no one can do the miracles you do unless God is with him" (John 3:2 NCV).

Jesus disregards the compliment. "I tell you the truth, unless you are born again, you cannot be in God's kingdom" (v. 3 NCV).

Straight to the point. Jesus knows the heart of the legalist is hard. You can't crack it with feathery accolades. So Jesus hammers away:

You can't help the blind by turning up the light, Nicodemus.

You can't help the deaf by turning up the music, Nicodemus.

You can't change the inside by decorating the outside, Nicodemus.

You can't grow fruit without seed, Nicodemus.

You must be born again.

The meeting between Jesus and Nicodemus was more than an encounter between two religious figures. It was a collision between two philosophies. Two opposing views on salvation.

Nicodemus thought the person did the work; Jesus says God does the work. Nicodemus thought it was a trade-off. Jesus says it is a gift. Nicodemus thought man's job was to earn it. Jesus says man's job is to accept it.

These two views encompass all views. All the world religions can be placed in one of two camps: legalism or grace. Humankind does it or God does it. Salvation as a wage based on deeds done—or salvation as a gift based on Christ's death.

A legalist believes the supreme force behind salvation is you. If you look right, speak right, and belong to the right segment of the right group, you will be saved. The brunt of responsibility doesn't lie within God; it lies within you.

The result? The outside sparkles. The talk is good and the step is true. But look closely. Listen carefully. Something is missing. What is it? Joy. What's there? Fear. Arrogance. Failure.

Legalism is slow torture, suffocation of the spirit, amputation of one's dreams. Legalism is just enough religion to keep you but not enough to nourish you.

Legalism doesn't need God. Legalism is the search for innocence—not forgiveness. It's a systematic process of defending self, explaining self, exalting self, and justifying self. Legalists are obsessed with self—not God.

Nicodemus knew how to march, but he longed to sing. He knew there was something more, but he didn't know where to find it. So he went to Jesus.

He went at night because he feared the displeasure of his peers. Legalism puts the fear of man in you. It makes you approval hungry. You become keenly aware of what others will say and think, and you do what it takes to please them. Conformity is not fun, but it's safe. The uniform doesn't fit, but it's approved, so you wear it. You don't know why you are marching or where you are going—but who are you to ask questions? So you stay in step and plod down the path of least resistance.

And if you dare explore another trail, you must do so at night, like Nicodemus did. In the conversation, Nicodemus, the renowned teacher of the law, speaks only three times: once to compliment and twice to question. After a lifetime of weighing the tittles of Scripture in the scale of logic, the scholar becomes suddenly silent as Jesus opens the gate and the light of grace floods the catacomb.

Jesus begins by revealing the source of spirituality: "Human life comes from human parents, but spiritual life comes from the Spirit" (v. 6 NCV).

Spiritual life is not a human endeavor. It is rooted in and orchestrated by the Holy Spirit. Every spiritual achievement is created and energized by God.

Spirituality, Jesus says, comes not from church attendance or good deeds or correct doctrine, but from heaven itself. Such words must have set Nicodemus back on his heels. But Jesus was just getting started.

"The wind blows where it wants to and you hear the sound of it, but you don't know where the wind comes from or where it is going. It is the same with every person who is born from the Spirit" (v. 8 NCV).

Ever had a gust of wind come to you for help? Ever seen a windstorm on the side of the road catching its breath? No, you haven't. The wind doesn't seek our aid. Wind doesn't even reveal its destiny. It's silent and invisible, and so is the Spirit.

By now Nicodemus was growing edgy.

Salvation is God's business. Grace is his idea, his work, and his expense. He offers it to whom he desires, when he desires. Our job in the process is to inform the people, not to screen the people.

The question must have been written all over Nicodemus's face. Why would God do this? What would motivate him to offer such a gift? What Jesus told Nicodemus, Nicodemus never could have imagined. The motive behind the gift of new birth? Love. "God loved the world so much that he gave his one and only Son so that whoever believes in him may not be lost, but have eternal life" (v. 16 NCV).

Nicodemus has never heard such words. He has had many discussions of salvation. But this is the first in which no rules were given. "Everyone who believes can have eternal life in him," Jesus told him. Could God be so generous? Even in the darkness of night, the amazement is seen on Nicodemus's face. Everyone who believes can have eternal life. Not "everyone who achieves." Not "everyone who succeeds." Not "everyone who agrees." But "everyone who believes."

Note how God liberates the legalist. Observe the tender firmness of his touch. Like a master farmer, he shoveled away the crusty soil until a moist, fertile spot was found,

and there he planted a seed, a seed of grace. Did it bear fruit? Read the following and see for yourself.

> Nicodemus, who earlier had come to Jesus at night, went with Joseph. He brought about seventy-five pounds of myrrh and aloes. These two men took Jesus' body and wrapped it with the spices in pieces of linen cloth, which is how [Jewish people] bury the dead. In the place where Jesus was crucified, there was a garden. In the garden was a new tomb that had never been used before. The men laid Jesus in that tomb. (John 19:39–42 NCV)

Strange how a man can go full circle in the kingdom. The one who'd come at night now appears in the day. The one who crept through the shadows to meet Jesus now comes to the cross to serve Jesus. And the one who'd received the seed of grace now plants the greatest seed of all—the seed of eternal life.

REFLECTION AND DISCUSSION

Read John 3:2. Why do you think Jesus ignored Nicodemus's comment and instead responded, "I tell you the truth, unless you are born again, you cannot be in God's kingdom" (v. 3 NCV)?

_____

_____

_____

_____

_____

Read Colossians 2:20-23. Why do you think we are so easily drawn back into legalism? What is the only way to stay free of it?

_____

_____

_____

_____

_____

_____

Read Galatians 5:1-6. How does this passage teach that salvation cannot be achieved through a mixture of faith and deeds?

_____

_____

_____

_____

_____

_____

How does John 19:39–42 prove that Nicodemus finally escaped the trap of legalism? How did he escape this grip?

_____

_____

_____

_____

_____

_____

_____

_____

_____

_____

_____

_____

_____

NOAH

NOAH

BEFORE YOU BEGIN

Read Genesis 8:6–11 NIV

After forty days Noah opened a window he had made in the ark and sent out a raven, and it kept flying back and forth until the water had dried up from the earth. Then he sent out a dove to see if the water had receded from the surface of the ground. But the dove could find nowhere to perch because there was water over all the surface of the earth; so it returned to Noah in the ark. He reached out his hand and took the dove and brought it back to himself in the ark. He waited seven more days and again sent out the dove from the ark. When the dove returned to him in the evening, there in its beak was a freshly plucked olive leaf! Then Noah knew that the water had receded from the earth.

Water. All Noah can see is water. The evening sun sinks into it. The clouds are reflected in it. His boat is surrounded by it. Water. Water to the north. Water to the south. Water to the east. Water to the west.

He can't remember when he's seen anything but. He and the boys had barely pushed the last hippo up the ramp when heaven opened a thousand fire hydrants. Within moments the boat was rocking, and for days the rain was pouring, and for weeks Noah has been wondering, how long is this going to last? For forty days it rained. For months they have floated. For months they have eaten the same food, smelled the same smell, and looked at the same faces. After a certain point you run out of things to say to each other.

Finally the boat bumped, and the rocking stopped. Mrs. Noah gave Mr. Noah a look, and Noah gave the hatch a shove and poked his head through. The hull of the ark was resting on ground, but the ground was still surrounded by water. "Noah," she yelled up at him, "what do you see?"

"Water."

He sent a raven on a scouting mission; it never returned. He sent a dove. It came back shivering and spent, having found no place to roost. Then, just this morning, he tried again. He pulled a dove out of the bowels of the ark and ascended the ladder. The morning sun caused them both to squint. As he kissed the breast of the bird, he felt a pounding heart. Had he put a hand on his chest, he would have felt another. With a prayer he let it go and watched until the bird was no bigger than a speck on a window.

All day he looked for the dove's return. In between chores he opened the hatch and searched. The boys wanted him to play a little pin the tail on the donkey, but he passed. He chose instead to climb into the crow's nest and look. The wind lifted his gray hair. The sun warmed his weather-beaten face. But nothing lifted his heavy heart. He had seen nothing.

Now the sun is setting, and the sky is darkening, and he has come to look one final time, but all he sees is water. Water to the north. Water to the south. Water to the east. Water to the . . .

You know the feeling. You have stood where Noah stood. You've known your share of floods. Flooded by sorrow at the cemetery, stress at the office, anger at the disability in your body or the inability of your spouse. You've seen the floodwater rise, and you've likely seen the sun set on your hopes as well. You've been on Noah's boat.

And you've needed what Noah needed; you've needed some hope. You're not asking for a helicopter rescue, but the sound of one would be nice. Hope doesn't promise an instant solution but rather the possibility of an eventual one. Sometimes all we need is a little hope.

That's all Noah needed. And that's all Noah received.

He's about to call it a day when he hears the cooing of the dove. Here is how the Bible describes the moment: "That evening it came back to him with a fresh olive leaf in its mouth" (Gen. 8:11 NCV).

An olive leaf. Noah would have been happy to have the bird but to have the leaf! This leaf was more than foliage; this was promise. The bird brought more than a piece of a tree; it brought hope. For isn't that what hope is? Hope is an olive leaf—evidence of dry land after a flood. Proof to the dreamer that dreaming is worth the risk.

Don't we love the olive leaves of life? What's more, don't we love the doves that bring them? When the father walks his son through his first broken heart, he gives him an olive leaf. When the wife of many years consoles the wife of a few months, when she tells her that conflicts come and all husbands are moody and these storms pass, you know what she is doing? She is giving an olive leaf.

We love olive leaves. And we love those who give them. Perhaps that's the reason so many loved Jesus.

He stands near a woman who was yanked from a bed of promiscuity. She's still dizzy from the raid. A door slammed open, covers were pulled back, and the fraternity of moral police barged in. And now here she stands. Noah could see nothing but water. She can see nothing but anger. She has no hope.

But then Jesus speaks, "Let any one of you who is without sin be the first to throw a stone at hear." (John 8:7 NIV). Silence. Both the eyes and the rocks of the accusers hit the ground. Within moments they have left, and Jesus is alone with the woman. The dove of heaven offers her a leaf.

"Woman, where are they? Has no one condemned you?"

"No one, sir," she said.

"Then neither do I condemn you," Jesus declared. "Go now and leave your life of sin" (vv. 10–11 NIV).

Into her shame-flooded world he brings a leaf of hope.

He does something similar for Martha. She is bobbing in a sea of sorrow. Her brother is dead. His body has been buried. And Jesus, well, Jesus is late. "If you had been here, my brother would not have died." Then I think she might have paused. "But I know that even now God will give you whatever you ask" (John 11:21–22 NIV). As Noah opened his hatch, so Martha opens her heart. As the dove brought a leaf, so Christ brings the same.

> "I am the resurrection and the life. He who believes in me will live, even though they die; and whoever lives by believing in me will never die. Do you believe this?"
>
> "Yes, Lord," she replied, "I believe that you are the Messiah, the Son of God, who is to come into the world." (vv. 25–27 NIV)

How could he get by with such words? Who was he to make such a claim? What qualified him to offer grace to one woman and a promise of resurrection to another? Simple. He had done what the dove did. He'd crossed the shoreline of the future land and journeyed among the trees. And from the grove of grace he plucked a leaf for the woman. And from the tree of life he pulled a sprig for Martha.

And from both he brings leaves to you. Grace and life. Forgiveness of sin. The defeat of death. This is the hope he gives. This is the hope we need.

To all the Noahs of the world, to all who search the horizon for a fleck of hope, he proclaims, "Yes!" And he comes. He comes as a dove. He comes bearing fruit from a distant land, from our future home. He comes with a leaf of hope.

Have you received yours? Don't think your ark is too isolated. Don't think your flood is too wide. Your toughest challenge is nothing more than bobby pins and rubber bands to God. Bobby pins and rubber bands?

My older sister used to give them to me when I was a child. I would ride my tricycle up and down the sidewalk, pretending that the bobby pins were keys and my trike was a truck. But one day I lost the "keys." Crisis! What was I going to do? My search yielded nothing but tears and fear. But when I confessed my mistake to my sister, she just smiled. Being a decade older, she had a better perspective.

God has a better perspective as well. With all due respect, our severest struggles are, in his view, nothing worse than lost bobby pins and rubber bands. He is not confounded, confused, or discouraged.

Receive his hope, won't you? Receive it because you need it. Receive it so you can share it.

What do you suppose Noah did with his? What do you think he did with the leaf? Did he throw it overboard and forget about it? Do you suppose he stuck it in his pocket and saved it for a scrapbook? Or do you think he let out a whoop and assembled the troops and passed it around like the Hope Diamond it was?

Certainly he whooped. That's what you do with hope. What do you do with olive leaves? You pass them around. You don't stick them in your pocket. You give them to the ones you love. Love always hopes. "Love . . . bears all things, believes all things, hopes all things, endures all things" (1 Cor. 13:4–7 NKJV).

Love has hope in you. Love extends an olive leaf to the loved one and says, "I have hope in you." Love is just as quick to say, "I have hope for you."

You can say those words. You are a flood survivor. By God's grace you have found your way to dry land. You know what it's like to see the waters subside. And since you do, since you passed through a flood and lived to tell about it, you are qualified to give hope to someone else.

What? Can't think of any floods in your past? Let me jog your memory.

How about adolescence? Remember the torrent of the teenage years? Remember the hormones and hemlines? The puberty and pimples? Those were tough times. *Yeah, you're thinking, but you get through them.* That's exactly what teenagers need to hear you say. They need an olive leaf from a survivor.

So do young couples. It happens in every marriage. The honeymoon ends, and the river of romance becomes the river of reality, and they wonder if they will survive. You can tell them they will. You've been through it. Wasn't easy, but you survived. You and your spouse found dry land. Why don't you pluck an olive leaf and take it to an ark?

Are you a cancer survivor? Someone in the cancer ward needs to hear from you. Have you buried a spouse and lived to smile again? Then find the recently widowed and walk with them. Your experiences have deputized you into the dove brigade. You have an opportunity to give hope to the ark bound.

Remember Paul's admonition?

What a wonderful God we have—he is the Father of our Lord Jesus Christ, the source of every mercy, and the one who so wonderfully comforts and strengthens us in our hardships and trials. And why does he do this? So that when others are troubled, needing our sympathy and encouragement, we can pass on to them this same help and comfort God has given us. (2 Cor. 1:3–4 TLB)

Encourage those who are struggling. Don't know what to say? Then open your Bible. The olive leaf for the Christian is a verse of Scripture. "For everything that was written in the past was written to teach us, so that through endurance taught in the Scriptures and the encouragement they provide we might have hope" (Rom. 15:4 NIV).

Do you have a Bible? Do you know a Noah? Then start passing out the leaves.

To the grief stricken: "God has said, 'Never will I leave you; never will I forsake you'" (Heb. 13:5 NIV).

To the guilt ridden: "There is now no condemnation for those who are in Christ Jesus" (Rom. 8:1 NIV).

To the jobless: "In all things God works for the good of those who love him" (Rom. 8:28 NIV).

To those who feel beyond God's grace: "Whoever believes in him shall not perish but have eternal life" (John 3:16 NIV).

Your Bible is a basket of leaves. Won't you share one? They have amazing impact. After receiving his, Noah was a changed man. "Then Noah knew that the water had receded from the earth" (Gen. 8:11 NIV). He went up the ladder with questions and came down the ladder with confidence.

What a difference one leaf makes.

REFLECTION AND DISCUSSION

How has hope rescued you from a "flood" in the past? Explain.

_____

_____

_____

_____

_____

_____

In what areas of your life do you need hope today?

_____

_____

_____

_____

_____

_____

"Hope doesn't promise an instant solution but rather the possibility of an eventual one. Sometimes all we need is a little hope." Who do you know who could use a little hope right now?

_____

_____

_____

_____

_____

In what ways can you "pass out an olive leaf" to your loved ones? If you told them you have hope in them and for them, what would that mean to them?

_____

_____

_____

_____

_____

Why did Paul not grumble about his present struggles? (Rom. 8:18)

_____

_____

_____

_____

_____

_____

How can Paul's understanding of hope (Rom. 8:24–25) help us in our difficult times?

_____

_____

_____

_____

_____

PARALYZED MAN

PARALYZED MAN

BEFORE YOU BEGIN

Read John 5:1–9 NLT

Afterward Jesus returned to Jerusalem for one of the Jewish holy days. Inside the city, near the Sheep Gate, was the pool of Bethesda, with five covered porches. Crowds of sick people—blind, lame, or paralyzed—lay on the porches. One of the men lying there had been sick for thirty-eight years. When Jesus saw him and knew he had been ill for a long time, he asked him, "Would you like to get well?"

"I can't, sir," the sick man said, "for I have no one to put me into the pool when the water bubbles up. Someone else always gets there ahead of me."

Jesus told him, "Stand up, pick up your mat, and walk!"

Instantly, the man was healed! He rolled up his sleeping mat and began walking! But this miracle happened on the Sabbath.

For the longest time I thought Jesus was too kind. I thought this story was too bizarre and too good to be true. Then I realized something. This story isn't about an invalid in Jerusalem. This story is about you. It's about me. The fellow isn't nameless. He has a name—yours. He has a face—mine. He has a problem—just like ours.

Jesus encounters the man near a large pool north of the temple in Jerusalem. It's 360 feet long, 130 feet wide, and 75 feet deep. A colonnade with five porches overlooks the body of water. It's a monument of wealth and prosperity, but its residents are people of sickness and disease.

It's called Bethesda. An underwater spring caused the pool to bubble occasionally. The people believed the bubbles were caused by the dipping of angels' wings. They also believed that the first person to touch the water after the angel did would be healed. Did healing occur? I don't know. But I do know crowds of invalids came to give it a try.

Picture a battleground strewn with wounded bodies, and you see Bethesda. Imagine a nursing home overcrowded and understaffed, and you see the pool. Call to mind the orphans in Bangladesh or the abandoned in New Delhi, and you will see what people saw when they passed Bethesda. As they passed, what did they hear? An endless wave of groans. What did they witness? A field of faceless need. What did they do? Most walked past, ignoring the people.

But not Jesus. He is in Jerusalem for a feast. He is alone. He's not there to teach the disciples or to draw a crowd. The people need him—so he's there.

What is he thinking? When an infected hand touches his ankle, what does he do? When a blind child stumbles in Jesus' path, does he reach down to catch the child? When a wrinkled hand extends for alms, how does Jesus respond?

"When they suffered, he suffered also," Isaiah wrote (Isa. 63:9 NCV). On this day Jesus must have suffered much.

Remember, I told you this story was about us? Remember, I said I found our faces in the Bible? Well, here we are, filling the white space between the letters of John 5:5: "A man was lying there who had been sick for thirty-eight years."

Maybe you don't like being described like that. Perhaps you'd rather find yourself in the courage of David or the devotion of Mary. We all would. But before you or I can be like them, we must admit we are like the paralytic. Invalids out of options. Can't walk. Can't work. Can't care for ourselves. Can't even roll down the bank to the pool to cash in on the angel water.

You may be holding this book with healthy hands and reading with strong eyes, and you can't imagine what you and this four-decade invalid have in common. How could he be you? What do we have in common with him?

Simple. Our predicament and our hope. What predicament? It is described in Hebrews 12:14: "Anyone whose life is not holy will never see the Lord" (NCV).

That's our predicament: Only the holy will see God. Holiness is a prerequisite to heaven. Perfection is a requirement for eternity. We wish it weren't so. We act like it isn't so. We act like those who are "decent" will see God. We suggest that those who try hard will see God. We act as if we're good if we never do anything too bad. And that goodness is enough to qualify us for heaven.

Sounds right to us, but it doesn't sound right to God. And he sets the standard. And the standard is high. "You must be perfect, just as your Father in heaven is perfect" (Matt. 5:48 NCV).

You see, in God's plan, God is the standard for perfection. We don't compare ourselves to others; they are just as fouled up as we are. The goal is to be like him; anything less is inadequate.

That's why I say the invalid is you and me. We, like the invalid, are paralyzed. We, like the invalid, are trapped. We, like the invalid, are stuck; we have no solution for our predicament.

That's you and me lying on the ground. That's us wounded and weary. When it comes to healing our spiritual condition, we don't have a chance. We might as well be told to pole-vault the moon. We don't have what it takes to be healed. Our only hope is that God will do for us what he did for the man at Bethesda—that he will step out of the temple and step into our ward of hurt and helplessness.

Which is exactly what he has done.

Read slowly and carefully Paul's description of what God has done for you:

When you were spiritually dead because of your sins and because you were not free from the power of your sinful self, God made you alive with Christ, and he forgave all our sins. He canceled the debt, which listed all the rules we failed to follow. He took away that record with its rules and nailed it to the cross. God stripped the spiritual rulers and powers of their authority. With the cross, he won the victory and showed the world that they were powerless. (Col. 2:13–15 NCV)

As you look at the words above, answer these questions. Who is doing the work? You or God? Who is active? You or God? Who is doing the saving? You or God? Who is the one with strength? And who is the one paralyzed?

God has thrown life jackets to every generation.

Such are the stories in the Bible. One near-death experience after another. Just when the neck is on the chopping block, just when the noose is around the neck, Calvary comes.

Angels pound on Lot's door—Genesis 19.

The whirlwind speaks to Job's hurt—Job 38–42.

The Jordan purges Naaman's plague—2 Kings 5.

An angel appears in Peter's cell—Acts 12.

God's efforts are strongest when our efforts are useless.

Go back to Bethesda for a moment. I want you to look at the brief but revealing dialogue between the paralytic and the Savior. Before Jesus heals him, he asks him a question: "Do you want to be well?" (v. 6 NCV).

"Sir, there is no one to help me get into the pool when the water starts moving. While I am coming to the water, someone else always gets in before me" (v. 7 NCV).

Is the fellow complaining? Is he feeling sorry for himself? Or is he just stating the facts? Who knows? But before we think about it too much, look what happens next.

"Stand up. Pick up your mat and walk."

"And immediately the man was well; he picked up his mat and began to walk" (vv. 8–9 NCV).

I wish we would do that; I wish we would take Jesus at his word. I wish, like heaven, that we would learn that when he says something, it happens. What is this peculiar paralysis that confines us? What is this stubborn unwillingness to be healed? When Jesus tells us to stand, let's stand.

When he says we're forgiven, let's unload the guilt.

When he says we're valuable, let's believe him.

When he says we're eternal, let's bury our fear.

When he says we're provided for, let's stop worrying.

When he says, "Stand up," let's do it.

Is this your story? It can be. All the elements are the same. A gentle stranger has stepped into your hurting world and offered you a hand. Now it's up to you to take it.

REFLECTION AND DISCUSSION

Max writes, "We must admit we are like the paralytic. Invalids out of options." What does he mean by this? Do you agree with him? Why or why not?

_____

_____

_____

_____

_____

_____

_____

Have you ever chosen to be among the suffering? Is Jesus' presence at the pool of Bethesda an encouragement to you or a rebuke—or both? Explain.

_____

_____

_____

_____

_____

_____

In what way is the sick man's story a tale about you and me?

_____

_____

_____

_____

_____

_____

Read Colossians 2:13–15. List the things Jesus accomplished for you on the cross, based on this passage.

_____

_____

_____

_____

_____

_____

Is Jesus telling you today, like the paralytic, to "stand up" in any area of your life? If so, in what area? And what do you plan to do about it?

_____

_____

_____

_____

_____

PAUL

PAUL

BEFORE YOU BEGIN

Read 2 Corinthians 11:23–27 NIV

Are they servants of Christ? (I am out of my mind to talk like this.) I am more. I have worked much harder, been in prison more frequently, been flogged more severely, and been exposed to death again and again. Five times I received from the Jews the forty lashes minus one. Three times I was beaten with rods, once I was pelted with stones, three times I was shipwrecked, I spent a night and a day in the open sea, I have been constantly on the move. I have been in danger from rivers, in danger from bandits, in danger from my fellow Jews, in danger from Gentiles; in danger in the city, in danger in the country, in danger at sea; and in danger from false believers. I have labored and toiled and have often gone without sleep; I have known hunger and thirst and have often gone without food; I have been cold and naked.

True heroes are hard to identify. They don't look like heroes. Here's an example. Step with me into a dank dungeon in Judea. Peer through the door's tiny window. Consider the plight of the man on the floor. He has just inaugurated history's greatest movement. His words have triggered a revolution that will span two millennia. Future historians will describe him as courageous, noble, and visionary.

At this moment he appears anything but. Cheeks hollow. Beard matted. Bewilderment etched on his face. He leans back against the cold wall, closes his eyes, and sighs.

John had never known doubt. Hunger, yes. Loneliness, often. But doubt? Never. Only raw conviction, ruthless pronouncements, and rugged truth. Such was John the Baptist. Conviction as fierce as the desert sun.

Until now. Now the sun is blocked. Now his courage wanes. Now the clouds come. And now, as he faces death, he doesn't raise a fist of victory; he raises only a question. His final act is not a proclamation of courage, but a confession of confusion: "Find out if Jesus is the Son of God or not."

The forerunner of the Messiah is afraid of failure. *Find out if I've told the truth. Find out if I've sent people to the right Messiah. Find out if I've been right or if I've been duped.*[16]

Doesn't sound too heroic, does he?

We'd rather John die in peace. We'd rather the trailblazer catch a glimpse of the mountain. Seems only right that the sailor be granted a sighting of the shore. After all, didn't Moses get a view of the valley? Isn't John the cousin of Jesus? If anybody deserves to see the end of the trail, doesn't he?

Apparently not. The miracles he prophesied, he never saw. The kingdom he announced, he never knew. And the Messiah he proclaimed, he now doubts. John doesn't look like the prophet who would be the transition between law and grace. He doesn't look like a hero.

Can I take you to another prison for a second example?

This time the jail is in Rome. The man is named Paul. What John did to present Christ, Paul did to explain him. John cleared the path; Paul erected signposts.

Like John, Paul shaped history. And like John, Paul would die in the jail of a despot. No headlines announced his execution. No observer recorded the events. When the ax struck Paul's neck, society's eyes didn't blink. To them Paul was a peculiar purveyor of an odd faith.

Peer into the prison and see him for yourself: bent and frail, shackled to the arm of a Roman guard. Behold the apostle of God. Who knows when his back last felt a bed or his mouth knew a good meal? Three decades of travel and trouble, and what's he got to show for it?

There's squabbling in Philippi, competition in Corinth, the legalists are swarming in Galatia. Crete is plagued by money-grabbers. Ephesus is stalked by womanizers. Even some of Paul's own friends have turned against him. Dead broke. No family. No property. Nearsighted and worn out.

Doesn't look like a hero. Doesn't sound like one either. He introduced himself as the worst sinner in history. He was a Christian-killer before he was a Christian leader. At times his heart was so heavy, Paul's pen drug itself across the page. "What a miserable man I am! Who will save me from this body that brings me death?" (Rom. 7:24 NCV).

Only heaven knows how long he stared at the question before he found the courage to defy logic and write, "I thank God for saving me through Jesus Christ our Lord!" (v. 25 NCV).

One minute he's in charge; the next he's in doubt. One day he's preaching; the next he's in prison. And that's where I'd like you to look at him. Look at him in the prison.

Pretend you don't know him. You're a guard or a cook or a friend of the hatchet man, and you've come to get one last look at the guy while they sharpen the blade. What you see shuffling around in his cell isn't too much. But what I lean over and tell you is: "That man will shape the course of history."

You chuckle, but I continue. "Nero's fame will fade in this man's light." You turn and stare. I continue. "His churches will die. But his thoughts? Within two hundred years his thoughts will influence the teaching of every school on this continent."

You shake your head. "See those letters? Those letters scribbled on parchment? They'll be read in thousands of languages and will impact every major creed and constitution of the future. Every major figure will read them. Every single one."

That would be your breaking point. "No way. He's an old man with an odd faith. He'll be killed and forgotten before his head hits the floor."

Who could disagree? What rational thinker would counter? Paul's name would blow like the dust his bones would become.

Just like John's. No levelheaded observer would think otherwise. Both were noble, but passing. Courageous, but small. Radical, yet unnoticed. Their peers simply had no way of knowing—and neither do we.

For that reason, a hero could be next door and you wouldn't know it. The fellow who changes the oil in your car could be one. A hero in coveralls? Maybe. Maybe as he works he prays, asking God to do with the heart of the driver what he does with the engine.

The daycare worker where you drop off the kids? Perhaps her morning prayers include the name of each child and the dream that one of them will change the world. Who's to say God isn't listening?

The parole officer downtown? Could be a hero. She could be the one who challenges the ex-con to challenge the teens to challenge the gangs.

I know, I know. These folks don't fit our image of a hero. They look too, too . . . well, normal. Give us four stars, titles, and headlines. But something tells me that for every hero in the spotlight, there are dozens in the shadows. They don't get press. They don't draw crowds.

But behind every avalanche is a snowflake. Behind a rockslide is a pebble. An atomic explosion begins with one atom. And a revival can begin with one sermon.

History proves it. John Egglen had never preached a sermon in his life.

Wasn't that he didn't want to, just never needed to. But then one morning he did. The snow left his town of Colchester, England, buried in white. When he awoke on that January Sunday in 1850, he thought of staying home. Who would go to church in such weather?

But he reconsidered. He was, after all, a deacon. And if the deacons didn't go, who would? So he put on his boots, hat, and coat and walked the six miles to the Methodist church.

He wasn't the only member who considered staying home. In fact, he was one of the few who came. Only thirteen people were present. Twelve members and one visitor. Even the minister was snowed in. Someone suggested they go home. Egglen would hear none of that. They'd come this far; they would have a service. Besides, they had a visitor. A thirteen-year-old boy.

But who would preach? Egglen was the only deacon. It fell to him.

And so he did. His sermon lasted only ten minutes. It drifted and wandered and made no point in an effort to make several. But at the end, an uncharacteristic courage settled upon the man. He lifted his eyes and looked straight at the boy and challenged: "Young man, look to Jesus. Look! Look! Look!"

Did the challenge make a difference? Let the boy, now a man, answer. "I did look, and then and there the cloud on my heart lifted, the darkness rolled away, and at that moment I saw the sun."

The boy's name? Charles Haddon Spurgeon. England's prince of preachers.[17]

Did Egglen know what he'd done? No. Do heroes know when they are heroic? Rarely. Are historic moments acknowledged when they happen?

You know the answer to that one. We seldom see history in the making, and we seldom recognize heroes. Which is just as well, for if we knew either, we might mess up both.

But we'd do well to keep our eyes open. Tomorrow's Spurgeon might be mowing your lawn. And the hero who inspires him might be nearer than you think. He might be in your mirror.

REFLECTION AND DISCUSSION

What's your own concept of a hero?

_____

_____

_____

_____

_____

In what way do actual heroes seldom look like heroes?

_____

_____

_____

_____

What "heroes out of the spotlight" do you know? What makes them heroes?

_____

_____

_____

_____

Have you been a hero to anyone? Could you be a hero to anyone? In what circumstances has God surfaced your own heroism for someone else?

_____

_____

_____

_____

Read Mark 1:1–8. How would you describe John in modern terms? How did his appearance and lifestyle help him accomplish his mission? In what way was he a hero?

_____

_____

_____

_____

_____

_____

Read 2 Corinthians 4:7–11; 6:4–10; 11:22–28. What do you learn about Paul from these passages? What in them describes the kind of hero he was? Do these passages encourage or discourage you? Why?

_____

_____

_____

_____

_____

_____

PETER

PETER

BEFORE YOU BEGIN
Read Psalm 23:5-6 NKJV

You prepare a table before me in the presence
    of my enemies;
You anoint my head with oil;
My cup runs over.
Surely goodness and mercy shall follow me
All the days of my life;
And I will dwell in the house of the Lord
Forever.

See the fellow in the shadows? That's Peter. Peter the apostle. Peter the impetuous. Peter the passionate. He once walked on water. Stepped right out of the boat onto the lake. He'll soon preach to thousands. Fearless before friends and foes alike. But tonight the one who stepped on the water has hurried into hiding. The one who will speak with power is weeping in pain.

Not sniffling or whimpering, but weeping. Bearded face buried in thick hands. His howl echoing in the Jerusalem night. What hurts more? The fact that he did it? Or the fact that he swore he never would?

"Lord, I am ready to go with you to prison and even to die with you!" he pledged only hours earlier. "But Jesus said, 'Peter, before the rooster crows this day, you will say three times that you don't know me'" (Luke 22:33–34 NCV).

Denying Christ on the night of his betrayal was bad enough, but did he have to boast that he wouldn't? And one denial was pitiful, but three? Three denials were horrific, but did he have to curse? "Peter began to place a curse on himself and swear, 'I don't know the man'" (Matt. 26:74 NCV).

And now, awash in a whirlpool of sorrow, Peter is hiding. Peter is weeping. And soon Peter will be fishing.

We wonder why he goes fishing. We know why he goes to Galilee. He had been told that the risen Christ would meet the disciples there. The arranged meeting place is not the sea, however, but a mountain (Matt. 28:16). If the followers were to meet Jesus on a mountain, what are they doing in a boat? No one told them to fish, but that's what they did. "Simon Peter said, 'I am going out to fish.' The others said, 'We will go with you'" (John 21:3 NCV). Besides, didn't Peter quit fishing? Two years earlier, when Jesus called him to fish for men, didn't he drop his net and follow? We haven't seen him fish since. We never see him fish again. Why is he fishing now? Jesus has risen from the dead. Peter has seen the empty tomb. Who could fish at a time like this?

Were they hungry? Perhaps that's the sum of it. Maybe the expedition was born out of growling stomachs. Or then again, maybe it was born out of a broken heart.

You see, Peter could not deny his denial. The empty tomb did not erase the crowing rooster. Christ had returned, but Peter wondered, he must have wondered, *After what I did, would he return for someone like me?*

We've wondered the same. Is Peter the only person to do the very thing he swore he'd never do?

"Infidelity is behind me!" "From now on, I'm going to bridle my tongue." "No more shady deals. I've learned my lesson." Oh, the volume of our boasting. And, oh, the heartbreak of our shame.

Rather than resist the flirting, we return it. Rather than ignore the gossip, we share it. Rather than stick to the truth, we shade it.

And the rooster crows, and conviction pierces, and Peter has a partner in the shadows. We weep as Peter wept, and we do what Peter did. We go fishing. We go back to our old lives. We return to our pre-Jesus practices. We do what comes naturally, rather than what comes spiritually. And we question whether Jesus has a place for folks like us.

Jesus answers that question. He answers it for you and me and all who tend to "Peter out" on Christ. His answer came on the shore of the sea in a gift to Peter. You know what Jesus did? Split the waters? Turn the boat to gold and the nets to silver? No, Jesus did something much more meaningful. He invited Peter to breakfast. Jesus prepared a meal.

Of course, the breakfast was one special moment among several that morning. There was the great catch of fish and the recognition of Jesus. The plunge of Peter and the paddling of the disciples. And there was the moment they reached the shore and found Jesus next to a fire of coals. The fish were sizzling, and the bread was waiting, and the defeater of hell and the ruler of heaven invited his friends to sit down and have a bite to eat.

No one could have been more grateful than Peter. The one Satan had sifted like wheat was eating bread at the hand of God. Peter was welcomed to the meal of Christ. Right there for the devil and his tempters to see, Jesus "prepared a table in the presence of his enemies."

Okay, so maybe Peter didn't say it that way. But David did. "You prepare a table before me in the presence of my enemies" (Ps. 23:5 NKJV). What the shepherd did for the sheep sounds a lot like what Jesus did for Peter.

At this point in the psalm, David's mind seems to be lingering in the high country with the sheep. Having guided the flock through the valley to the alp lands for greener grass, he remembers the shepherd's added responsibility. He must prepare the pasture.

This is new land, so the shepherd must be careful. Ideally, the grazing area will be flat, a mesa or tableland. The shepherd searches for poisonous plants and ample water. He looks for signs of wolves, coyotes, and bears.

Of special concern to the shepherd is the adder, a small brown snake that lives underground. Adders are known to pop out of their holes and nip the sheep on the nose. The bite often infects and can even kill. As defense against the snake, the shepherd pours a circle of oil at the top of each adder's hole. He also applies the oil to the noses of the animals. The oil on the snake's hole lubricates the exit, preventing the snake from climbing out. The smell of the oil on the sheep's nose drives the serpent away. The shepherd, in a very real sense, has prepared the table.[18]

What if your Shepherd did for you what the shepherd did for his flock? Suppose he dealt with your enemy, the devil, and prepared for you a safe place of nourishment? What if Jesus did for you what he did for Peter? Suppose he, in the hour of your failure, invited you to a meal?

What would you say if I told you he has done exactly that? On the night before his death, Jesus prepared a table for his followers.

On the first day of the Festival of Unleavened Bread, the day the lambs for the Passover meal were killed, Jesus' disciples asked him, "Where do you want us to go and get the Passover meal ready for you?"

Then Jesus sent two of them with these instructions: "Go into the city, and a man carrying a jar of water will meet you. Follow him to the house he enters, and say to the owner of the house: 'The Teacher says, Where is the room where my disciples and I will eat the Passover meal?' Then he will show you a large upstairs room, fixed up and furnished, where you will get everything ready for us." (Mark 14:12–15 GNT)

Look who did the "preparing" here. Jesus reserved a large room and arranged for the guide to lead the disciples. Jesus made certain the room was furnished and the food set out. What did the disciples do? They faithfully complied and were fed.

The Shepherd prepared the table. Not only that, he dealt with the snakes. You'll remember that only one of the disciples didn't complete the meal that night. "The devil had already persuaded Judas Iscariot, the son of Simon, to turn against Jesus" (John 13:2 NCV). Judas started to eat, but Jesus didn't let him finish. On the command of Jesus, Judas left the room. "'The thing that you will do—do it quickly.' . . . Judas took the bread Jesus gave him and immediately went out. It was night" (vv. 27, 30).

There is something dynamic in this dismissal. Jesus prepared a table in the presence of the enemy. Judas was allowed to see the supper, but he wasn't allowed to stay there.

You are not welcome here. This table is for my children. You may tempt them. You may trip them. But you will never sit with them. This is how much he loves us.

And if any doubt remains, lest there be any "Peters" who wonder if there is a place at the table for them, Jesus issues a tender reminder as he passes the cup. "Every one of you drink this. This is my blood which is the new agreement that God makes with his people. This blood is poured out for many to forgive their sins" (Matt. 26:27–28 NCV).

"*Every one* of you drink this." Those who feel unworthy, drink this. Those who feel ashamed, drink this. Those who feel embarrassed, drink this.

May I share a time when I felt all three?

By the age of eighteen I was well on my way to a drinking problem. My system had become so resistant to alcohol that a six-pack of beer had little or no impact on me. At the age of twenty, God not only saved me from hell after this life, he saved me from hell during it. Only he knows where I was headed, but I have a pretty good idea.

For that reason, part of my decision to follow Christ included no more beer. So I quit. But, curiously, the thirst for beer never left. It hasn't hounded me or consumed me, but two or three times a week the thought of a good beer sure entices me. Proof to me that I have to be careful is this—nonalcoholic beers have no appeal. It's not the flavor of the drink; it's the buzz. But for more than twenty years, drinking has never been a major issue.

A couple of years ago, however, it nearly became one. I lowered my guard a bit. *One beer with barbecue won't hurt.* Then another time with Mexican food. Then a time or two with no food at all. Over a period of two months I went from no beers to maybe one or two a week. Again, for most people, no problem, but for me it could become one.

You know when I began to smell trouble? One hot Friday afternoon I was on my way to speak at our annual men's retreat. Did I say the day was hot? Brutally hot. I was thirsty. Soda wouldn't do. So I began to plot. Where could I buy a beer and not be seen by anyone I knew?

With that thought, I crossed a line. What's done in secret is best not done at all. But I did it anyway. I drove to an out-of-the-way convenience store, parked, and waited until all patrons had left. I entered, bought my beer, held it close to my side, and hurried to the car. That's when the rooster crowed.

It crowed because I was sneaking around. It crowed because I knew better. It crowed because, and this really hurt, the night before I'd scolded one of my daughters for keeping secrets from me. And now, what was I doing?

I threw the beer in the trash and asked God to forgive me. A few days later I shared my struggle with the elders and some members of the congregation and was happy to chalk up the matter to experience and move on.

But I couldn't. The shame plagued me. So many could be hurt by my stupidity. And of all the times to do such a thing. En route to minister at a retreat. What hypocrisy!

And, to make matters worse, Sunday rolled around. I found myself on the front row of the church, awaiting my turn to speak. Again, I had been honest with God, honest with the elders, honest with myself. But still, I struggled. Would God want a guy like me to preach?

The answer came in the Supper. The Lord's Supper. The same Jesus who'd prepared a meal for Peter had prepared one for me. The same Shepherd who had trumped the devil trumped him again. The same Savior who had built a fire on the shore stirred a few embers in my heart.

"Every one of you drink this." And so I did. It felt good to be back at the table.

REFLECTION AND DISCUSSION

Describe a time you followed Peter's example and did the very thing you swore you'd never do. What happened?

Have you ever "gone fishing" or returned to your pre-Jesus practices after a spiritual failure? If so, how did you feel at that time?

_____

_____

_____

_____

_____

Why do we question whether Jesus has a place for people like us? Have you ever felt that way? Explain.

_____

_____

_____

_____

Why do you think Jesus allowed Judas to see the Lord's Supper? Why not banish him before the disciples gathered?

_____

_____

_____

_____

_____

How do the stories of both Peter and Max show true repentance? How does Jesus always respond to true repentance? Why is this important to understand?

_____

_____

_____

_____

_____

PHILIP

PHILIP

BEFORE YOU BEGIN
Read Acts 8:36–37 NKJV

Now as they went down the road, they came to some water. And the eunuch said, "See, here is water. What hinders me from being baptized?"

Then Philip said, "If you believe with all your heart, you may."

And he answered and said, "I believe that Jesus Christ is the Son of God."

D o any walls bisect your world? There you stand on one side. And on the other? The person you've learned to disregard, perhaps even disdain. The teen with the tattoos. The boss with the money. The immigrant with the heavy accent. The person with opposing political views.

Or the Samaritans outside Jerusalem.

Talk about a wall, ancient and tall. "Jews," as John wrote in his gospel, "refuse to have anything to do with Samaritans" (John 4:9 NLT). The two cultures had hated each other for a thousand years. The feud involved claims of defection, intermarriage, and disloyalty to the temple. Samaritans were blacklisted. Their beds, utensils—even their spittle—were considered unclean. No orthodox Jew would travel into the region. Most Jews would gladly double the length of their trip rather than go through Samaria.

Jesus, however, played by a different set of rules. He spent the better part of a day on the turf of a Samaritan woman, drinking water from her ladle, discussing her questions (John 4:1–26). He stepped across the cultural taboo as if it were a sleeping dog in the doorway. Jesus loves to break down walls. That's why he sent Philip to Samaria.

> Then Philip went down to the city of Samaria and preached Christ to them. And the multitudes with one accord heeded the things spoken by Philip, hearing and seeing the miracles which he did. For unclean spirits, crying with a loud voice, came out of many who were possessed; and many who were paralyzed and lame were healed. . . .
>
> When they believed Philip as he preached the things concerning the kingdom of God and the name of Jesus Christ, both men and women were baptized. (Acts 8:5–7, 12 NKJV)

The city broke out into a revival. Peter and John heard about the response and traveled from Jerusalem to Samaria to confirm it. "When they had come down, [they] prayed for them that they might receive the Holy Spirit. For as yet He had fallen upon none of them. They had only been baptized in the name of the Lord Jesus. Then they laid hands on them, and they received the Holy Spirit" (vv. 15–17 NKJV).

This is a curious turn of events. Why hadn't the Samaritans received the Holy Spirit? On the Day of Pentecost, Peter promised the gift of the Spirit to those who repented and were baptized. How then can we explain the baptism of the Samaritans, which, according to Luke, was not accompanied by the Spirit? Why delay the gift?

Simple. To celebrate the falling of a wall. The gospel, for the first time, was breaching an ancient bias. God marked the moment with a ticker-tape parade of sorts. He rolled out the welcome mat and sent his apostles to verify the revival and place hands on the Samaritans. Let any doubt be gone: God accepts all people.

But he wasn't finished. He sent Philip on a second cross-cultural mission.

> Now an angel of the Lord spoke to Philip, saying, "Arise and go toward the south along the road which goes down from Jerusalem to Gaza." This is desert. So he arose and

went. And behold, a man of Ethiopia, a eunuch of great authority under Candace the queen of the Ethiopians, who had charge of all her treasury, and had come to Jerusalem to worship, was returning. And sitting in his chariot, he was reading Isaiah the prophet. Then the Spirit said to Philip, "Go near and overtake this chariot." (vv. 26–29 NKJV)

Walls separated Philip from the eunuch. The Ethiopian was dark skinned; Philip was light. The official hailed from distant Africa; Philip grew up nearby. The traveler was rich enough to travel. And who was Philip but a simple refugee, banished from Jerusalem? And don't overlook the delicate matter of differing testosterone levels. Philip, we later learn, was the father of four girls (Acts 21:9). The official was a eunuch. No wife or kids or plans for either. The lives of the two men could not have been more different.

But Philip didn't hesitate. He "preached Jesus to him. Now as they went down the road, they came to some water. And the eunuch said, 'See, here is water. What hinders me from being baptized?' " (Acts 8:35–36 NKJV).

No small question. A dark-skinned, influential, effeminate official from Africa turns to the light-skinned, simple, virile Christian from Jerusalem and asks, "Is there any reason I can't have what you have?"

What if Philip had said, "Now that you mention it, yes. Sorry. We don't take your type"?

But Philip, charter member of the bigotry-demolition team, blasted through the wall and invited, "'If you believe with all your heart, you may.' And he answered and said, 'I believe that Jesus Christ is the Son of God'" (v. 37 NKJV).

Next thing you know, the eunuch is stepping out of the baptism waters, whistling "Jesus Loves Me," Philip is on to his next assignment, and the church has her first non-Jewish convert.

And we are a bit dizzy. What do we do with a chapter like this? Samaria. Peter and John arriving. Holy Spirit falling. Gaza. Ethiopian official. Philip. What do these events teach us?

They teach us how God feels about the person on the other side of the wall.

He tore down the wall we used to keep each other at a distance. . . . Instead of continuing with two groups of people separated by centuries of animosity and suspicion, he created a new kind of human being, a fresh start for everybody.

"Christ brought us together through his death on the cross. The Cross got us to embrace, and that was the end of the hostility" (Eph. 2:14–16 MSG).

The cross of Christ creates a new people, a people unhindered by skin color or family feud. A new citizenry based not on common ancestry or geography but on a common Savior.

What walls are in your world? We can't outlive our lives if we can't get beyond our biases. Who are your Samaritans? Ethiopian eunuchs? Whom have you been taught to distrust and avoid?

It's time to remove a few bricks. Welcome the day God takes you to your Samaria—not so distant in miles but different in styles, tastes, tongues, and traditions.

And if you meet an Ethiopian eunuch, so different yet so sincere, don't refuse that person. Don't let class, race, gender, politics, geography, or culture hinder God's work. For the end of the matter is this: when we cross the field and cheer for the other side, everyone wins.

REFLECTION AND DISCUSSION

Philip went to Samaria, and the grace of God blasted the walls between the Jews and Samaritans. Max asks you, "Do any walls bisect your world?" What divisions do you see dominating your culture? What unspoken rules of separation promote a subconscious prejudice? How long has this wall been there? What are the root causes? What keeps it going?" Explain.

_____

_____

_____

As Christians, how well do we live out Galatians 3:28–29 and erase the divisions between us? Where have we succeeded? Where have we failed?

_____

_____

_____

_____

_____

_____

How could you tell a person on the other side of a dividing wall that he or she matters to you? What could you do to show you care?

_____

_____

_____

_____

_____

_____

Be honest with yourself about your prejudices. Spend some quiet time thinking about this. Make a list of groups of people you tend to prejudge or categorize. Pray over that list, asking God to change your heart.

_____

_____

_____

_____

_____

_____

_____

_____

_____

_____

_____

RAHAB

RAHAB

BEFORE YOU BEGIN
Read Hebrews 11:30–31 NIV

By faith the walls of Jericho fell, after the army had marched around them for seven days.

By faith the prostitute Rahab, because she welcomed the spies, was not killed with those who were disobedient.

Some kids in Cateura, on the outskirts of Asunción, Paraguay, are making music with their trash. They're turning washtubs into kettledrums and drainpipes into trumpets. Other orchestras fine-tune their maple cellos or brass tubas. Not this band. They play Beethoven sonatas with plastic buckets.

On their side of Asunción, garbage is the only crop to harvest. Garbage pickers sort and sell refuse for pennies a pound. Many of them have met the same fate as the trash; they've been tossed out and discarded.

But now, thanks to two men, they are making music.

Favio Chavez is an environmental technician who envisioned a music school as a welcome reprieve for the kids. Don Cola Gomez is a trash worker and carpenter. He had never seen, heard, or held a violin in his life. Yet when someone described the instrument, this untutored craftsman took a paint can and an oven tray into his tiny workshop and made a violin. His next instrument was a cello. He fashioned the body out of an oil barrel and made tuning knobs from a hairbrush, the heel of a shoe, and a wooden spoon.

Thanks to this Stradivarius, the junk gets a mulligan, and so do the kids who live among it. Since the day their story hit the news, they've been tutored by maestros, featured on national television programs, and taken a world tour. They've been called the Landfill Harmonic and also the Recycled Orchestra of Cateura.[19]

We could also call them a picture of God's grace.

God makes music out of riffraff. Heaven's orchestra is composed of the unlikeliest of musicians. Peter, first-chair trumpeter, cursed the name of the Christ, who saved him. Paul plays the violin. But there was a day when he played the religious thug. And the guy on the harp? That's David. King David. Womanizing David. Conniving David. Bloodthirsty David. Repentant David.

Take special note of the woman with the clarinet. Her name is Rahab. Her story occupies the second chapter of Joshua. "Now Joshua the son of Nun sent out two men from Acacia Grove to spy secretly, saying, 'Go, view the land, especially Jericho.' So they went, and came to the house of a harlot named Rahab, and lodged there" (v. 1 NKJV).

The time had come for the Hebrew people to enter the promised land. Jericho, a formidable town that sat just north of the Dead Sea, was their first challenge. Canaanites indwelled the city. To call the people barbaric is to describe the North Pole as nippy. These people turned temple worship into orgies. They buried babies alive. The people of Jericho had no regard for human life or respect for God.

It was into this city that the two spies of Joshua crept. It was in this city that the spies met Rahab, the harlot.

Much could be said about Rahab without mentioning her profession. She was a Canaanite. She provided cover for the spies of Joshua. She came to believe in the God of Abraham before she ever met the children of Abraham. She was spared in the destruction of her city. She was grafted into the Hebrew culture. She married a contemporary of Joshua's, bore a son named Boaz, had a great-grandson named Jesse, a great-great-grandson named David, and a descendant named Jesus. Yes, Rahab's name appears on the family tree of the Son of God.

Her résumé needn't mention her profession. Yet in five of the eight appearances of her name in Scripture, she is presented as a "harlot."[20] Five! Wouldn't one suffice? And couldn't that one reference be nuanced in a euphemism such as "Rahab, the best hostess in Jericho" or "Rahab, who made everyone feel welcome"? It's bad enough that the name Rahab sounds like "rehab." Disguise her career choice. Veil it. Mask it. Put a little concealer on this biblical blemish. Drop the reference to the brothel, please.

But the Bible doesn't. Just the opposite. It points a neon sign at it. It's even attached to her name in the book of Hebrews Hall of Fame. The list includes Abel, Noah, Abraham, Isaac, Jacob, Joseph, Moses . . . and then, all of a sudden, "the harlot Rahab" (11:31 NKJV). No asterisk, no footnote, no apology. Her history of harlotry is part of her testimony.

Her story begins like this: "And it was told the king of Jericho, saying, 'Behold, men have come here tonight from the children of Israel to search out the country'" (Josh. 2:2 NKJV). The king could see the multitude of Hebrews camped on Jordan's eastern banks. As Rahab would later disclose, the people of Jericho were scared. Word on the street was that God had his hand on the newcomers and woe be unto anyone who got in their way. When the king heard that the spies were hiding at Rahab's house, he sent soldiers to fetch them.

I'm seeing half a dozen men squeeze down the narrow cobblestoned path in the red-light district. It's late at night. The torch-lit taverns are open, and the patrons are a few sheets to the wind. They yell obscenities at the king's men, but the soldiers don't react. The guards keep walking until they stand before the wooden door of a stone building that abuts the famous Jericho walls. The lantern is unlit, leaving the soldiers to wonder if anyone is home. The captain pounds on the door. There is a shuffling inside. Rahab answers.

"Sorry, boys, we're booked for the night."

"We aren't here for that," the captain snaps. "We're here for the Hebrews."

"Hebrews?" She cocks her head. "I thought you were here for fun."

"We came for the spies. Where are they?"

She steps out onto the porch, looks to the right and left, and then lowers her voice to a whisper. "You just missed them. They snuck out before the gates were shut. If you get a move on, you can catch them."

The king's men turn and run. As they disappear around the corner, Rahab hurries up the brothel stairs to the roof, where the two spies have been hiding. She tells them the coast is clear.

Her words must have stunned the spies. They never expected to find cowards in Jericho. And, even more, they never expected to find faith in a brothel. But they did. Read what Jericho's shady lady said to them:

I know that the LORD has given you the land . . . [W]e have heard how the LORD dried up the water of the Red Sea . . . and what you did to the two kings . . . who were on the other side of the Jordan . . . [T]he LORD your God, He is God in heaven above and on earth beneath. (vv. 9–11 NKJV)

Rahab found God. Or, better worded, God found Rahab. He spotted a tender heart in this hard city and reached out to save her. He would have saved the entire city, but no one else made the request. Then again, Rahab had an advantage over the other people. She had nothing to lose.

Perhaps that is where you are as well.

You've sold out. We all have. We've wondered, we've all wondered, *Glory Days? Perhaps for him or for her. But not for me. I am too . . . soiled, dirty, afflicted. I have sinned too much, stumbled too often, floundered too long. I'm on the garbage heap of society. No Glory Days for me.*

God's one-word reply for such doubt? *Rahab!*

Lest we think God's promised land is promised to a chosen few, he positions her story in the front of the book. The narrator gives her an entire chapter, for heaven's sake! She gets more inches of type than do the priests, the spies, or Joshua's right-hand man. If quantity and chronology mean anything in theology, then Rahab's headline position announces this: God has a place for the Rahabs of the world.

The Hebrew spies, as it turns out, were actually missionaries. They thought they were on a reconnaissance trip. They weren't. God needed no scouting report. His plan was to collapse the city walls like a stack of dominoes. He didn't send the men to collect data. He sent the spies to reach Rahab. They told her to "bind this line of scarlet cord in the window" so they could identify her house (Josh. 2:18 NKJV). Without hesitation she bound the scarlet cord in the window.

The spies escaped and Rahab made preparation. She told her family to get ready. She kept an eye out for the coming army. She checked the cord to make sure it was tied securely and dangling from the window.

When the Hebrews came and the walls fell, when everyone else perished, Rahab and her family were saved. "By faith the harlot Rahab did not perish" (Heb. 11:31 NKJV). Her profession of faith mattered more than her profession as a harlot.

Maybe your past is a checkered one. Maybe your peers don't share your faith. Maybe your pedigree is one of violence, your ancestry one of rebellion. If so, then Rahab is your model.

We don't drop scarlet cords from our windows. But we trust the crimson thread of Christ's blood. We don't prepare for the coming of the Hebrews, but we do live with an eye toward the second coming of our Joshua—Jesus Christ.

Ultimately we will all see what the people of Asunción are discovering. Our mess will become music, and God will have a heaven full of rescued Rahabs in his symphony. That'll be me on the tuba. And you? What will you be playing? One thing is for sure. We will all know "Amazing Grace" by heart.

REFLECTION AND DISCUSSION

How has God used the "garbage" in your life and turned it into something beautiful like music?

_____

_____

_____

What has been the result for you and those around you?

_____

_____

_____

_____

_____

_____

Max says, "God has a place for the Rahabs of the world." What does he mean?

_____

_____

_____

_____

_____

_____

Do you know a Rahab? How has he or she impacted others? Are you a Rahab?

_____

_____

_____

_____

_____

_____

_____

_____

_____

_____

_____

_____

_____

RICH YOUNG RULER

RICH YOUNG RULER

BEFORE YOU BEGIN

Read Matthew 19:16–26 NIV

Just then a man came up to Jesus and asked, "Teacher, what good thing must I do to get eternal life?"

"Why do you ask me about what is good?" Jesus replied. "There is only One who is good. If you want to enter life, keep the commandments."

"Which ones?" he inquired.

Jesus replied, "'You shall not murder, you shall not commit adultery, you shall not steal, you shall not give false testimony, honor your father and mother,' and 'love your neighbor as yourself.'"

"All these I have kept," the young man said. "What do I still lack?"

Jesus answered, "If you want to be perfect, go, sell your possessions and give to the poor, and you will have treasure in heaven. Then come, follow me."

When the young man heard this, he went away sad, because he had great wealth.

Then Jesus said to his disciples, "Truly I tell you, it is hard for someone who is rich to enter the kingdom of heaven. Again I tell you, it is easier for a camel to go through the eye of a needle than for someone who is rich to enter the kingdom of God."

When the disciples heard this, they were greatly astonished and asked, "Who then can be saved?"

Jesus looked at them and said, "With man this is impossible, but with God all things are possible."

We could begin with Sarai laughing. Her wrinkled face buried in bony hands. Her shoulders shaking. Her lungs wheezing. She knows she shouldn't laugh; it's not kosher to laugh at what God says. But just as she catches her breath and wipes away the tears, she thinks about it again—and a fresh wave of hilarity doubles her over.

We could begin with Peter staring. It's a stunned stare. His eyes are the size of grapefruits. He's oblivious to the fish piled to his knees and to the water lapping over the edge of the boat. He's deaf to the demands that he snap out of it and help. Peter is numb, absorbed in one thought—a thought too zany to say aloud.

We could begin with Paul resting. For three days he has wrestled; now he rests. He sits on the floor, in the corner. His face is haggard. His stomach is empty. His lips are parched. Bags droop beneath the blinded eyes. But there is a slight smile on his lips. A fresh stream is flowing into a stagnant pool, and the water is sweet.

But let's not begin with these. Let's begin elsewhere.

Let's begin with the New Testament yuppie negotiating.

He's rich. Italian shoes. Tailored suit. His money is invested. His plastic is golden. He lives like he flies—first class. He's young. He pumps away fatigue at the gym and slam-dunks old age on the court. His belly is flat, his eyes sharp. Energy is his trademark, and death is an eternity away.

He's powerful. If you don't think so, just ask him. You got questions? He's got answers. You got problems? He's got solutions. You got dilemmas? He's got opinions.

He knows where he's going, and he'll be there tomorrow. He's the new generation. So the old had better pick up the pace or pack their bags.

He has mastered the three "Ps" of yuppiedom. Prosperity. Posterity. Power. He's the rich . . . young . . . ruler.[21]

Till today, life for him has been a smooth cruise down a neon avenue. But today he has a question. A casual concern or a genuine fear? We don't know. We do know he has come for some advice.

For one so used to calling the shots, calling on this carpenter's son for help must be awkward. For a man of his pedigree to seek the counsel of a country rube is not standard procedure. But this is no standard question.

"Teacher," he asks, "what good thing must I do to get eternal life?" The wording of his question betrays his misunderstanding. He thinks he can get eternal life as he gets everything else—by his own strength.

"What must I do?" What are the requirements, Jesus?

Jesus' answer is intended to make him wince. "If you want to enter life, obey the commandments."

A man with half a conscience would have thrown up his hands at that point. "Keep the commandments? Keep the commandments! Do you know how many commandments there are? Have you read the Law lately? I've tried—honestly, I've tried—but I can't."

That is what the ruler should say, but confession is the furthest thing from his mind. Instead of asking for help, he grabs a pencil and paper and asks for the list.

Jesus indulges him. "Do not murder, do not commit adultery, do not steal, do not give false testimony, honor your father and mother, and love your neighbor as yourself." (Matt.19:18–19 TLV, paraphrase)

"Great!" thinks the yuppie as he finishes the notes. "Murder? Of course not. Adultery? Well, nothing any red-blooded boy wouldn't do. Stealing? A little extortion, but all justifiable. False testimony? Hmmmm . . . let's move on. Honor your father and mother? Sure, I see them on holidays. Love your neighbor as yourself . . . ?"

"Hey," he grins, "a piece of cake. I've done all of these. In fact, I've done them since I was a kid." He swaggers a bit and hooks a thumb in his belt. "Got any other commandments you want to run past me?"

How Jesus keeps from laughing—or crying—is beyond me. The question that was intended to show the ruler how he falls short only convinces him that he stands tall. Jesus gets to the point. "If you want to be perfect, then go sell your possessions and give to the poor, and you will have treasure in heaven" (Matt. 19:21, paraphrase).

The statement leaves the young man distraught and the disciples bewildered.

Their question could be ours: "Who then can be saved?" (Luke 18:26 NIV).

Jesus' answer shellshocks the listeners, "With man this is impossible . . ." (Matt. 19:26 NIV).

He doesn't say improbable. He doesn't say unlikely. He doesn't even say it will be tough. He says it is "impossible." No chance. No way. No loopholes. No hope. And unless somebody does something, you don't have a chance of going to heaven.

Does that strike you as cold? All your life you've been rewarded according to your performance. You get grades according to your study. You get commendations according to your success. You get money in response to your work.

That's why the rich young ruler thought heaven was just a payment away. You work hard, you pay your dues, and "zap"—your account is credited as paid in full. Jesus says, "No way." What you want costs far more than what you can pay. You don't need a system, you need a Savior. You don't need a resume, you need a Redeemer. For "what is impossible with men is possible with God" (Luke 18:27 NIV).

Don't miss the thrust of this verse: You cannot save yourself. Not through the right rituals. Not through the right doctrine. Not through the right devotion. Jesus' point is crystal clear. It is impossible for human beings to save themselves.

You see, it wasn't the money that hindered the rich man; it was the self-sufficiency. It wasn't the possessions; it was the pomp. It wasn't the big bucks; it was the big head. "How hard it is for the rich to enter the kingdom of God!" (Mark 10:23 NIV). It's not just the rich who have difficulty. So do the educated, the strong, the good-looking, the popular, the religious. So do you if you think your piety or power qualifies you as a kingdom candidate.

And if you have trouble digesting what Jesus said to the rich young ruler, then his description of the judgment day will stick in your throat.

It's a prophetic picture of the final day: "Many will say to me on that day, 'Lord,

Lord, did we not prophesy in your name, and in your name drive out demons and perform many miracles?'" (Matt. 7:22 NIV).

These people are standing before the throne of God and bragging about themselves. The great trumpet has sounded, and they are still tooting their own horns. Rather than sing his praises, they sing their own. Rather than worship God, they read their résumés. When they should be speechless, they speak. In the very aura of the King they boast of self. What is worse—their arrogance or their blindness?

You don't impress the officials at NASA with a paper airplane. You don't boast about your crayon sketches in the presence of Picasso. You don't claim equality with Einstein because you can write "H2O." And you don't boast about your goodness in the presence of the Perfect.

"Then I will tell them plainly, 'I never knew you. Away from me, you evildoers'" (v. 23 NIV).

Mark it down. God does not save us because of what we've done. Only a puny god could be bought with tithes. Only an egotistical god would be impressed with our pain. Only a temperamental god could be satisfied by sacrifices. Only a heartless god would sell salvation to the highest bidders.

And only a great God does for his children what they can't do for themselves. That is the message of Paul: "For what the law was powerless to do . . . God did" (Rom. 8:3 NIV).

And that is the message of the first beatitude from Christ's Sermon on the Mount. "Blessed are the poor in spirit, for theirs is the kingdom of heaven" (Matt. 5:3 NIV).

The jewel of joy is given to the impoverished spirits, not the affluent.[22] God's delight is received upon surrender, not awarded upon conquest. The first step to joy is a plea for help, an acknowledgment of moral destitution, an admission of inward paucity. Those who taste God's presence have declared spiritual bankruptcy and are aware of their spiritual crisis. Their cupboards are bare. Their pockets are empty. Their options are gone. They have long since stopped demanding justice; they are pleading for mercy.[23]

They ask God to do for them what they can't do without him. They have seen how holy God is and how sinful they are and have agreed with Jesus' statement, "Salvation is impossible."

Oh, the irony of God's delight—born in the parched soil of destitution rather than the fertile ground of achievement.

It's a different path, a path we're not accustomed to taking. We don't often declare our impotence. Admission of failure is not usually admission into joy. Complete confession is not commonly followed by total pardon. But then again, God has never been governed by what is common.

REFLECTION AND DISCUSSION

How does this chapter interpret being "poor in spirit"? How does this compare with any previous ideas you had about what this beatitude means?

_____

_____

_____

_____

_____

_____

_____

Read Luke 6:20, 24. Luke's version of this beatitude omits the "in spirit" idea entirely; it simply states that the "rich" have their reward here and therefore cannot expect a reward in heaven.

_____

_____

_____

_____

_____

_____

Now read Matthew 19:23–24. Jesus tells the rich young ruler directly that "it is hard for someone who is rich to enter the kingdom of heaven" (NIV). Do you think the first beatitude applies especially to those who are poor in material possessions? If not, why does Matthew make these specific comments about material wealth?

_____

_____

_____

_____

_____

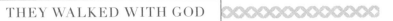

What do you think are the motives behind the rich young ruler's self-justification and overachievement? What is the difference between trying to achieve salvation and trying to please God?

_____

_____

_____

_____

_____

"Those who taste God's presence have declared spiritual bankruptcy and are aware of their spiritual crisis." Have you ever declared yourself spiritually bankrupt? If so, have you asked God to do for you what you can't do without him?

_____

_____

_____

_____

SAMARITAN
WOMAN

SAMARITAN WOMAN

BEFORE YOU BEGIN

Read John 4:6-7, 9-19, 25-26, 28-29 NLT

Jacob's well was there; and Jesus, tired from the long walk, sat wearily beside the well about noontime. Soon a Samaritan woman came to draw water, and Jesus said to her, "Please give me a drink."

The woman was surprised, for Jews refuse to have anything to do with Samaritans. She said to Jesus, "You are a Jew, and I am a Samaritan woman. Why are you asking me for a drink?"

Jesus replied, "If you only knew the gift God has for you and who you are speaking to, you would ask me, and I would give you living water."

"But sir, you don't have a rope or a bucket," she said, "and this well is very deep. Where would you get this living water? And besides, do you think you're greater than our ancestor Jacob, who gave us this well? How can you offer better water than he and his sons and his animals enjoyed?"

Jesus replied, "Anyone who drinks this water will soon become thirsty again. But those who drink the water I give will never be thirsty again. It becomes a fresh, bubbling spring within them, giving them eternal life."

"Please, sir," the woman said, "give me this water! Then I'll never be thirsty again, and I won't have to come here to get water."

"Go and get your husband," Jesus told her.

"I don't have a husband," the woman replied.

Jesus said, "You're right! You don't have a husband—for you have had five husbands, and you aren't even married to the man you're living with now. You certainly spoke the truth!"

"Sir," the woman said, "you must be a prophet.

The woman said, "I know the Messiah is coming—the one who is called Christ. When he comes, he will explain everything to us."

Then Jesus told her, "I am the Messiah!"

The woman left her water jar beside the well and ran back to the village, telling everyone, "Come and see a man who told me everything I ever did! Could he possibly be the Messiah?"

How many people will die in the loneliness in which they are living? The homeless in Atlanta. The happy-hour hopper in LA. A bag lady in Miami. Any person who doubts whether the world needs him. Any person who is convinced that no one really cares. These are the victims of futility.

That's why the story you are about to read is significant. She is a Samaritan; she knows the sting of racism. She is a woman; she's bumped her head on the ceiling of sexism. She's been married to five men. Five different marriages. Five different beds. Five different rejections. She knows the sound of slamming doors.

She knows what it means to love and receive no love in return. Her current mate won't even give her his name. He only gives her a place to sleep.

On this day, she came to the well at noon. She expected silence. She expected solitude. Instead, she found one who knew her better than she knew herself.

He was seated on the ground: legs outstretched, hands folded, back resting against the well. His eyes were closed. She stopped and looked at him. She looked around. No one was near. She looked back at him. He was obviously Jewish. What was he doing here? His eyes opened and hers ducked in embarrassment. She went quickly about her task.

Sensing her discomfort, Jesus asked her for water. But she was too streetwise to think that all he wanted was a drink. "Since when does an uptown fellow like you ask a girl like me for water?" She wanted to know what he really had in mind. Her intuition was partly correct. He was interested in more than water. He was interested in her heart.

They talked. Who could remember the last time a man had spoken to her with respect? He told her about a spring of water that would quench not the thirst of the throat, but of the soul. That intrigued her. "Sir, give me this water so that I won't get thirsty and have to keep coming here to draw water."

"Go, call your husband and come back." Her heart must have sunk. Here was a Jew who didn't care if she was a Samaritan. Here was a man who didn't look down on her as a woman. "I have no husband."

You probably know the rest of the story. This woman wondered what Jesus would do. She must have wondered if the kindness would cease when the truth was revealed. *He will be angry. He will leave. He will think I'm worthless.*

"You're right. You have had five husbands and the man you are with now won't even give you a name." The woman was amazed.

"I can see that you are a prophet." Translation? "There is something different about you. Do you mind if I ask you something?" Then she asked the question that revealed the gaping hole in her soul. "Where is God? My people say he is on the mountain. Your people say he is in Jerusalem. I don't know where he is" (John 4:20).

I'd give a thousand sunsets to see the expression on Jesus' face as he heard those words. Did his eyes water? Did he smile? Did he look up into the clouds and wink at his Father? Of all the places to find a hungry heart—Samaria?

Of all the Samaritans to be searching for God—a woman? Of all the women to have an insatiable appetite for God—a five-time divorcée?

"I am the Messiah."

The most important phrase in the chapter is one easily overlooked. "The woman left her water jar beside the well and ran back to the village, telling everyone, 'Come and see a man who told me everything I ever did! Could he possibly be the Messiah?'" (John 4:28–29 NLT).

Don't miss the drama of the moment. Look at her eyes, wide with amazement. Listen to her as she struggles for words. "Y-y-y-you a-a-a-are the M-m-m-messiah!" And watch as she scrambles to her feet, takes one last look at this grinning Nazarene, turns and runs right into the burly chest of Peter. She almost falls, regains her balance, and hotfoots it toward her hometown.

Did you notice what she forgot? She forgot her water jar. She left behind the jug that had caused the sag in her shoulders. She left behind the burden she brought.

Suddenly the shame of the tattered romances disappeared. Suddenly the insignificance of her life was swallowed by the significance of the moment. "God is here! God has come! God cares . . . for me!"

That is why she forgot her water jar. That is why she ran to the city. That is why she grabbed the first person she saw and announced her discovery.

The disciples offered Jesus some food. He refused it—he was too excited! He had just done what he does best. He had taken a life that was drifting and given it direction. "Look!" he announced to disciples, pointing at the woman who was running to the village. "Vast fields of human souls are ripening all around us, and are ready now for the reaping" (John 4:35 TLB). Who could eat at a time like this?

For some of you the story of the Samaritan woman is touching but distant. You belong. You are needed and you know it.

But others of you are different. You know why the Samaritan woman was avoiding people. You do the same thing.

You know what it's like to have no one sit by you at the cafeteria. You've wondered what it would be like to have one good friend. You've been in love and you wonder if it is worth the pain to do it again. And you, too, have wondered where in the world God is.

Again, I would give a thousand sunsets to have seen Jesus' face as this tiny prayer reached his throne. For indeed that is what it was—a prayer.

An earnest prayer that a good God in heaven would remember a forgotten soul on earth. A prayer to do what God does best: take the common and make it spectacular. To take a rejected woman and make her a missionary.

REFLECTION AND DISCUSSION

Read John 4:4–42. How did Jesus use his own needs as tools for evangelism (vv. 6–15)? What can we learn from this?

_____

_____

_____

_____

_____

What is the "living water" Jesus talks about in verse 10? What does it do?

_____

_____

_____

_____

_____

Identify the single greatest lesson you have learned from this story of the Samaritan woman.

_____

_____

_____

_____

_____

_____

Spend some time considering what it is that gives your life purpose and meaning. Describe it in detail; make a list and read it often. Be specific. Next time you feel overwhelmed or insignificant, read your list and thank God for the gift of life and purpose.

_____

_____

_____

_____

_____

_____

SAPPHIRA

SAPPHIRA

A false witness will not go unpunished,

And he who speaks lies shall perish.

Sapphira and her husband sat at the kitchen table and stared at the check for $15,000. The silence was a respite. The last half hour had been twelve rounds of verbal jabs and uppercuts. She blamed him for the idea. "You just had to give the money away."

He snapped back, "You didn't complain when everyone clapped for you at church, now did you?"

"Who would have thought that piece of dirt would bring this kind of price?"

Ananias hadn't expected to get $15,000. Ten thousand at best. Eight thousand at least. But fifteen thousand for an undeveloped acre off a one-lane road south of Jerusalem? He had inherited the property from his Uncle Ernie, who had left this note with the will: "Hang on to the land, Andy. You never know. If the road expands from one lane to four, you've got a nest egg."

So Ananias had taken the advice, locked the deed in a safe, and never thought about it until Sapphira, his wife, got wind of a generous deed done by Barnabas.

Ananias knew Barnabas from Rotary. Of course, everyone knew Barnabas. The guy had more friends than the temple had priests. Ananias couldn't help but notice the tone people used when discussing Barnabas's gift. Respect. Appreciation. It would be nice to be thought of that way.

So he mentioned the acre to Sapphira. "We're never going to build on it. I'm sure we can get $8,000. Let's give the money to the church."

"All of it?"

"Why not?"

They would have been better off just doing it, just keeping their mouths shut and giving the gift. They didn't need to tell a soul. But Ananias never excelled at mouth management.

During the next Sunday's worship service, the apostle Peter opened the floor for testimonials and prayer requests. Ananias popped up and took his place at the front. "Sapphira and I've been blessed beyond words since coming here to the Jerusalem church. We want to say thank you. We are selling an acre, and we pledge to give every mite to the Widows' Fund."

The congregation, several thousand members strong, broke into applause. Ananias gestured for Sapphira to wave . . . she did. She stood and turned a full circle and blew a kiss toward Ananias. He returned the gesture and then saluted Peter. But Peter was not smiling. Ananias chose not to think much of it and stepped back to his seat. Later that night he called a real-estate agent and listed the property. He fell asleep with the thought of a foyer named after him.

Uncle Ernie's hunch about road expansion was spot-on. Two land developers wanted the property. Neither winced at the $10,000 price tag. By the time the bidding was finished, the couple had a check for $15,000.

So they sat at their kitchen table in silence. Ananias stared at the check. It was Sapphira who first suggested the plan.

"What if we tell them we sold the property for just $10,000?"

"What?"

"Who has to know?"

Ananias thought for a moment. "Yeah, we'll just let everyone think we closed at $10,000. That way we get credit for the gift and a little cash for something special."

She smiled. "Like a $5,000 down payment on a Jaffa condo?"

"No harm in that."

"No harm at all."

And so on the following Sunday, Ananias stood in front of the church again. He waved a check and announced, "We sold the property for $10,000!" and he placed the check in the offering basket. He basked in the applause and signaled for Sapphira to stand. She did.

They thought their cover-up was a success. On Sunday afternoon the apostles called Ananias to a meeting. "They surely want to thank us," he told Sapphira as he tightened his necktie. "Probably wondering if we'd be self-conscious at a recognition banquet."

"I'd be okay with one," she assured him.

He smiled and walked out the door, never thinking he wouldn't return.

According to Luke the meeting lasted only long enough for Peter to ask four questions and render a single verdict.

Question 1: "Ananias, why has Satan filled your heart to lie to the Holy Spirit and keep back part of the price of the land for yourself?" (Acts 5:3 NKJV). So much for the cover-up. Luke's phrase for keep back means "misappropriate." The apostles sniffed out the couple's scheme for what it was: financial fraud.

Question 2: "While it remained, was it not your own?" (v. 4 NKJV). No one forced the couple to sell the property. They acted of their own accord and free will.

Question 3: "After it was sold, was it not in your own control?" (v. 4 NKJV). At any point the couple could have changed their minds or altered their contribution. The sin was not in keeping a portion of the proceeds but in pretending they gave it all. They wanted the appearance of sacrifice without the sacrifice.

Question 4: "Why have you conceived this thing in your heart?" (v. 4 NKJV). This deceitful act was not an impulsive stumble but a calculated, premeditated swindle.

Ananias had every intention of misleading the church. Did he not realize he was lying to God?

Peter made it clear with this verdict: "'You have not lied to men but to God.' Then Ananias, hearing these words, fell down and breathed his last" (vv. 4–5 NKJV).

The body of Ananias was wrapped and buried before Sapphira had any clue what had happened. When she came to meet with Peter, she expected a word of appreciation. Peter gave her a chance to come clean.

"Tell me whether you sold the land for so much" (v. 8 NKJV).

"Yes, for so much" (v. 8 NKJV).

"How is it that you have agreed together to test the Spirit of the Lord? Look, the feet of those who have buried your husband are at the door, and they will carry you out" (v. 9 NKJV).

As they carry Sapphira to join her husband in the cemetery, we shake our heads. Dare we wonder out loud what we're wondering inside? Ask the question we all think? Since no one else will ask it, I will.

Was that really necessary?

Ananias and Sapphira deserved punishment, for sure. But the death sentence? Does the punishment fit the crime? Let's think about it.

They used the church for self-promotion. They leveraged God's family for personal gain. They attempted to turn a congregation into a personal stage across which they could strut.

God has a strong word for such behavior: *hypocrisy*. When Jesus used it, people ducked for cover. He lambasted the Pharisees with this blowtorch:

All their works they do to be seen by men . . . They love the best places at feasts, the best seats in the synagogues, greetings in the marketplaces, and to be called by men, "Rabbi, Rabbi." . . . But woe to you, scribes and Pharisees, hypocrites! For you shut up the kingdom of heaven against men . . . Woe to you, scribes and Pharisees, hypocrites! For you devour widows' houses, and for a pretense make long prayers . . . You cleanse the outside of the cup and dish, but inside they are full of extortion and self-indulgence. (Matt. 23:5–7, 13–14, 25 NKJV)

Jesus never spoke to anyone else with such intensity. But when he saw the religious hypocrite, he flipped on the spotlight and exposed every self-righteous mole and pimple. "They love to pray standing in the synagogues and on the corners of the streets, that they may be seen by men" (Matt. 6:5 NKJV).

This is the working definition of *hypocrisy*: "to be seen by men." The Greek word for hypocrite, *hupokrites*, originally meant "actor." First-century actors wore masks. A hypocrite, then, is one who puts on a mask, a false face.

Jesus did not say, "Do not do good works." Nor did he instruct, "Do not let your works be seen." We must do good works, and some works, such as benevolence or teaching, must be seen in order to have an impact. So let's be clear. To do a good thing is a good thing. To do good to be seen is not. In fact, to do good to be seen is a serious offense. Here's why.

Hypocrisy turns people away from God. When God-hungry souls walk into a congregation of wannabe superstars, what happens? When God seekers see singers strut like Las Vegas entertainers . . . when they hear the preacher—a man of slick words, dress, and hair—play to the crowd and exclude God . . . when other attendees dress to be seen and make much to-do over their gifts and offerings . . . when people enter a church to see God yet can't see God because of the church, don't think for a second that God doesn't react. "Be especially careful when you are trying to be good so that you don't make a performance out of it. It might be good theater, but the God who made you won't be applauding" (Matt. 6:1 MSG).

Hypocrisy turns people against God. So God has a no-tolerance policy. Let the cold, lifeless bodies of the embezzling couple issue their intended warning. Let's take hypocrisy as seriously as God does. How can we?

1. Expect no credit for good deeds. None. If no one notices, you aren't disappointed. If someone does, you give the credit to God.

Ask yourself this question: "If no one knew of the good I do, would I still do it?" If not, you're doing it to be seen by people.

2. Give financial gifts in secret. Money stirs the phony within us. We like to be seen earning it. And we like to be seen giving it. So "when you give to someone in need, don't let your left hand know what your right hand is doing" (Matt. 6:3 NLT).

3. Don't fake spirituality. When you go to church, don't select a seat just to be seen or sing just to be heard. If you raise your hands in worship, raise holy ones, not showy ones. When you talk, don't doctor your vocabulary with trendy religious terms. Nothing nauseates more than a fake "Praise the Lord" or a shallow "Hallelujah" or an insincere "Glory be to God."

"First wash the inside of the cup and the dish, and then the outside will become clean, too" (Matt. 23:26 NLT). Focus on the inside, and the outside will take care of itself. Lay your motives before God daily, hourly. "Search me, O God, and know my heart; test me and know my anxious thoughts. Point out anything in me that offends you, and lead me along the path of everlasting life" (Ps. 139:23–24 NLT).

Do good things. Just don't do them to be noticed. You can be too good for your own good, you know.

REFLECTION AND DISCUSSION

Why are we tempted to display our good deeds? Have you ever struggled with giving back and expecting to receive something in return? If so, how do you overcome that desire?

_____

_____

_____

_____

_____

Do you think we long for the approval from others because we need the approval of our Creator? How can you become closer to God and his love?

_____

_____

_____

_____

_____

Why do you think Ananias and Sapphira decided to keep the money? Do you think they were wrong? Why or why not?

_____

_____

_____

_____

_____

How does our culture tempt us to flaunt our good deeds and ideals?

_____

_____

_____

_____

_____

_____

_____

_____

_____

_____

_____

_____

SARAH

SARAH

BEFORE YOU BEGIN
Read Genesis 18:10–12 NIV

One of them said, "I will surely return to you about this time next year, and Sarah your wife will have a son."

Now Sarah was listening at the entrance to the tent, which was behind him. Abraham and Sarah were already very old, and Sarah was past the age of childbearing. So Sarah laughed to herself as she thought, "After I am worn out and my lord is old, will I now have this pleasure?"

The kingdom of heaven. Its citizens are drunk on wonder.

Consider the case of Sarai.[24] Read Genesis 16–18, 21 so you can better understand her situation.

She is in her golden years, but God promises her a son. She gets excited. She visits the maternity shop and buys a few dresses. She plans her shower and remodels her tent . . . but no son. She eats a few birthday cakes and blows out a lot of candles . . . still no son. She goes through a decade of wall calendars . . . still no son.

So Sarai decides to take matters into her own hands. ("Maybe God needs me to take care of this one.")

She convinces Abram that time is running out. ("Face it, Abe, you ain't getting any younger either.") She commands her maid, Hagar, to go into Abram's tent and see if he needs anything. ("And I mean 'anything'!") Hagar goes in a maid. She comes out a mom. And the problems begin.

Hagar is haughty. Sarai is jealous. Abram is dizzy from the dilemma. And God calls the baby boy a "wild donkey"—an appropriate name for one born out of stubbornness and destined to kick his way into history.

It isn't the cozy family Sarai expected. And it isn't a topic Abram and Sarai bring up very often at dinner.

Finally, fourteen years later, when Abram is pushing a century of years and Sarai ninety . . . when Abram has stopped listening to Sarai's advice, and Sarai has stopped giving it . . . when the wallpaper in the nursery is faded and the baby furniture is several seasons out of date . . . when the topic of the promised child brings sighs and tears and long looks into a silent sky . . . God pays them a visit and tells them they had better select a name for their new son.

Abram and Sarai have the same response: laughter. They laugh partly because it is too good to happen and partly because it might. They laugh because they have given up hope, and hope born anew is always funny before it is real.

They laugh at the lunacy of it all.

Abram looks over at Sarai—toothless and snoring in her rocker, head back and mouth wide open, as fruitful as a pitted prune and just as wrinkled. And he cracks up. He tries to contain it, but he can't. He has always been a sucker for a good joke.

Sarai is just as amused. When she hears the news, a cackle escapes before she can contain it. She mumbles something about her husband's needing a lot more than what he's got and then laughs again.

They laugh because that is what you do when someone says he can do the impossible. They laugh a little at God, and a lot with God—for God is laughing too. Then, with the smile still on his face, he gets busy doing what he does best—the unbelievable.

He changes a few things—beginning with their names. Abram, the father of one, will now be Abraham, the father of a multitude. Sarai, the barren one, will now be Sarah, the mother.

But their names aren't the only things God changes. He changes their minds. He changes their faith. He changes the number of their tax deductions. He changes the way they define the word *impossible.*

But most of all, he changes Sarah's attitude about trusting God. Were she to hear Jesus' statement about being poor in spirit, she could give a testimony: "He's right. I do things my way, I get a headache. I let God take over, I get a son. You try to figure that out. All I know is I am the first lady in town to pay her pediatrician with a Social Security check."

Have you ever tried to rush God's plans or question his promises? Trusting God means relinquishing what we think is the way and allowing God to take the wheel.

REFLECTION AND DISCUSSION

When Sarai said, "No way," God would say, "My way." Has this ever happened to you? If so, explain.

_____

_____

_____

_____

_____

What is getting in your way of seeing the world with spiritual eyes? Why are you hesitant to believe that God can do the impossible?

_____

_____

_____

_____

_____

Sarai and Abram stumbled but they still had faith in God. Can you relate to their faith journey? What circumstances have caused your heart to forget God's promises to you?

_____

_____

_____

_____

_____

SIMON AND MARY

SIMON AND MARY

BEFORE YOU BEGIN
Read John 12:3 NKJV

Then Mary took a pound of very costly oil of spikenard, anointed the feet of Jesus, and wiped His feet with her hair. And the house was filled with the fragrance of the oil.

Artful Eddie lacked nothing. He was the slickest of the slick lawyers. A crony of Al Capone, he ran the gangster's dog tracks. He mastered the simple technique of fixing the race by overfeeding seven dogs and betting on the eighth. Wealth. Status. Style. Artful Eddie lacked nothing.

Then why did he turn himself in? Why did he offer to squeal on Capone? What was his motive?

His son. Eddie had spent his life with the despicable. For his son, he wanted more. He wanted to give his son a name and that meant he would have to clear his own. Eddie was willing to take a risk so that his son could have a clean slate. After Eddie squealed, the mob remembered. Two shotgun blasts silenced him forever.

Was it worth it? For the son it was. Artful Eddie's boy lived up to the sacrifice. His is one of the best-known names in the world. But before we talk about the son, let's talk about the principle: risky love. Love that takes a chance. Love that makes a statement and leaves a legacy. Sacrificial love. Acts of love that are never forgotten.

Such an act of love was seen in the last week of the life of Jesus. A demonstration of devotion that the world will never forget. An act of extravagant tenderness in which Jesus wasn't the giver; he was the receiver.

A cluster of friends encircle Jesus. They are at the table. The city is Bethany and the house is Simon's.

He was known as Simon the leper. We don't know when Jesus healed him. But we do know what he was like before Jesus healed him. Stooped shoulders. Fingerless hand. Scabbed arm and infected back draped in rags. A tattered wrap that hides all of the face except for two screaming white eyes.

But that was before Jesus' touch. Was Simon the one Jesus healed after he delivered the Sermon on the Mount? Was he the one in the ten who returned to say thank you? Was he one of the four thousand Jesus helped in Bethsaida? Or was he one of the nameless myriads the Gospel writers didn't take time to mention? We don't know. But we know he had Jesus and his disciples over for dinner.

A simple act, but it must have meant a lot to Jesus.

Simon didn't forget what Jesus had done. Where there had been a nub, there was now a finger for his daughter to hold. Where there had been ulcerous sores, there was now skin for his wife to stroke. And where there had been lonely hours in quarantine, there were now happy hours such as this—a house full of friends, a table full of food.

Simon knew what it was like to stare death in the face. He knew what it was like to have no home to call your own, and he knew what it was like to be misunderstood. He wanted Jesus to know that if he ever needed a meal and a place to lay his head, there was one house in Bethany to which he could go.

Other homes will not be as gracious as Simon's. Before the week is up, Jesus will spend some time in the high priest's house, the nicest in Jerusalem. Three barns in the back and a beautiful view of the valley. But Jesus won't see the view; he'll see only the false witnesses, hear the lies, and feel the slaps on his face.

Before the week is up, Jesus will visit the chambers of Herod. Elegant chambers. Plenty of servants. Perhaps there is fruit and wine on the table. But Herod won't offer any to Jesus. Herod wants a trick. "Show me a miracle, country boy," he will jab. The guards will snicker.

Before the week is up, Jesus will visit the home of Pilate. Rare opportunity to stand before the couch of the procurator of all Israel. Should be a moment to remember, but it won't be. It's a moment the world would rather forget. Pilate has an opportunity to perform the world's greatest act of mercy—and he doesn't. God is in his house and Pilate doesn't see him.

What if Pilate had come to the defense of the innocent? What if Herod had asked Jesus for help and not entertainment? What if the high priest had been as concerned with truth as he was his position? What if one of them had turned his back on the crowd and his face toward the Christ and made a stand?

But Simon did. Risky love seizes the moment. He gave Jesus a good meal. Not much, but more than most. And when the priests accused and the soldiers slapped, perhaps Jesus remembered what Simon did and was strengthened. And when he remembered Simon's meal, perhaps he remembered Mary's gesture.

She was the only one who believed him. Whenever he spoke of his death the others shrugged, the others doubted, but Mary believed. Mary believed because he spoke with a firmness she'd heard before.

"Lazarus, come out!" he'd demanded, and her brother came out. After four days in a stone-sealed grave he walked out.

And as Mary kissed the now-warm hands of her just-dead brother, she turned and looked. Jesus was smiling. Tear streaks were dry and the teeth shone from beneath the beard. He was smiling. And in her heart, she knew she would never doubt his words. So when he spoke of his death, she believed.

And when she saw the three together, she couldn't resist. Simon, the healed leper, head thrown back in laughter. Lazarus, the resurrected corpse, leaning in to see what Jesus has said. And Jesus, the source of life for both, beginning his joke a second time.

"Now is the right time," she told herself. It wasn't an act of impulse. She'd carried the large vial of perfume from her house to Simon's. It wasn't a spontaneous gesture. But it was an extravagant one. The perfume was worth a year's wages. It wasn't a logical thing to do, but since when has love been led by logic?

Logic hadn't touched Simon. Common sense hadn't wept at Lazarus's tomb. Practicality didn't feed the crowds or love the children. Love did. Extravagant, risky, chance-taking love. And now someone needs to show the same to the giver of such love.

So Mary did. She stepped up behind him and stood with the jar in her hand. Within a couple of moments every mouth was silent and every eye wide as they watched her nervous fingers remove the ornate cover.

Only Jesus was unaware of her presence. Just as he noticed everyone looking behind him, she began to pour. The fragrance rushed through the room. Smells of cooked lamb and herbs were lost in the aroma of the sweet ointment. "Wherever you go," the gesture spoke, "breathe the aroma and remember one who cares."

On his skin the fragrance of faith. In his clothing the balm of belief. Even as the soldiers divided his garments, her gesture brought a bouquet into a cemetery.

The other disciples mocked her extravagance. They, the recipients of exorbitant love, chastised her generosity. "Why waste that perfume? It could have been sold for a great deal of money that could be given to the poor," they smirk.

Don't miss Jesus' prompt defense of Mary: "Why are you troubling this woman? She did an excellent thing for me" (Matt. 26:10 NCV).[25]

Jesus' message is just as powerful today as it was then. Don't miss it: "There is a time for risky love. There is a time for extravagant gestures. There is a time to pour out your affections on one you love. And when the time comes—seize it, don't miss it."

Some days never come. And the price of practicality is sometimes higher than extravagance. But the rewards of risky love are always greater than its cost.

Go to the effort. Invest the time. Write the letter. Make the apology. Take the trip. Purchase the gift. Do it. The seized opportunity renders joy. The neglected brings regret.

The reward was great for Simon. He was privileged to give rest to the one who made the earth. Simon's gesture will never be forgotten.

Neither will Mary's. Jesus promised, "Wherever the Good News is preached in all the world, what this woman has done will be told, and people will remember her" (v. 13 NCV).

Simon and Mary: examples of the risky gift given at the right time.

Which brings us back to Artful Eddie, the Chicago mobster who squealed on Al Capone so his son could have a fair chance. Had Eddie lived to see his son Butch grow up, he would have been proud.

He would have been proud of Butch's appointment to Annapolis. He would have been proud of the commissioning as a World War II navy pilot. He would have been proud as he read of his son downing five bombers in the Pacific night and saving the lives of hundreds of crewmen on the carrier Lexington. The name was cleared. The Congressional Medal of Honor that Butch received was proof.

When people say the name O'Hare in Chicago, they don't think gangsters—they think aviation heroism. And now when you say his name, you have something else to think about.

REFLECTION AND DISCUSSION

Describe your initial reaction to Mary's action. Did you think it foolish? Exorbitant? Profound? Moving? Explain.

_____

_____

_____

_____

_____

_____

What are some appropriate times for risky love? Describe them. When have you chosen to demonstrate risky love? What was the outcome? Would you do it again? Why?

_____

_____

_____

_____

In what way does practicality sometimes cost more than extravagance? Do you agree that "the rewards of risky love are always greater than its cost"? Why or why not?

_____

_____

_____

Read Matthew 26:6–13. In what way was the woman's action a beautiful thing? Why do you suppose Jesus said what he did in verse 13?

_____

_____

_____

_____

THE
CANAANITE
WOMAN

THE CANAANITE WOMAN

BEFORE YOU BEGIN

Read Matthew 15:21–28 NIV

Leaving that place, Jesus withdrew to the region of Tyre and Sidon. A Canaanite woman from that vicinity came to him, crying out, "Lord, Son of David, have mercy on me! My daughter is demon-possessed and suffering terribly."

Jesus did not answer a word. So his disciples came to him and urged him, "Send her away, for she keeps crying out after us."

He answered, "I was sent only to the lost sheep of Israel."

The woman came and knelt before him. "Lord, help me!" she said.

He replied, "It is not right to take the children's bread and toss it to the dogs."

"Yes it is, Lord," she said. "Even the dogs eat the crumbs that fall from their master's table."

Then Jesus said to her, "Woman, you have great faith! Your request is granted." And her daughter was healed at that moment.

We don't know a thing about her. We don't know her name . . .her background . . . her looks . . . her hometown. She came from nowhere and went nowhere. She disappeared the same way that she appeared, like a puff of smoke.

But what a delightful puff she was.

The disciples, during two years of training, hadn't done what she did in a few moments of conversing. She impressed God with her faith. The disciples' hearts may have been good. Their desire may have been sincere. But their faith didn't turn God's head.

Hers did. For all we don't know about her, we do know one remarkable truth: she impressed God with her faith. After that, anything else she ever did was insignificant.

"Woman, you have great faith!" Jesus stated.

Some statement. Especially when you consider God said it. The God who can put a handful of galaxies into his palm. The one who creates Everests as a hobby. The one who paints rainbows without a canvas. The one who can measure the thickness of mosquito wings with one hand and level a mountain with the other.

One would think that the Creator would not be easily impressed. But something about this woman brought a sparkle to his eyes and . . . most likely . . . a smile to his face.

Matthew called her a "Canaanite woman" and, in doing so, called strikes one and two. Strike one? A Canaanite. An outsider. A foreigner. An apple in a family tree of oranges. Strike two? A woman. Might as well have been a junkyard dog. She lived in a culture that had little respect for women outside the bedroom and kitchen.

But she met the Teacher, who had plenty of respect for her.

Oh, it doesn't appear that way. In fact, the dialogue between the two seems harsh. It's not an easy passage to understand unless you're willing to concede that Jesus knew how to smile. If you have trouble with the sketch of the smiling Jesus hanging in my office, you'll have trouble with this story. But if you don't, if the thought of God smiling brings you a bit of relief, then you'll like the next few paragraphs.

Here's my interpretation.

The woman is desperate. Her daughter is demon possessed.

The Canaanite woman has no right to ask anything of Jesus. She is not a Jew. She is not a disciple. She offers no money for the ministry. She makes no promises to devote herself to missionary service. You get the impression that she knows as well as anybody that Jesus doesn't owe her anything, and she is asking him for everything. But that doesn't slow her down. She persists in her plea.

"Have mercy on me!"

Matthew notes that Jesus says nothing at first. Nothing. He doesn't open his mouth. Why?

To test her? Most commentators suggest this. Maybe, they say, he is waiting to see how serious she is about her plea. My dad used to make me wait a week from the day I asked him for something to the day he gave me his answer. Most of the time, I forgot that I ever made the request. Time has a way of separating whims from needs. Is Jesus doing that?

I have another opinion. I think that he was admiring her. I think that it did his heart good to see some spunky faith for a change. I think that it refreshed him to see someone asking him to do the very thing he came to do—give great gifts to unworthy children.

How strange that we don't allow him to do it more often for us.

Perhaps the most amazing response to God's gift is our reluctance to accept it. We want it. But on our terms. For some odd reason, we feel better if we earn it. So we create religious hoops and hop through them—making God a trainer, us his pets, and religion a circus.

The Canaanite woman knew better. She had no resume. She claimed no heritage. She had no earned degrees. She knew only two things: her daughter was weak, and Jesus was strong.

The disciples are annoyed. As Jesus sits in silence, they grow smugger. "Send her away," they demand. The spotlight is put on Jesus. He looks at the disciples, then looks at the woman. And what follows is one of the most intriguing dialogues in the New Testament.

"I was sent only to the lost sheep of Israel," he says.

"Lord, help me!"

"It is not right to take the children's bread and toss it to their dogs," he answers.

"But even the dogs eat the crumbs that fall from their masters' table," she responds.

Is Jesus being rude? Is he worn-out? Is he frustrated? Is he calling this woman a dog? How do we explain this dialogue?

Bible commentaries give us three options.

Some say that Jesus was trapped. He could not help the woman because he had been sent first to the lost sheep of Israel. Neat theory, but full of problems. One is the Samaritan woman. Another is the centurion. Jesus had already helped Gentiles and stayed faithful to the focus of his mission. So why couldn't he do it now?

Others think that Jesus was rude. Who can blame him? He was tired. It had been a long trip. The disciples were coming along slowly. And this request was the straw that broke the camel's back.

Like that explanation? I don't either. The one who had had compassion on the five thousand men . . . who had wept over the city of Jerusalem . . . who had come to seek and save ones like this one . . . would not snap so abruptly at such a needy woman.

The most popular theory is that he was testing her . . . again. Just to be sure that she was serious about her request. Just to make sure that her faith was real.

But by insinuating that she was a dog?

I don't think Jesus would do that either. Let me suggest another alternative.

Could it be that Jesus' tongue is poking his cheek? Could it be that he and the woman are engaging in satirical banter? Is it a wry exchange in which God's unlimited grace is being highlighted? Could Jesus be so delighted to have found one who is not bartering with a religious system or proud of a heritage that he can't resist a bit of satire?

He knows he can heal her daughter. He knows he isn't bound by a plan. He knows her heart is good. So he decides to engage in a humorous moment with a faithful woman. In essence, here's what they said:

"Now, you know that God only cares about Jews," he says, smiling.

And when she catches on, she volleys back, "But your bread is so precious, I'll be happy to eat the crumbs."

In a spirit of exuberance, he bursts out, "Never have I seen such faith! Your daughter is healed."

This story does not portray a contemptuous God. It portrays a willing one who delights in a sincere seeker.

Aren't you glad he does?

The story is told about the time Napoleon's steed got away from him. An alert private jumped on his own horse and chased down the emperor's horse. When he presented the reins of the animal to Napoleon, the ruler took them, smiled at this willing private, and said, "Thank you, Captain."

The soldier's eyes widened at what he had heard. He then straightened. Saluted. And snapped, "Thank you, sir!"

He immediately went to the barracks. Got his bags. Moved into the officers' quarters. Took his old uniform to the quartermaster and exchanged it for that of a captain. By the emperor's word, he had become a private-turned-commissioned-officer. He didn't argue. He didn't shrug. He didn't doubt. He knew that the one who had the power to do it had done it. And he accepted that.

If only we would do the same. If only we would have the faith of the private and the trust of the Canaanite woman. If only, when God smiles and says we are saved, we'd salute him, thank him, and live like those who have just received a gift from the commander in chief.

We seldom do that, though. We prefer to get salvation the old fashioned way: we earn it. To accept grace is to admit failure, a step we are hesitant to take. We opt to impress God with how good we are rather than confessing how great he is. We dizzy ourselves with doctrine. Burden ourselves with rules. Think that God will smile on our efforts.

He doesn't.

God's smile is not for the healthy hiker who boasts that he made the journey alone. It is, instead, for the crippled leper who begs God for a back on which to ride.

Such were the woman's words. She knew that her request was ludicrous. But she also knew that Jesus was Lord.

Daniel's words could have been hers: "We do not make requests of you because we are righteous, but because of your great mercy" (Daniel 9:18 NIV).

She came, banking on the hope that Jesus would answer her prayer based on his goodness and not her worthiness.

And he did. With a smile.

When I think about the prayers God has answered for me despite the life I've lived, I think he must be smiling still.

So I think I'll keep his picture on the wall.

After reading the opening Scripture verses, what were your first thoughts about the Canaanite woman?

_____

_____

_____

_____

Do you think Jesus was testing the Canaanite woman? Why or why not?

_____

_____

_____

_____

Max writes, "We opt to impress God with how good we are rather than confessing how great he is." Can you think of an example in your life, where this is true?

_____

_____

_____

_____

_____

What can you do to also have the faith of the private and trust of the Canaanite woman in your life?

_____

_____

_____

_____

_____

_____

THE CRIPPLED MAN AT THE GATE

THE CRIPPLED MAN
AT THE GATE

BEFORE YOU BEGIN

Read Acts 3:4, 7 MSG

When he saw Peter and John about to enter the Temple, he asked for a handout.

He grabbed him by the right hand and pulled him up.

A gate called Beautiful. The man was anything but. He couldn't walk but had to drag himself about on his knees. He passed his days among the contingent of real and pretend beggars who coveted the coins of the worshippers entering Solomon's court. Peter and John were among them.

The needy man saw the apostles, lifted his voice, and begged for money. They had none to give, yet still they stopped. "Peter and John looked straight at him and said, 'Look at us!'" (Acts 3:4). They locked their eyes on his with such compassion that "he gave them his attention, expecting to receive something from them" (v. 5 NKJV). Peter and John issued no embarrassed glance, irritated shrug, or cynical dismissal but an honest look.

It is hard to look suffering in the face. Wouldn't we rather turn away? Stare in a different direction? Fix our gaze on fairer objects? Human hurt is not easy on the eyes. The dusty cheeks of the Pakistani refugee. The wide-eyed stare of the Peruvian orphan. Or the salt-and-pepper tangle of a beard worn by the drifter Stanley and I met in Pennsylvania.

Stanley Shipp served as a father to my young faith. He was thirty years my senior and blessed with a hawkish nose, thin lips, a rim of white hair, and a heart as big as the Midwest. His business cards, which he gave to those who requested and those who didn't, read simply, "Stanley Shipp—Your Servant."

I spent my first post college year under his tutelage. One of our trips took us to a small church in rural Pennsylvania for a conference. He and I happened to be the only two people at the building when a drifter, wearing alcohol like a cheap perfume, knocked on the door. He recited his victim spiel. Overqualified for work. Unqualified for pension. Lost bus ticket. Bad back. His kids in Kansas didn't care. I crossed my arms, smirked, and gave Stanley a *get-a-load-of-this-guy* glance.

Stanley didn't return it. He devoted every optic nerve to the drifter. Stanley saw no one else but him. How long, I remember wondering, since anyone looked this fellow square in the face?

The meandering saga finally stopped, and Stanley led the man into the church kitchen and prepared him a plate of food and a sack of groceries. As we watched him leave, Stanley blinked back a tear and responded to my unsaid thoughts. "Max, I know he's probably lying. But what if just one part of his story was true?"

We both saw the man. I saw right through him. Stanley saw deep into him. There is something fundamentally good about taking time to see a person. Simon the Pharisee once disdained Jesus' kindness toward a woman of questionable character. So Jesus tested him: "Do you see this woman?" (Luke 7:44 NKJV). Simon didn't.

What do we see? "When He saw the multitudes, He was moved with compassion for them, because they were weary and scattered, like sheep having no shepherd" (Matt. 9:36 NKJV).

This word *compassion* is one of the oddest in Scripture. The New Testament Greek lexicon says this word means "to be moved as to one's bowels . . . (for the bowels were thought to be the seat of love and pity)."[26] It shares a root system with *splanchnology*, the study of the visceral parts. Compassion, then, is a movement deep within—a kick in the gut.

Perhaps that is why we turn away. Who can bear such an emotion? Especially when we can do nothing about it. Why look suffering in the face if we can't make a difference? Yet what if we could? What if our attention could reduce someone's pain? This is the promise of the encounter.

> Then Peter said, "Silver and gold I do not have, but what I do have I give you: In the name of Jesus Christ of Nazareth, rise up and walk." And he took him by the right hand and lifted him up, and immediately his feet and ankle bones received strength. So he, leaping up, stood and walked and entered the temple with them—walking, leaping, and praising God. (Acts 3:6–8 NKJV)

The thick, meaty hand of the fisherman reached for the frail, thin one of the beggar. Think Sistine Chapel and the high hand of God. One from above, the other from below. A holy helping hand. Peter lifted the man toward himself. The cripple swayed like a newborn calf finding its balance. It appeared as if the man would fall, but he didn't. He stood. And as he stood, he began to shout, and passersby began to stop. They stopped and watched the cripple skip.

Don't you think he did? Not at first, mind you. But after a careful step, then another few, don't you think he skipped a jig? Parading and waving the mat on which he had lived?

The crowd thickened around the trio. The apostles laughed as the beggar danced. Other beggars pressed toward the scene in their ragged coverings and tattered robes and cried out for their portion of a miracle. "I want my healing! Touch me! Touch me!"

So Peter complied. He escorted them to the clinic of the Great Physician and invited them to take a seat. "His name, . . . faith in His name, has made this man strong. . . . Repent therefore and be converted, that your sins may be blotted out, so that times of refreshing may come from the presence of the Lord" (vv. 16, 19 NKJV).

Blotted out is a translation of a Greek term that means "to obliterate" or "erase completely." Faith in Christ, Peter explained, leads to a clean slate with God. What Jesus did for the legs of this cripple, he does for our souls. Brand new!

Let's be the people who stop at the gate. Let's look at the hurting until we hurt with them. No hurrying past, turning away, or shifting of eyes. No pretending or glossing over. Let's look at the face until we see the person.

Could this be God's strategy for human hurt? First, kind eyes meet desperate ones. Next, strong hands help weak ones. Then, the miracle of God. We do our small part, he does the big part, and life at the Beautiful Gate begins to be just that.

REFLECTION AND DISCUSSION

"Human hurt is not easy on the eyes." Tell of a time you encountered suffering that was painful to observe. Describe a time you were hurting and someone made you think he or she really saw you.

What does it communicate to people in need, especially those who are not beautiful, when you look directly at them, in their eyes?

_____

_____

_____

_____

_____

_____

Take note of each meaningful touch you find in the following miracles of Jesus: Matthew 9:20-22; Mark 1:40-45; Mark 7:32-35; Luke 8:51-55; Luke 13:11-13; John 9:1-7. Did Jesus need to touch people to heal them? Why do you think some form of touch was part of each healing?

_____

_____

_____

_____

_____

Peter and John gave more than the money the crippled beggar asked for in Acts 3. What resources do you have—beyond money—that you could give to people in need?

_____

_____

_____

_____

_____

For Peter and John the strategy of kind eyes meeting desperate ones and strong hands helping weak ones unleashed a miracle of God. How could you live out this strategy?

_____

_____

_____

_____

_____

THE
GADARENE
DEMONIAC

THE GADARENE DEMONIAC

BEFORE YOU BEGIN
Read Mark 5:2–5 NASB

When He got out of the boat, immediately a man from the tombs with an unclean spirit met Him. He lived among the tombs; and no one was able to bind him anymore, not even with a chain, because he had often been bound with shackles and chains, and the chains had been torn apart by him and the shackles broken in pieces; and no one was strong enough to subdue him. Constantly, night and day, he was screaming among the tombs and in the mountains, and cutting himself with stones.

Wiry, clumpy hair. A beard to the chest, ribboned with blood. Furtive eyes, darting in all directions, refusing to fix. Naked. No sandals to protect feet from the rocks of the ground or clothing to protect skin from the rocks of his hand. He beats himself with stones. Bruises blotch his skin like ink stains. Open sores and gashes attract flies.

His home is a limestone mausoleum, a graveyard of Galilean shoreline caves cut out of the cliffs. Apparently, he feels more secure among the dead than the living.

Which pleases the living. He baffles them. See the cracked shackles on his legs and broken chains on his wrists? They can't control the guy. Nothing holds him. How do you manage chaos? Travelers skirt the area out of fear (Matt. 8:28). The villagers were left with a problem, and we are left with a picture—a picture of the work of Satan.

How else do we explain our bizarre behavior? The violent rages, secret binges, sudden rebellion, and insensitive words. Satan does not sit still. A glimpse of the wild man reveals Satan's goals for you and me.

Self-imposed pain. The demoniac used rocks. We are more sophisticated; we use drugs, sex, work, violence, and food.

Obsession with death and darkness. Even unchained, the wild man loitered among the dead. Evil feels at home there. Communing with the deceased, sacrificing the living, a morbid fascination with death and dying—this is not the work of God.

Endless restlessness. The man on the eastern shore screamed day and night (Mark 5:5). Satan begets raging frenzy. "The evil spirit . . . wanders . . ." Jesus says, "looking for rest" (Matt. 12:43 PHILLIPS).

Isolation. The man is all alone in his suffering. Such is Satan's plan. "The devil prowls around like a roaring lion, seeking some *one* to devour" (1 Peter 5:8 RSV, emphasis added). Fellowship foils his work.

And Jesus? Jesus wrecks his work. Christ steps out of the boat with both pistols blasting. "Come out of the man, unclean spirit!" (Mark 5:8 NKJV).

Demons deserve no tolerance. They throw themselves at the feet and mercy of Christ. The leader of the horde begs for the others:

"What have you to do with me, Jesus, Son of the Most High God? I adjure you by God, do not torment me." . . . Jesus asked him, "What is your name?" He replied, "My name is Legion; for we are many." He begged him earnestly not to send them out of the country. (vv. 7, 9–10 NRSV)

Legion is a Roman military term. A Roman legion involved six thousand soldiers. To envision that many demons inhabiting this man is frightening but not unrealistic. What bats are to a cave, demons are to hell—too many to number.

The demons are not only numerous, they are equipped. A legion is a battalion in arms. Satan and his friends come to fight. Hence, we are urged to "take up the full armor of God, so that you will be able to resist in the evil day, and having done everything, to stand firm" (Eph. 6:13 NASB).

Well, we should, for they are organized. "We are fighting against forces and authorities and against rulers of darkness and powers in the spiritual world" (Eph. 6:12 CEV). Jesus spoke of the "gates of hell" (Matt. 16:18 KJV), a phrase that suggests the "council of hell." Our enemy has a complex and conniving spiritual army. Dismiss any image of a red-suited Satan with pitchfork and pointy tail. The devil is a strong devil.

But, and this is the point of the passage, in God's presence, the devil is a wimp. Satan is to God what a mosquito is to an atomic bomb.

> Now a large herd of swine was feeding there near the mountains. So all the demons begged Him, saying, "Send us to the swine, that we may enter them." And at once Jesus gave them permission. Then the unclean spirits went out and entered the swine (there were about two thousand); and the herd ran violently down the steep place into the sea, and drowned in the sea. (Mark 5:11–13 NKJV)

How hell's court cowers in Christ's presence! Demons bow before him, solicit him, and obey him. They can't even lease a pig without his permission. Then how do we explain Satan's influence?

Natalie must have asked that question a thousand times.[27] In the list of characters for a modern-day Gerasene story, her name is near the top. She was raised in a tormented world.

The community suspected nothing. Her parents cast a friendly facade. Each Sunday they paraded Natalie and her sisters down the church aisle. Her father served as an elder. Her mom played the organ. The congregation respected them. Natalie despised them. To this day she refuses to call her parents "Mom" and "Dad." A "warlock" and "witch" don't deserve the distinction.

When she was six months old, they sexually sacrificed Natalie on hell's altar, tagging her as a sex object to be exploited by men in any place, anytime. Cultists bipolarized her world: dressing her in white for Sunday service and, hours later, stripping her at the coven. If she didn't scream or vomit during the attack, Natalie was rewarded with an ice cream cone. Only by "crawling down deep" inside herself could she survive.

Natalie miraculously escaped the cult but not the memories. Well into her adult years, she wore six pairs of underpants as a wall of protection. Dresses created vulnerability; she avoided them. She hated being a woman; she hated seeing men; she hated being alive. Only God could know the legion of terrors that dogged her. But God did know.

Hidden within the swampland of her soul was an untouched island. Small but safe. Built, she believes, by her heavenly Father during the hours the little girl sat on a church pew. Words of his love, hymns of his mercy—they left their mark. She learned to retreat to this island and pray. God heard her prayers. Counselors came. Hope began to offset horror. Her faith increasingly outweighed her fears. The healing process was lengthy and tedious but victorious, culminating in her marriage to a godly man.[28]

Her deliverance didn't include cliffs and pigs, but, make no mistake, she was delivered. And we are reminded. Satan can disturb us, but he cannot defeat us. The head of the serpent is crushed.

I saw a literal picture of this in a prairie ditch. A petroleum company was hiring strong backs and weak minds to lay a pipeline. Since I qualified, much of a high school summer was spent shoveling in a shoulder-high, multi-mile West Texas trough. A large digging machine trenched ahead of us. We followed, scooping out the excess dirt and rocks.

One afternoon the machine dislodged more than dirt. "Snake!" shouted the foreman. We popped out of that hole faster than a jack-in-the-box and looked down at the rattlesnake nest. One worker launched his shovel and beheaded the rattler. We stood on the higher ground and watched as she—now headless—writhed and twisted in the soft dirt below. Though defanged, the snake still spooked us.

That scene in the West Texas summer is a parable of where we are in life. Is the devil not a snake? John calls him "that old snake who is the devil" (Rev. 20:2 NCV).

Has he not been decapitated? Not with a shovel, but with a cross. "God disarmed the spiritual rulers and authorities. He shamed them publicly by his victory over them on the cross" (Col. 2:15 NLT).

So how does that leave us? Confident. The punch line of the passage is Jesus' power over Satan. One word from Christ, and the demons are swimming with the swine and the wild man is "clothed and in his right mind" (Mark 5:15 NASB). Just one command! Jesus "commands . . . evil spirits, and they obey him" (Mark 1:27 NCV). The snake in the ditch and Lucifer in the pit—both have met their match.

And yet, both stir up dust long after their defeat. For that reason, though confident, we are still careful. For a toothless ol' varmint, Satan sure has some bite! He spooks our work, disrupts our activities, and leaves us thinking twice about where we step. Which we need to do. "Be alert and of sober mind. Your enemy the devil prowls around like a roaring lion looking for someone to devour" (1 Peter 5:8 NIV). Alertness is needed. Panic is not. The serpent still wiggles and intimidates, but he has no poison. He is defeated, and he knows it! "He knows his time is short" (Rev. 12:12 CEV).

"Greater is He who is in you than he who is in the world" (1 John 4:4 NASB). Believe it. Trust the work of your Savior. "Resist the devil and he will flee from you" (James 4:7 NASB). In the meantime, the best he can do is squirm.

REFLECTION AND DISCUSSION

Max says, "A glimpse of the wild man reveals Satan's goals for you and me. Self-imposed pain. The demoniac used rocks. We are more sophisticated; we use drugs, sex, work, violence, and food." How have you seen people around you suffer from self-imposed pain? In what way(s) has hell made you hurt yourself?

Read Mark 5:1–20. Why could Christ control the demons with a single command? What does it mean for you that Christ has such power over hell?

_____

_____

_____

_____

_____

Why do you think the demon-possessed man came out to meet Jesus when the Lord got out of the boat (Mark 5:2)? Why wouldn't he just run away?

_____

_____

_____

_____

_____

What did the cured man request of Jesus (Mark 5:18)? What answer did Jesus give (v. 19)? Why do you think he gave this answer?

_____

_____

_____

_____

_____

Read 1 Peter 5:8–10. How do you steady yourself so that you stand "strong in your faith"? Why does it help to remember that you are not alone in suffering and temptation (v. 9)? From where does all spiritual strength ultimately come (v. 10)?

_____

_____

_____

_____

_____

THE LEPER
JESUS HEALED

THE LEPER JESUS
HEALED

BEFORE YOU BEGIN
Read Colossians 3:12 TLB

Since you have been chosen by God who has given you this new kind of life, and because of his deep love and concern for you, you should practice tenderhearted mercy and kindness to others. Don't worry about making a good impression on them, but be ready to suffer quietly and patiently.

May I ask you to look at your hand for a moment? Look at the back, then the palm. Reacquaint yourself with your fingers. Run a thumb over your knuckles. What if someone were to film a documentary about your hands? What if a producer were to tell your story based on the life of your hands? What would we see? As with all of us, the film would begin with an infant's fist, then a close-up of a tiny hand wrapped around mommy's finger. Then what? Holding on to a chair as you learned to walk? Handling a spoon as you learned to eat?

We aren't too long into the feature before we see your hand being affectionate, stroking daddy's face or petting a puppy. Nor is it too long before we see your hand acting aggressively: pushing big brother or yanking back a toy. All of us learned early that the hand is suited for more than survival—it's a tool of emotional expression. The same hand can help or hurt, extend or clench, lift someone up or shove someone down.

Were you to show the documentary to your friends, you'd be proud of certain moments: your hand extending with a gift, placing a ring on another's finger, doctoring a wound, preparing a meal, or folding in prayer. And then there are other scenes. Shots of accusing fingers, abusive fists. Hands taking more often than giving, demanding instead of offering, wounding rather than loving. Oh, the power of our hands. Leave them unmanaged and they become weapons: clawing for power, strangling for survival, seducing for pleasure. But manage them and our hands become instruments of grace— not just tools in the hands of God, but God's very hands. Surrender them and these five-fingered appendages become the hands of heaven.

That's what Jesus did. Our Savior completely surrendered his hands to God. The documentary of his hands has no scenes of greedy grabbing or unfounded finger pointing. It does, however, have one scene after another of people longing for his compassionate touch: parents carrying their children, the poor bringing their fears, the sinful shouldering their sorrow. And each who came was touched. And each one touched was changed. But none was touched or changed more than the unnamed leper of Matthew 8.

When Jesus came down from the hill, great crowds followed him. Then a man with a skin disease came to Jesus. The man bowed down before him and said, "Lord, you can heal me if you will."

Jesus reached out his hand and touched the man and said, "I will. Be healed!" And immediately the man was healed from his disease. Then Jesus said to him, "Don't tell anyone about this. But go and show yourself to the priest and offer the gift Moses commanded for people who are made well. This will show the people what I have done." (vv. 1–4 NCV)

Mark and Luke chose to tell this same story. But with apologies to all three writers, I must say none tell enough. Oh, we know the man's disease and his decision, but as to the rest? We are left with questions. The authors offer no name, no history, no description.

Sometimes my curiosity gets the best of me, and I wonder out loud. That's what I'm about to do here—wonder out loud about the man who felt Jesus' compassionate touch. He makes one appearance, has one request, and receives one touch. But that one touch changed his life forever. And I wonder if his story went something like this:

For five years no one touched me. No one. Not one person. Not my wife. Not my child. Not my friends. No one touched me. They saw me. They spoke to me. I sensed love in their voices. I saw concern in their eyes. But I didn't feel their touch.

What is common to you, I coveted. Handshakes. Warm embraces. A tap on the shoulder to get my attention. A kiss on the lips to steal a heart. Such moments were taken from my world. No one touched me. No one bumped into me. What I would have given to be bumped into, to be caught in a crowd, for my shoulder to brush against another's. But for five years it has not happened. How could it? I was not allowed on the streets. Even the rabbis kept their distance from me. I was not permitted in my synagogue. Not even welcome in my own house.

I was untouchable. I was a leper. And no one touched me. Until today.

I wonder about this man because in New Testament times leprosy was the most dreaded disease. The condition rendered the body a mass of ulcers and decay. Fingers would curl and gnarl. Blotches of skin would discolor and stink. Certain types of leprosy would numb nerve endings, leading to a loss of fingers, toes, even a whole foot or hand. Leprosy was death by inches.

The social consequences were as severe as the physical. Considered contagious, the leper was banished to a leper colony.

In Scripture the leper is symbolic of the ultimate outcast: infected by a condition he did not seek, rejected by those he knew, avoided by people he did not know, condemned to a future he could not bear. And in the memory of each outcast must have been the day he was forced to face the truth: life would never be the same.

One year during harvest my grip on the scythe seemed weak. The tips of my fingers numbed. First one finger, then another. Within a short time I could grip the tool but scarcely feel it. By the end of the season, I felt nothing at all. The hand grasping the handle might as well have belonged to someone else—the feeling was gone. I said nothing to my wife, but I know she suspected something. How could she not? I carried my hand against my body like a wounded bird.

One afternoon I plunged my hands into a basin of water intending to wash my face. The water reddened. My finger was bleeding, bleeding freely. I didn't even know I was wounded. How did I cut myself? On a knife? Did my hand slide across the sharp edge of metal? It must have, but I didn't feel anything.

"It's on your clothes too," my wife said softly. She was behind me. Before looking at her, I looked down at the crimson spots on my robe. For the longest time I stood over the basin, staring at my hand. Somehow I knew my life was being forever altered.

"Shall I go with you to tell the priest?" she asked. "No," I sighed, "I'll go alone."

I turned and looked into her moist eyes. Standing next to her was our three-year-old daughter. Squatting, I gazed into her face and stroked her cheek, saying nothing. What could I say? I stood and looked again at my wife. She touched my shoulder, and with my good hand, I touched hers. It would be our final touch.

Five years have passed, and no one has touched me since, until today. The priest didn't touch me. He looked at my hand, now wrapped in a rag. He looked at my face, now shadowed in sorrow. I've never faulted him for what he said. He was only doing as he was instructed. He covered his mouth and extended his hand, palm forward. "You are unclean," he told me. With one pronouncement I lost my family, my farm, my future, my friends.

My wife met me at the city gates with a sack of clothing and bread and coins. She didn't speak. By now friends had gathered. What I saw in their eyes was a precursor to what I've seen in every eye since: fearful pity. As I stepped out, they stepped back. Their horror of my disease was greater than their concern for my heart—so they, and everyone else I have seen since, stepped back.

The banishing of a leper seems harsh, unnecessary. The Ancient East hasn't been the only culture to isolate their wounded, however. We may not build colonies or cover our mouths in their presence, but we certainly build walls and duck our eyes.

One of my sadder memories involves my fourth-grade friend Jerry.[29] He and a half-dozen of us were an ever-present, inseparable fixture on the playground. One day I called his house to see if we could play. The phone was answered by a cursing, drunken voice telling me Jerry could not come over that day or any day. I told my friends what had happened. One of them explained that Jerry's father was an alcoholic. I don't know if I knew what the word meant, but I learned quickly. Jerry, the second baseman; Jerry, the kid with the red bike; Jerry, my friend on the corner was now "Jerry, the son of a drunk." Kids can be hard, and for some reason we were hard on Jerry. He was infected. Like the leper, he suffered from a condition he didn't create. Like the leper, he was put outside the village.

The handicapped know this feeling. The unemployed have felt it, as have the less educated. We keep our distance from the depressed and avoid the terminally ill. We have residential areas for the poor, convalescent homes for the elderly, schools for the simple, centers for the addicted, and prisons for the criminals.

The rest simply try to get away from it all. Only God knows how many Jerrys are in voluntary exile—individuals living quiet, lonely lives infected by their fear of rejection and their memories of the last time they tried. They choose not to be touched at all rather than risk being hurt again.

Oh, how I repulsed those who saw me. Five years of leprosy had left my hands gnarled. Tips of my fingers were missing as were portions of an ear and my nose. At the sight of me, fathers grabbed their children. Mothers covered their faces. Children pointed and stared.

The rags on my body couldn't hide my sores. Nor could the wrap on my face hide the rage in my eyes. I didn't even try to hide it. How many nights did I shake my crippled fist at the silent sky? "What did I do to deserve this?" But never a reply.

Some think I sinned. Some think my parents sinned. All I know is that I grew so tired of it all: sleeping in the colony, smelling the stench. I grew so tired of the damnable bell I was required to wear around my neck to warn people of my presence. As if I needed it. One glance and the announcements began, "Unclean! Unclean! Unclean!"

Several weeks ago I dared walk the road to my village. I had no intent of entering. Heaven knows I only wanted to look again upon my fields. Gaze again upon my home. And see, perchance, the face of my wife. I did not see her. But I saw some children playing in a pasture. I hid behind a tree and watched them scamper and run. Their faces were so joyful and their laughter so contagious that for a moment, for just a moment, I was no longer a leper. I was a farmer. I was a father. I was a man.

Infused with their happiness, I stepped out from behind the tree, straightened my back, breathed deeply . . . and they saw me. Before I could retreat, they saw me. And they screamed. And they scattered. One lingered, though, behind the others. One paused and looked in my direction. I don't know, and I can't say for sure, but I think, I really think, she was my daughter. And I don't know, I really can't say for sure. But I think she was looking for her father.

That look is what made me take the step I took today. Of course it was reckless. Of course it was risky. But what did I have to lose? He calls himself God's Son. Either he will hear my complaint and kill me or accept my demands and heal me. Those were my thoughts. I came to him as a defiant man. Moved not by faith but by a desperate anger. God had wrought this calamity on my body, and he would either fix it or end it.

But then I saw him, and when I saw him, I was changed. You must remember, I'm a farmer, not a poet, so I cannot find the words to describe what I saw. All I can say is that the Judean mornings are sometimes so fresh and the sunrises so glorious that to look at them is to forget the heat of the day before and the hurt of times past. When I looked at his face, I saw a Judean morning.

Before he spoke, I knew he cared. Somehow I knew he hated this disease as much as, no—more—than I hate it. My rage became trust, and my anger became hope. From behind a rock, I watched him descend a hill. Throngs of people followed him. I waited until he was only paces from me, then I stepped out.

"Master!" He stopped and looked in my direction, as did dozens of others. A flood of fear swept across the crowd. Arms flew in front of faces. Children ducked behind parents. "Unclean!" someone shouted. Again, I don't blame them. I was a huddled mass of death. But I scarcely heard them. I scarcely saw them. Their panic I'd seen a thousand times. His compassion, however, I'd never beheld. Everyone stepped back except him. He stepped toward me.

Five years ago my wife had stepped toward me. She was the last to do so. Now he *did. I did not move. I just spoke. "Lord, you can heal me if you will." Had he healed me with a word, I would have been thrilled. Had he cured me with a prayer, I would have rejoiced. But he wasn't satisfied with speaking to me. He drew near me. He touched me.*

"I will." His words were as tender as his touch. "Be healed!"

Energy flooded my body like water through a furrowed field. In an instant, in a moment, I felt warmth where there had been numbness. I felt strength where there had been atrophy. My back straightened, and my head lifted. Where I had been eye level with his belt, I now stood eye level with his face. His smiling face.

He cupped his hands on my cheeks and drew me so near I could feel the warmth of his breath and see the wetness in his eyes. "Don't tell anyone about this. But go and show yourself to the priest and offer the gift Moses commanded for people who are made well. This will show the people what I have done."

And so that is where I am going. I will show myself to my priest and embrace him. I will show myself to my wife, and I will embrace her. I will pick up my daughter, and I will embrace her. And I will never forget the one who dared to touch me. He wanted to honor me, to validate me, to christen me. Imagine that . . . unworthy of the touch of a man, yet worthy of the touch of God.

The touch did not heal the disease, you know. Matthew is careful to mention that it was the pronouncement and not the touch of Christ that cured the condition. "Jesus reached out his hand and touched the man and said, 'I will. Be healed!' And immediately the man was healed from his disease" (Matt. 8:3 NCV).

The infection was banished by a word from Jesus. The loneliness, however, was treated by a touch from Jesus.

Oh, the power of a godly touch. Haven't you known it? The doctor who treated you, or the teacher who dried your tears? Was there a hand holding yours at a funeral? Another on your shoulder during a trial? A handshake of welcome at a new job? A pastoral prayer for healing? Haven't we known the power of a godly touch? Can't we offer the same?

Many of you already do. Some of you have the master touch of the Physician himself. You use your hands to pray over the sick and minister to the weak. If you aren't

touching them personally, your hands are writing letters, dialing phones, baking pies. You have learned the power of a touch.

But others of us tend to forget. Our hearts are good; it's just that our memories are bad. We forget how significant one touch can be. We fear saying the wrong thing or using the wrong tone or acting the wrong way. So rather than do it incorrectly, we do nothing at all.

Aren't we glad Jesus didn't make the same mistake? If your fear of doing the wrong thing prevents you from doing anything, keep in mind the perspective of the lepers of the world. They aren't picky. They aren't finicky. They're just lonely. They are yearning for a godly touch.

Jesus touched the untouchables of the world. Will you do the same?

REFLECTION AND DISCUSSION

Have you ever built a boundary between you and someone from your life? If so, what was the situation that prompted your decision? What would cause you to include him or her again?

_____

_____

_____

_____

_____

Though Jesus' words cured the leper's disease, Max points out that only Christ's loving touch banished the man's loneliness. Describe a time in your life when no words came, but a touch said it all.

_____

_____

_____

_____

_____

Read again the story of the cleansed leper from Matthew 8:1–4. Why do you think Jesus thought it was important to physically touch the man? Would the story have been diminished without the touch? Explain.

_____

_____

_____

_____

_____

Read Mark 1:40–45. The cleansed leper, though having been warned not to tell the story to anyone, instead went out and began to talk freely. Would you have been able to keep quiet if such a marvelous thing had happened to you? Explain.

_____

_____

_____

_____

_____

_____

Think of someone who has a compassionate spirit. How is this spirit expressed through his or her actions, speech, and demeanor? With the Lord's help, how can you work at better showing compassion?

_____

_____

_____

_____

_____

_____

THE WOMAN CAUGHT IN ADULTERY

THE WOMAN CAUGHT
IN ADULTERY

BEFORE YOU BEGIN
Read John 8:1–11 NIV

Jesus went to the Mount of Olives.

At dawn he appeared again in the temple courts, where all the people gathered around him, and he sat down to teach them. The teachers of the law and the Pharisees brought in a woman caught in adultery. They made her stand before the group and said to Jesus, "Teacher, this woman was caught in the act of adultery. In the Law Moses commanded us to stone such women. Now what do you say?" They were using this question as a trap, in order to have a basis for accusing him.

But Jesus bent down and started to write on the ground with his finger. When they kept on questioning him, he straightened up and said to them, "Let any one of you who is without sin be the first to throw a stone at her." Again he stooped down and wrote on the ground.

At this, those who heard began to go away one at a time, the older ones first, until only Jesus was left, with the woman still standing there. Jesus

straightened up and asked her, "Woman, where are they? Has no one condemned you?"

"No one, sir," she said.

"Then neither do I condemn you," Jesus declared. "Go now and leave your life of sin."

Rebecca Thompson fell twice from the Fremont Canyon Bridge. She died both times. The first fall broke her heart; the second broke her neck.

She was only eighteen years of age when she and her eleven-year-old sister were abducted by a pair of hoodlums near a store in Casper, Wyoming. They drove the girls forty miles southwest to the Fremont Canyon Bridge, a one-lane, steel-beamed structure rising 112 feet above the North Platte River.

The men brutally beat and raped Rebecca. She somehow convinced them not to do the same to her sister Amy. Both were thrown over the bridge into the narrow gorge. Amy died when she landed on a rock near the river, but Rebecca slammed into a ledge and was ricocheted into deeper water.

With a hip fractured in five places, she struggled to the shore. To protect her body from the cold, she wedged herself between two rocks and waited until the dawn. But the dawn never came for Rebecca. Oh, the sun came up, and she was found. The physicians treated her wounds, and the courts imprisoned her attackers. Life continued, but the dawn never came.

The blackness of her night of horrors lingered. She was never able to climb out of the canyon. So in September 1992, nineteen years later, she returned to the bridge.

Against her boyfriend's pleadings, she drove seventy miles per hour to the North Platte River. With her two-year-old daughter and boyfriend at her side, she sat on the edge of the Fremont Canyon Bridge and wept. Through her tears she retold the story. The boyfriend didn't want the child to see her mother cry, so he carried the toddler to the car.

That's when he heard her body hit the water. And that's when Rebecca Thompson

died her second death. The sun never dawned on Rebecca's dark night. Why? What eclipsed the light from her world?

Fear? Perhaps. She had testified against the men, pointing them out in the court-room. One of the murderers had taunted her by smirking and sliding his finger across his throat. On the day of her death, the two had been up for parole. Perhaps the fear of a second encounter was too great.

Was it anger? Anger at her rapists? Anger at the parole board? Anger at herself for the thousand falls in the thousand nightmares that followed? Or anger at God for a canyon that grew ever deeper and a night that grew ever blacker and a dawn that never came?

Was it guilt? Some think so. Despite Rebecca's attractive smile and appealing personality, friends say that she struggled with the ugly fact that she had survived and her little sister had not.

Was it shame? Everyone she knew and thousands she didn't had heard the humiliating details of her tragedy. The stigma was tattooed deeper with the newspaper ink of every headline. She had been raped. She had been violated. She had been shamed. And try as she might to outlive and outrun the memory . . . she never could.

So nineteen years later she went back to the bridge.

Canyons of shame run deep. Gorges of never-ending guilt. If it were your fault, it would be different. If you were to blame, you could apologize. If the tumble into the canyon were your mistake, you could respond. But you weren't a volunteer. You were a victim.

Sometimes your shame is private. No one else knows. But you know. And that's enough.

Sometimes it's public. Branded by a divorce you didn't want. Contaminated by a disease you never expected. Marked by a handicap you didn't create. And whether it's actually in their eyes or just in your imagination, you have to deal with it—you are marked: a divorcée, an invalid, an orphan, an AIDS patient.

Whether private or public, shame is always painful. And unless you deal with it, it is permanent. Unless you get help—the dawn will never come.

You're not surprised when I say there are Rebecca Thompsons in every city and

Fremont Bridges in every town. But there is one woman whose story embodies them all. A story of failure. A story of abuse. A story of shame. And a story of grace.

That's her, the woman standing in the center of the circle. Those men around her are religious leaders. Pharisees, they are called. Self-appointed custodians of conduct. And the other man, the one in the simple clothes, the one sitting on the ground, the one looking at the face of the woman, that's Jesus.

Jesus has been teaching. The woman has been cheating. And the Pharisees are out to stop them both.

"Teacher, this woman was caught in the act of adultery" (John 8:4 NIV). The accusation rings off the courtyard walls. "Caught in the act of adultery." The words alone are enough to make you blush. Doors slammed open. Covers jerked back.

"In the act." In the arms. In the moment. In the embrace. "Caught." Aha! What have we here? This man is not your husband. We know what to do with women like you!

In an instant she is yanked from private passion to public spectacle. Heads poke out of windows as the posse pushes her through the streets. The city sees. Clutching a thin robe around her shoulders, she hides her nakedness. But nothing can hide her shame.

From this second on, she'll be known as an adulteress. When she goes to the market, women will whisper. When she passes, heads will turn. When her name is mentioned, the people will remember.

Moral failure finds easy recall.

The greater travesty, however, goes unnoticed. What the woman did is shameful, but what the Pharisees did is despicable. According to the law, adultery was punishable by death, but only if two people witnessed the act. There had to be two eyewitnesses.

Question: How likely are two people to be eyewitnesses to adultery? What are the chances of two people stumbling upon an early morning flurry of forbidden embraces? Unlikely. But if you do, odds are it's not a coincidence.

So we wonder. How long did the men peer through the window before they barged in? How long did they lurk behind the curtain before they stepped out?

And what of the man? Adultery requires two participants. What happened to him? Could it be that he slipped out? The evidence leaves little doubt. It was a trap. She's been caught. But she'll soon see that she is not the catch—she's only the bait.

"The law of Moses commands that we stone to death every woman who does this. What do you say we should do?" (v. 5 NCV).

Pretty cocky, this committee of high ethics. Pretty proud of themselves, these agents of righteousness. This will be a moment they long remember, the morning they foil and snag the mighty Nazarene.

As for the woman? Why, she's immaterial. Merely a pawn in their game. Her future? It's unimportant. Her reputation? Who cares if it's ruined? She is a necessary, yet dispensable, part of their plan.

The woman stares at the ground. Her sweaty hair dangles. Her tears drip hot with hurt. Her lips are tight; her jaw is clenched. She knows she's been framed. No need to look up. She'll find no kindness. She looks at the stones in their hands. Squeezed so tightly that fingertips turn white.

The woman has nowhere to turn. You'd expect Jesus to stand and proclaim judgment on the hypocrites. He doesn't. You'd hope that he would snatch the woman and the two would be beamed to Galilee. That's not what happens either. You'd imagine that an angel would descend or heaven would speak or the earth would shake.

Once again, his move is subtle and unmistakable. Jesus writes in the sand.

He stoops down and draws in the dirt. The same finger that engraved the commandments on Sinai's peak and scared the warning on Belshazzar's wall now scribbles on the courtyard floor. And as he writes, he speaks: "Anyone here who has never sinned can throw the first stone at her" (v. 7 NCV).

The young look to the old. The old look in their hearts. They are the first to drop their stones. And as they turn to leave, the young who were cocky with borrowed convictions do the same. The only sound is the thud of rocks and the shuffle of feet.

Jesus and the woman are left alone. With the jury gone, the courtroom becomes the judge's chambers, and the woman awaits his verdict.

"Woman, where are they? Has no one judged you guilty?" She answers, "No one, sir."

Then Jesus says, "I also don't judge you guilty. You may go now, but don't sin anymore" (vv. 10–11 NCV).

If you have ever wondered how God reacts when you fail, frame these words and hang them on the wall. Or better still, take him with you to your canyon of shame.

Invite Christ to journey with you back to the Fremont Bridge of your world. Let him stand beside you as you retell the events of the darkest nights of your soul.

And then listen. He's speaking. "I don't judge you guilty." And watch. He's writing. He's leaving a message. Not in the sand, but on a cross. Not with his hand, but with his blood. His message has two words: *not guilty.*

REFLECTION AND DISCUSSION

With what character in the story of John 8 do you identify most closely? The woman? The guilty (but absent) man? The Pharisees? The men in the crowd? Explain your choice.

_____

_____

_____

_____

Jesus told the woman, "I also don't judge you guilty. You may go now, but don't sin anymore" (John 8:11 NCV). Does any part of this statement bother you? Is it what you would have expected Jesus to say? Why?

_____

_____

_____

Do the words *not guilty* apply to you? Explain your answer. How do those words make you feel?

_____

_____

_____

_____

_____

_____

What does the word *shame* mean to you? What does the word *grace* mean to you? Which is the stronger term? Why?

_____

_____

_____

_____

_____

_____

THE WOMAN
WHO WASHED
JESUS' FEET

THE WOMAN WHO WASHED JESUS' FEET

BEFORE YOU BEGIN

Read Luke 7:36–39, 47 NLT

One of the Pharisees asked Jesus to have dinner with him, so Jesus went to his home and sat down to eat. When a certain immoral woman from that city heard he was eating there, she brought a beautiful alabaster jar filled with expensive perfume. Then she knelt behind him at his feet, weeping. Her tears fell on his feet, and she wiped them off with her hair. Then she kept kissing his feet and putting perfume on them.

When the Pharisee who had invited him saw this, he said to himself, "If this man were a prophet, he would know what kind of woman is touching him. She's a sinner!"

"I tell you, her sins—and they are many—have been forgiven, so she has shown me much love. But a person who is forgiven little shows only little love."

Could two people be more different? He is looked up to. She is looked down on. He is a church leader. She is a streetwalker. He makes a living promoting standards. She's made a living breaking them. He's hosting the party. She's crashing it.

Ask the other residents of Capernaum to point out the more pious of the two, and they'll pick Simon. Why, after all, he's a student of theology, a man of the cloth. Anyone would pick him. Anyone, that is, except Jesus. Jesus knew them both and picked the woman. What's more, he tells Simon why.

Simon is angry. Just look at her—groveling at Jesus' feet. Kissing them, no less! Why, if Jesus were who he says he is, he would have nothing to do with this woman.

One of the lessons Simon learned that day was this: Don't think thoughts you don't want Jesus to hear. For Jesus heard them, and when he did, he chose to share a few of his own.

"Simon," he said to the Pharisee, "I have something to say to you."

"Go ahead, Teacher," Simon replied.

Then Jesus told him this story: "A man loaned money to two people—500 pieces of silver to one and 50 pieces to the other. But neither of them could repay him, so he kindly forgave them both, canceling their debts. Who do you suppose loved him more after that?"

Simon answered, "I suppose the one for whom he canceled the larger debt."

"That's right," Jesus said. Then he turned to the woman and said to Simon, "Look at this woman kneeling here. When I entered your home, you didn't offer me water to wash the dust from my feet, but she has washed them with her tears and wiped them with her hair. You didn't greet me with a kiss, but from the time I first came in, she has not stopped kissing my feet. You neglected the courtesy of olive oil to anoint my head, but she has anointed my feet with rare perfume.

"I tell you, her sins—and they are many—have been forgiven, so she has shown me much love. But a person who is forgiven little shows only little love." (Luke 7:40–47 NLT)

Simon invites Jesus to his house but treats him like an unwanted step uncle. No customary courtesies. Or, in modern terms, no one opened the door for him, took his coat, or shook his hand.

Simon does nothing to make Jesus feel welcome. The woman, however, does everything that Simon didn't. We aren't told her name. Just her reputation—a sinner. A prostitute most likely. She has no invitation to the party and no standing in the community.

But people's opinions didn't stop her from coming. It's not for them she has come. It's for him. Her every move is measured and meaningful. Each gesture extravagant. She puts her cheek to his feet, still dusty from the path. She has no water, but she has tears. She has no towel, but she has her hair. She uses both to bathe the feet of Christ. As one translation reads, "she rained tears" on his feet (v. 44 MSG). She opens a vial of perfume, perhaps her only possession of worth, and massages it into his skin. The aroma is as inescapable as the irony.

You'd think Simon of all people would show such love. Is he not the reverend of the church, the student of Scripture? But he is harsh, distant. You'd think the woman would avoid Jesus. Simon's "love" is calibrated and stingy. Her love, on the other hand, is extravagant and risky.

How do we explain the difference between the two? Training? Education? Money? No, for Simon has outdistanced her in all three.

But there is one area in which the woman leaves him eating dust. Think about it. What one discovery has she made that Simon hasn't? What one treasure does she cherish that Simon doesn't? Simple. God's love. We don't know when she received it. We aren't told how she heard about it. Did she overhear Jesus' words "your Father is merciful"? (Luke 6:36 ESV). Was she nearby when Jesus had compassion on the widow of Nain? Did someone tell her how Jesus touched lepers and turned tax collectors into disciples? We don't know. But we know this. She came thirsty. Thirsty from guilt. Thirsty from regret. Thirsty from countless nights of making love and finding none. She came thirsty.

And when Jesus hands her the goblet of grace, she drinks. She doesn't just taste or nip. She doesn't dip her finger and lick it or take the cup and sip it. She lifts the liquid to her lips and drinks, gulping and swallowing like the parched pilgrim she is. She drinks until the mercy flows down her chin and onto her neck and chest. She drinks until every inch of her soul is moist and soft. She comes thirsty and she drinks. She drinks deeply.

Simon, on the other hand, doesn't even know he is thirsty. People like Simon don't need grace; they analyze it. They don't request mercy; they debate and prorate it. It wasn't that Simon couldn't be forgiven; he just never asks to be.

So while she drinks up, he puffs up. While she has ample love to give, he has no love to offer. Why? The 7:47 Principle. Read again verse 47 of Luke chapter 7: "A person who is forgiven little shows only little love." Just like the jumbo jet, the 7:47 Principle has wide wings. Just like the aircraft, this truth can lift you to another level. Read it one more time. "A person who is forgiven little shows only little love" (NLT). In other words, we can't give what we've never received. If we've never received love, how can we love others?

But, oh, how we try! As if we can conjure up love by the sheer force of will. As if there is within us a distillery of affection that lacks only a piece of wood or a hotter fire. We poke it and stoke it with resolve. What's our typical strategy for treating a troubled relationship? Try harder.

"My spouse needs my forgiveness? I don't know how, but I'm going to give it."

"I don't care how much it hurts, I'm going to be nice to that bum."

"I'm supposed to love my neighbor? Okay. By golly, I will."

So we try. Teeth clinched. Jaw firm. We're going to love if it kills us! And it may do just that.

Could it be we are missing a step? Could it be that the first step of love is not toward them but toward him? Could it be that the secret to loving is receiving? You give love by first receiving it. "We love, because He first loved us" (1 John 4:19 NASB).

Long to be more loving? Begin by accepting your place as a dearly loved child. "Follow God's example, therefore, as dearly loved children and walk in the way of love, just as Christ loved us and gave himself up for us as a fragrant offering and sacrifice to God" (Eph. 5:1–2 NIV).

Want to learn to forgive? Then consider how you've been forgiven. "Be kind and compassionate to one another, forgiving each other, just as in Christ God forgave you" (Eph. 4:32 NIV).

Finding it hard to put others first? Think of the way Christ put you first. "Though he was God, he did not think of equality with God as something to cling to" (Phil. 2:6 NLT).

Need more patience? Drink from the patience of God (2 Peter 3:9). Is generosity an elusive virtue? Then consider how generous God has been with you (Rom. 5:8). Having trouble putting up with ungrateful relatives or cranky neighbors? God puts up with you when you act the same. "He is kind to the ungrateful and wicked" (Luke 6:35 NIV).

Can't we love like this?

Not without God's help we can't. Oh, we may succeed for a time. We, like Simon, may open a door. But our relationships need more than a social gesture. Some of our spouses need a foot washing. A few of our friends need a flood of tears. Our children need to be covered in the oil of our love.

But if we haven't received these things ourselves, how can we give them to others? Apart from God, "the heart is deceitful above all things" (Jer. 17:9 NIV). A marriage-saving love is not within us. A friendship-preserving devotion cannot be found in our hearts. We need help from an outside source. A transfusion. Would we love as God loves? Then we start by receiving God's love.

The secret to loving is living loved. This is the forgotten first step in relationships. Remember Paul's prayer? "Your roots will grow down into God's love and keep you strong" (Eph. 3:17 NLT). As a tree draws nutrients from the soil, we draw nourishment from the Father. But what if the tree has no contact with the soil?

Many people tell us to love. Only God gives us the power to do so.

We know what God wants us to do. "This is what God commands: . . . that we love each other" (1 John 3:23 NCV). But how can we? How can we be kind to the vow breakers? To those who are unkind to us? How can we be patient with people who have the warmth of a vulture and the tenderness of a porcupine? How can we forgive the moneygrubbers and backstabbers we meet, love, and marry? How can we love as God loves? We want to. We long to. But how can we?

By living loved. By following the 7:47 Principle: receive first, love second.

REFLECTION AND DISCUSSION

Read Luke 7:36–50. What principle did Jesus develop in verse 47? How does this principle relate to you? Explain.

_____

_____

_____

_____

_____

How does someone "receive" love? How does someone "refuse" love?

_____

_____

_____

_____

_____

Have you experienced purposeful love toward someone who seemed hard to love? How did this active love change your own heart?

_____

_____

_____

_____

_____

Think of the person closest to you (spouse, friend, child, parent, etc.). Create a list of actions by responding to the question _How can I do a better job of showing love to this person?_ Today, do one of the actions on your list. Keep a journal of how your active love toward this person affects your relationship.

_____

_____

_____

_____

_____

THE WOMAN WITH THE ISSUE OF BLOOD

THE WOMAN WITH THE
ISSUE OF BLOOD

BEFORE YOU BEGIN
Read Mark 5:24-34 NIV

So Jesus went with him.

A large crowd followed and pressed around him. And a woman was there who had been subject to bleeding for twelve years. She had suffered a great deal under the care of many doctors and had spent all she had, yet instead of getting better she grew worse. When she heard about Jesus, she came up behind him in the crowd and touched his cloak, because she thought, "If I just touch his clothes, I will be healed." Immediately her bleeding stopped and she felt in her body that she was freed from her suffering.

At once Jesus realized that power had gone out from him. He turned around in the crowd and asked, "Who touched my clothes?"

"You see the people crowding against you," his disciples answered, "and yet you can ask, 'Who touched me?' "

But Jesus kept looking around to see who had done it. Then the woman, knowing what had happened to her, came and fell at his feet and, trembling with fear, told him the whole truth. He said to her, "Daughter, your faith has healed you. Go in peace and be freed from your suffering."

A clock for Christmas is not the kind of gift that thrills an eight-year-old boy, but I said thank you and took it to my bedroom, put it on the nightstand, and plugged it in.

It was a square-faced Bulova. It didn't have moving numbers—it had rotating hands. It didn't play tapes or CDs, but over the years it developed a slight, soothing hum that could be heard when the room was quiet.

But still, over time, I grew attached to it. Not because of its accuracy; it was always a bit slow. Nor the hum, which I didn't mind. I liked it because the clock glowed in the dark.

All day, every day, it soaked up the light. It sponged up the sun. The hands were little sticks of ticks and time and sunshine. And when the night came, the clock was ready. When I flicked off the light to sleep, the little clock flicked on its light and shined. Not much light, but when your world is dark, just a little seems like a lot.

Somewhat like the light a woman got when she met Jesus. We don't know her name, but we know her situation. Read these three verses and see what I mean:

A large crowd followed Jesus and pushed very close around him. Among them was a woman who had been bleeding for twelve years. She had suffered very much from many doctors and had spent all the money she had, but instead of improving, she was getting worse. (Mark 5:24–26 NCV)

She was a bruised reed: "bleeding for twelve years," "suffered very much," "spent all the money she had," and "getting worse." Such a condition would be difficult for any woman of any era. But for a Jewess, nothing could be worse. No part of her life was left unaffected.

Sexually . . . she could not touch her husband.

Maternally . . . she could not bear children.

Domestically . . . anything she touched was considered unclean. No washing dishes. No sweeping floors.

Spiritually . . . she was not allowed to enter the temple.

She was physically exhausted and socially ostracized.

She had sought help "under the care of many doctors" (v. 26 NIV). The Talmud gives no fewer than eleven cures for such a condition. No doubt she had tried them all. Some were legitimate treatments. Others, such as carrying the ashes of an ostrich egg in a linen cloth, were hollow superstitions.

She "had spent all she had" (v. 26 NIV). To dump financial strain on top of the physical strain is to add insult to injury. A friend battling cancer told me that the hounding of the creditors who demand payments for ongoing medical treatment is just as devastating as the pain.

"Instead of getting better she grew worse" (v. 26 NIV). She was a bruised reed. She awoke daily in a body that no one wanted. She is down to her last prayer. And on the day we encounter her, she's about to pray it.

By the time she gets to Jesus, he is surrounded by people. He's on his way to help the daughter of Jairus, the most important man in the community. What are the odds that he will interrupt an urgent mission with a high official to help the likes of her? Very few. But what are the odds that she will survive if she doesn't take a chance? Fewer still. So she takes a chance.

"If I can just touch his clothes," she thinks, "I will be healed" (v. 28 NCV).

Risky decision. To touch him, she will have to touch the people. If one of them recognizes her . . . hello rebuke, good-bye cure. But what choice does she have? She has no money, no clout, no friends, no solutions. All she has is a crazy hunch that Jesus can help and a high hope that he will.

Maybe that's all you have: a crazy hunch and a high hope. You have nothing to give. But you are hurting. And all you have to offer him is your hurt.

Maybe that has kept you from coming to God. Oh, you've taken a step or two in his direction. But then you saw the other people around him. They seemed so clean, so neat, so trim and fit in their faith. And when you saw them, they blocked your view of him. So you stepped back.

If that describes you, note carefully, only one person was commended that day for having faith. It wasn't a wealthy giver. It wasn't a loyal follower. It wasn't an acclaimed teacher. It was a shame-struck, penniless outcast who clutched onto her hunch that he could and her hope that he would.

Which, by the way, isn't a bad definition of faith: A conviction that he can and a hope that he will. Sounds similar to the definition of faith given by the Bible. "Without faith no one can please God. Anyone who comes to God must believe that he is real and that he rewards those who truly want to find him" (Heb. 11:6 NCV).

Not too complicated, is it? Faith is the belief that God is real and that God is good. Faith is not a mystical experience or a midnight vision or a voice in the forest . . . it is a choice to believe that the one who made it all hasn't left it all and that he still sends light into shadows and responds to gestures of faith.

There was no guarantee, of course. She hoped he'd respond . . . she longed for it . . . but she didn't know if he would. All she knew was that he was there and that he was good. That's faith.

Faith is not the belief that God will do what you want. Faith is the belief that God will do what is right.

"Blessed are the dirt-poor, nothing-to-give, trapped-in-a-corner, destitute, diseased," Jesus said, "for theirs is the kingdom of heaven" (Matt. 5, paraphrase).

God's economy is upside down (or right side up and ours is upside down!). God says that the more hopeless your circumstance, the more likely your salvation. The greater your cares, the more genuine your prayers. The darker the room, the greater the need for light.

Which takes us back to my clock. When it was daylight, I never appreciated my little Bulova's capacity to glow in the dark. But as the shadows grew, so did my gratitude.

A healthy lady never would have appreciated the power of a touch of the hem of his robe. But this woman was sick . . . and when her dilemma met his dedication, a miracle occurred.

Her part in the healing was very small. All she did was extend her arm through the crowd. What's important is not the form of the effort but the fact of the effort. The fact is, she did something. She refused to settle for sickness another day and resolved to make a move.

Healing begins when we do something. Healing begins when we reach out. Healing starts when we take a step.

God's help is near and always available, but it is only given to those who seek it. Nothing results from apathy. The great work in this story is the mighty healing that occurred. But the great truth is that the healing began with her touch. And with that small, courageous gesture, she experienced Jesus' tender power.

Compared to God's part, our part is minuscule but necessary. We don't have to do much, but we do have to do something.

Write a letter. Ask forgiveness. Call a counselor. Confess. Call Mom. Visit a doctor. Be baptized. Feed a hungry person. Pray. Teach. Go.

Do something that demonstrates faith. For faith with no effort is no faith at all. God will respond. He has never rejected a genuine gesture of faith. Never. God honors radical, risk-taking faith.

When arks are built, lives are saved. When soldiers march, Jerichos tumble. When staffs are raised, seas still open. When a lunch is shared, thousands are fed. And when a garment is touched—whether by the hand of an anemic woman in Galilee or by the prayers of a beggar in Bangladesh—Jesus stops and responds.

Mark can tell you. When this woman touched Christ, two things happened that happen nowhere else in the Bible. He recorded them both.

First, Jesus heals before he knows it. The power left automatically and instantaneously. It's as if the Father short-circuited the system and the divinity of Christ was a step ahead of the humanity of Christ.

Her need summoned his help. No neon lights or loud shouts. Just help.

Just like my dark room brought out the light of my clock, our dark world brings out the light of God.

Second, he calls her daughter. "Daughter, your faith has made you well" (Mark 5:34 NKJV). It's the only time Jesus calls any woman anywhere daughter. Imagine how that made her feel! Who could remember the last time she received a term of affection? Who knew the last time kind eyes had met hers?

Tradition holds that she never forgot what Jesus did. Legend states that she stayed with Jesus and followed him as he carried his cross up Calvary. Some believe she was

Veronica, the woman who walked the road to the cross with him. And when the sweat and blood were stinging his eyes, she wiped his forehead.

She, at an hour of great need, received his touch—and he, at an hour of pain, received hers. We don't know if the legend is true, but we know it could be. And I don't know if the same has happened to you, but I know it can.

REFLECTION AND DISCUSSION

What was the crazy hunch and the high hope of the woman in Mark 5? In specific terms, how can she be an example for us today?

_____

_____

_____

_____

Max writes, "Faith is not the belief that God will do what you want. Faith is the belief that God will do what is right." How should this change the way you pray? Why?

_____

_____

_____

_____

Is it true that "faith with no effort is no faith at all"? Explain your answer.

_____

_____

_____

_____

_____

_____

What is significant about Jesus calling the afflicted woman "daughter"?
Does this mean anything for your relationship with Jesus?

_____

_____

_____

_____

_____

_____

TWO
CRIMINALS

TWO CRIMINALS

BEFORE YOU BEGIN
Read Luke 23:32-33 NIV

Two other men, both criminals, were also led out with him to be executed. When they came to the place called the Skull, they crucified him there, along with the criminals—one on his right, the other on his left.

Meet Edwin Thomas, a master of the stage. During the latter half of the 1800s, this small man with the huge voice had few rivals. Debuting in *Richard III* at the age of fifteen, he quickly established himself as a premier Shakespearean actor. In New York he performed *Hamlet* for one hundred consecutive nights. In London he won the approval of the tough British critics. When it came to tragedy on the stage, Edwin Thomas was in a select group.

When it came to tragedy in life, the same could be said as well.

Edwin had two brothers, John and Junius. Both were actors, although neither rose to his stature. In 1863, the three siblings united their talents to perform *Julius Caesar.*

The fact that Edwin's brother John took the role of Brutus was an eerie harbinger of what awaited the brothers—and the nation—two years hence.

For this John who played the assassin in Julius Caesar is the same John who took the role of assassin in Ford's Theatre. On a crisp April night in 1865, he stole quietly into the rear of a box in the Washington theater and fired a bullet at the head of Abraham Lincoln. Yes, the last name of the brothers was Booth—Edwin Thomas Booth and John Wilkes Booth.

Edwin was never the same after that night. Shame from his brother's crime drove him into retirement. He might never have returned to the stage had it not been for a twist of fate at a New Jersey train station. Edwin was awaiting his coach when a well-dressed young man, pressed by the crowd, lost his footing and fell between the platform and a moving train. Without hesitation, Edwin locked a leg around a railing, grabbed the man, and pulled him to safety. After the sighs of relief, the young man recognized the famous Edwin Booth.

Edwin, however, didn't recognize the young man he'd rescued. That knowledge came weeks later in a letter, a letter he carried in his pocket to the grave. A letter from General Adams Budeau, chief secretary to General Ulysses S. Grant. A letter thanking Edwin Booth for saving the life of the child of an American hero, Abraham Lincoln. How ironic that while one brother killed the president, the other brother saved the president's son. The boy Edwin Booth yanked to safety? Robert Todd Lincoln.[30]

Edwin and James Booth. Same father, mother, profession, and passion—yet one chooses life, the other, death. How could it happen? I don't know, but it does. Though their story is dramatic, it's not unique.

Abel and Cain, both sons of Adam. Abel chooses God. Cain chooses murder. And God lets him.

Abraham and Lot, both pilgrims in Canaan. Abraham chooses God. Lot chooses Sodom. And God lets him.

David and Saul, both kings of Israel. David chooses God. Saul chooses power. And God lets him.

Peter and Judas, both deny their Lord. Peter seeks mercy. Judas seeks death. And God lets him.

In every age of history, on every page of Scripture, the truth is revealed: God allows us to make our own choices.

And no one delineates this more clearly than Jesus. According to him, we can choose:

a narrow gate or a wide gate (Matt. 7:13–14)
a narrow road or a wide road (Matt. 7:13–14)
the big crowd or the small crowd (Matt. 7:13–14)

We can choose to:

build on rock or sand (Matt. 7:24–27)
serve God or riches (Matt. 6:24)
be numbered among the sheep or the goats (Matt. 25:32–33)

"Then they [those who rejected God] will go away to eternal punishment, but the righteous to eternal life" (Matt. 25:46 NIV).

God gives eternal choices, and these choices have eternal consequences.

Isn't this the reminder of Calvary's trio? Ever wonder why there were two crosses next to Christ? Why not six or ten? Ever wonder why Jesus was in the center? Why not on the far right or far left? Could it be that the two crosses on the hill symbolize one of God's greatest gifts? The gift of choice.

The two criminals have so much in common. Convicted by the same system. Condemned to the same death. Surrounded by the same crowd. Equally close to the same Jesus. In fact, they begin with the same sarcasm: "The two criminals also said cruel things to Jesus" (Matt. 27:44 CEV). But one changed.

One of the criminals on a cross began to shout insults at Jesus: "Aren't you the Christ? Then save yourself and us." But the other criminal stopped him and said, "You should fear God! You are getting the same punishment he is. We are punished justly, getting what we deserve for what we did. But this man has done nothing wrong." Then he said, "Jesus, remember me when you come into your kingdom." Jesus said to him, "I tell you the truth, today you will be with me in paradise" (Luke 23:39–43).

Much has been said about the prayer of the penitent thief, and it certainly warrants our admiration. But while we rejoice at the thief who changed, dare we forget the one who didn't? What about him, Jesus? Wouldn't a personal invitation be appropriate? Wouldn't a word of persuasion be timely?

Does not the shepherd leave the ninety-nine sheep and pursue the one lost? Does not the housewife sweep the house until the lost coin is found? Yes, the shepherd does, the housewife does, but the father of the prodigal, remember, does nothing.

The sheep was lost innocently. The coin was lost irresponsibly. But the prodigal son left intentionally. The father gave him the choice. Jesus gave both criminals the same.

There are times when God sends thunder to stir us. There are times when God sends blessings to lure us. But then there are times when God sends nothing but silence as he honors us with the freedom to choose where we spend eternity.

And what an honor it is! In so many areas of life we have no choice. Think about it. You didn't choose your gender. You didn't choose your siblings. You didn't choose your race or place of birth.

Sometimes our lack of choices angers us. "It's not fair," we say. It's not fair that I was born in poverty or that I sing so poorly or that I run so slowly. But the scales of life were forever tipped on the side of fairness when God planted a tree in the garden of Eden. All complaints were silenced when Adam and his descendants were given free will, the freedom to make whatever eternal choice we desire. Any injustice in this life is offset by the honor of choosing our destiny in the next.

Wouldn't you agree? Would you have wanted it otherwise? Would you have preferred the opposite? You choose everything in this life, and he chooses where you spend the next? You choose the size of your nose, the color of your hair, and your DNA structure, and he chooses where you spend eternity? Is that what you would prefer?

It would have been nice if God had let us order life like we order a meal. I'll take good health and a high IQ. I'll pass on the music skills, but give me a fast metabolism . . . Would've been nice. But it didn't happen. When it came to your life on earth, you weren't given a voice or a vote.

But when it comes to life after death, you were. In my book that seems like a good deal. Wouldn't you agree?

Have we been given any greater privilege than that of choice? Not only does this privilege offset any injustice, the gift of free will can offset any mistakes.

Think about the thief who repented. Though we know little about him, we know this: He made some bad mistakes in life. He chose the wrong crowd, the wrong morals, the wrong behavior. But would you consider his life a waste? Is he spending eternity reaping the fruit of all the bad choices he made? No, just the opposite. He is enjoying the fruit of the one good choice he made. In the end all his bad choices were redeemed by a solitary good one.

You've made some bad choices in life, haven't you? You've chosen the wrong friends, maybe the wrong career, even the wrong spouse. You look back over your life and say, "If only . . . if only I could make up for those bad choices." You can. One good choice for eternity offsets a thousand bad ones on earth.

The choice is yours.

How can two brothers be born of the same mother, grow up in the same home, and one choose life and the other choose death? I don't know, but they do.

How could two men see the same Jesus and one choose to mock him and the other choose to pray to him? I don't know, but they did.

And when one prayed, Jesus loved him enough to save him. And when the other mocked, Jesus loved him enough to let him. He allowed him the choice. He does the same for you.

REFLECTION AND DISCUSSION

Why do you think God allows us to make our own choices?

_____

_____

_____

What "big" choices are facing you right now? How will you make them?

_____

_____

_____

_____

_____

_____

**"God gives eternal choices, and these choices have eternal consequences."
What does Max mean by "eternal choices"?**

_____

_____

_____

_____

_____

_____

"There are times when God sends thunder to stir us. There are times when God sends blessings to lure us. But then there are times when God sends nothing but silence as he honors us with the freedom to choose where we spend eternity." Describe a time when God sent thunder to stir you. Has God ever sent blessings to lure you? Explain. Why would God be silent when we're faced with such a huge choice?

_____

_____

_____

_____

_____

Read Deuteronomy 30:19–20 and Joshua 24:14–15. What choices are presented in these passages? Who is to do the choosing? What choice have you made in this crucial area of life? Explain.

_____

_____

_____

_____

_____

_____

NOTES

1. Ernest Gordon, *To End All Wars: A True Story About the Will to Survive and the Courage to Forgive* (Grand Rapids, MI: Zondervan, 2002), 105–6, 101.
2. Hans Wilhelm Hertzberg, *1 and 11 Samuel*, trans. J.S. Bowden (Philadelphia: Westminster John Knox Press, 1964), 199–200.
3. Gordon, *To End All Wars*, 101–2.
4. Not to be confused with the Ananias of Acts 5.
5. Gavan Daws, *Holy Man; Father Damien of Molokai* (Honolulu: University of Hawaii Press, 1984).
6. Alfred Edersheim, *The Life and Times of Jesus the Messiah*, unabridged edition (Peabody, MA: Hendrickson Publishers, 1993), 62–63.
7. Author's paraphrase.
8. See Exodus 9:22–23; Joshua 6:15–20; 1 Samuel 7:10.
9. Darren Brown, ed., *The Greatest Exploration Stories Ever Told: The Tales of Search and Discovery* (Guilford, CT: Lyons Press, 2003), 207–19.
10. Brown, *Greatest Exploration Stories*, 223.
11. Jerry Bridges, *The Pursuit of Holiness* (Colorado Springs: NavPress, 1978), 64.
12. Edward W. Goodrick and John R. Kohlenberger, *Zondervan NIV Exhaustive Concordance*, 2nd ed., James A. Swanson, ed. (Grand Rapids: Zondervan, 1999), 1487.
13. Arthur W. Pink, *Exposition of the Gospel of John* (Grand Rapids, MI: Zondervan, 1975), 1077.
14. William Barclay, *The Gospel of John*, vol. 2, rev. ed. (Philadelphia: Westminster Press, 1975), 267.
15. With appreciation to Stefan Richart-Willmes.
16. See Matthew 11:2.

17. *1,041 Sermon Illustrations, Ideas and Expositions*, compiled and edited by A. Gordon Nasby (Grand Rapids, MI: Baker, 1953), 180–81.

18. Charles W. Slemming, *He Leadeth Me: The Shepherd's Life in Palestine* (Fort Washington, PA: Christian Literature Crusade, 1964), quoted in Charles R. Swindoll, *Living Beyond the Daily Grind*, Book 1: Reflections on the Songs and Sayings in Scripture (Nashville: W Publishing Group, 1988), 77–78.

19. "Price of Success: Will the Recycled Orchestra Last?" CBSNews.com, November 17, 2013, www.cbsnews.com/news/price-of-success-will-the-recycled-orchestra-last/.

20. Joshua 2:1; 6:17, 25; Hebrews 11:31; James 2:25.

21. His story is told in Matthew 19, Mark 10, and Luke 18.

22. Frederick Dale Bruner clarifies this as he interprets Matthew 5:3: "Blessed are those who feel their poverty . . . and so cry out to heaven." *The Christbook: Matthew 1–12* (Waco, TX: Word Publishing, 1987), 135.

23. The word Jesus used for "poor" is a word which, when used in its most basic sense, "would not indicate the pauper, one so poor that he must daily work for his living, but the beggar, one who is dependent upon others for support." William Hendricksen, *Exposition of the Gospel of Matthew* (Grand Rapids, MI: Baker, 1973), 269.

24. See Genesis 16–18, 21.

25. Matthew waits until chapter 26 to tell a story that chronologically should appear in chapter 20. By referring to John's gospel we see the anointing by Mary in Bethany occurred on Saturday night (John 12:1). Why does Matthew wait until so late to record the story? It appears that he sometimes elevates theme over chronology. The last week of Christ's life is a week of bad news. Chapters 26 and 27 sing the woeful chorus of betrayal. First the leaders, then Judas, then the apostles, Peter, Pilate, and eventually all the people turn against Jesus. Perhaps with the desire to tell one good story of faith in the midst of so many ones of betrayal, Matthew waits until Matthew 26 to tell of Simon and Mary.

26. James Strong, *New Strong's Exhaustive Concordance* (Nashville: Thomas Nelson, 1996), s.v. "compassion."

27. Not her real name.

28. Linda Dillow and Lorraine Pintus, *Gift-Wrapped by God: Secret Answers to the Question, "Why Wait?"* (Colorado Springs, CO: WaterBrook Press, 2002), 59–64.

29. Not his real name.

30. Paul Aurandt, *Paul Harvey's the Rest of the Story* (New York: Bantam Press, 1977), 47.

Inspired by what you just read?

Connect with Max.

Listen to Max's teaching ministry, UpWords, on the radio and online. Visit www.MaxLucado.com to get FREE resources for spiritual growth and encouragement, including:

- Archives of *UpWords*, Max's daily radio program, and a list of radio stations where it airs
- Devotionals and emails from Max
- First look at book excerpts
- Downloads of audio, video, and printed material
- Mobile content

You will also find an online store and special offers.

www.MaxLucado.com

1-800-822-9673

UpWords Ministries
P.O. Box 692170
San Antonio, TX 78269-2170

Join the Max Lucado community:
Facebook.com/MaxLucado
Instagram.com/MaxLucado
Twitter.com/MaxLucado

Max Lucado

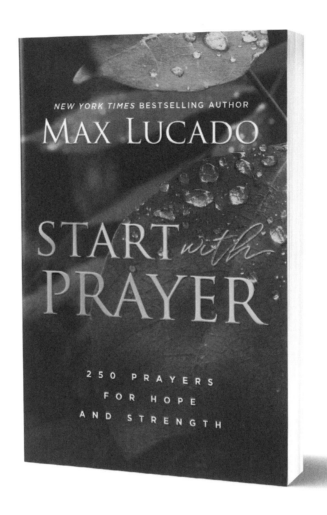

Start with Prayer is a special collection of 250 topically arranged prayers, designed to help you find the strength and hope you need before you try to solve the problem on your own. It is the perfect go-to when you want to pray but lack the words to do so.